Counselling Older People

Counselling Older People

Second edition

Steve Scrutton CQSW, BSc, MA, Cert Ed, Dip Ed

Social Work Team Leader, Northamptonshire Social Services Department, UK

A member of the Hodder Headline Group
LONDON · SYDNEY · AUCKLAND

First published in Great Britain in 1999 by
Arnold, a member of the Hodder Headline Group,
338 Euston Road, London NW1 3BH

http://www.arnoldpublishers.com

Whilst the advice and information in this book are believed to be true and accurate at the
date of going to press, neither the author nor the publisher can accept any legal responsibility
or liability for any errors or omissions that may be made.

British Library Cataloguing in Publication Data
A catalogue record for this book is available from the British Library

ISBN 0 340 71948 6 (pb)

1 2 3 4 5 6 7 8 9 10

Publisher: Cathy Peck
Production Editor: Wendy Rooke
Production Controller: Priya Gohil
Cover Design: Terry Griffiths

Typeset in 10/12 Palatino by Photoprint, Torquay
Printed and bound in Britain by J.W. Arrowsmith, Bristol

What do you think about this book? Or any other Arnold title?
Please send your comments to feedback.arnold@hodder.co.uk

Contents

Introduction

Mr Brown retired when he was 65 years old. His retirement was considered by many to be a privilege, and he was told that it was his right. However, Mr Brown enjoyed his work, and he was obliged to retire. So was his retirement a problem?

Mrs White was 80 years old when she lost her husband after 55 years of married life. He was slightly older than her, had been ill for some time, and his death was not unexpected. Many people felt that he had lived a full and rewarding life. So was his death a problem?

Mr Gray, after 70 years of almost unbroken good health, had a sudden and unexpected stroke. After several months, he had regained limited movement on his left side, and his speech was slurred. So was his debility a problem?

Mrs Black, now in her nineties, gradually lost control of her bladder. She is loved by her two daughters, who do not mind caring for her. So is her dependence on their help a problem?

Mr Green has developed severe arthritis, and has virtually lost his mobility. Despite his advancing years (his doctor told him that he must expect to be ill now that he is approaching his eightieth year), he had always enjoyed his social activities with his friends, and now he can no longer get out to see them. So is this a problem?

Mrs Amber, aged 85 years, always loved reading and sewing, but now her declining eyesight has left her unable to do either. So is her boredom a problem?

Mrs Scarlet has lived in this country for 45 years, since she was 25 years old. It was always her intention to return to her homeland, but she knows that this will never happen. Her family live around her. They are attentive, but they have become imbued with values that she cannot accept. Is her old age likely to be a problem?

The human race is unique among the animals in that we continue to live beyond the time when we have relinquished two vital roles – the ability to work for a living, and the ability to procreate and nurture offspring. Yet often it is this very uniqueness that brings problems which can be seen in the lives of many older people. This book addresses these problems, and the potential value of counselling in helping people come to terms with the many losses that old age involves.

The book is not a difficult, complicated or intellectually demanding treatise on the skills of counselling, beyond the reach of people who perceive their task to be straightforwardly to tend to the needs of older people. Counselling is often presented as a highly technical activity, to be practised only by professionally trained people who have a sound understanding of psychotherapy or some other psychological discipline. There are numerous 'schools' of counselling, all with differing styles and procedures. Arguments between proponents of these various schools can lead to the belief that counselling is a highly structured and complicated technique, with a 'right' and a 'wrong' way of setting about the task. Too often, 'counselling' seems to be the exclusive province of professionally trained people who, because of their qualifications and experience, assume that they are the only people able to use the technique. Some American literature (Landreth and Berg, 1980) would certainly suggest this is so. Sargent (1980) also acknowledges this when he refers to his less technical contributors as 'non-traditional' in order to distinguish their approach from the more technical, medicalized models.

This 'professionalization' of counselling denies that the techniques involved in counselling – good relationships, empathy, and clear two-way communication – are essentially a simple and very human means of helping people who are in trouble. This book presents counselling as a simple but effective technique that is practised by many caring people every day, and which can – and indeed should be – developed and used by many more in their daily care of older people. The book seeks to demystify counselling, and to present the counsellor as 'carer and friend', not as 'therapist and psycho-analyst'. It presents counselling as a set of techniques which can be mastered by all who genuinely care, and who are prepared to give some time and thought to what they are doing. Indeed, it is the simplicity and the basic humanity of counselling that make it such an attractive, powerful and valuable technique for those who care for older people.

The book is directed towards social workers, care managers, staff in residential and nursing homes and day centres for elderly people, home helps, health professionals, including nurses and general practitioners, as well as priests and parsons, and any other professional who comes into contact with older people.

However, it also makes the assumption that relatives and friends – by far the largest group of carers of older people – can find counselling a valuable technique. Talking to older people about their problems and difficulties, which is what counselling is about, has tended to be undervalued, and even neglected. Prior to the first edition of this book, there was no UK text dealing specifically with the subject. Yet many carers will know the value that older people place upon companionship and friendship, and how their commu-nication and support can help them to cope with the problems of ageing, and of being 'old' within our society. They may not be trained counsellors, and they may not even have 'volunteered' for their caring role. None the less, they find themselves in both situations. Often there is no one else who can, or perhaps will, take on the responsibility.

Many people have the idea that counselling requires a great deal of skill and is something rather difficult and complicated to learn. If that is what you believe, then stop and ask yourself a few questions. Have you ever comforted a child who is crying? Have you ever spent time sitting quietly with a friend who was terribly upset? Have you ever listened to somebody who was in a dilemma, and who did not know what to do?

(Geldard, 1989)

Training in counselling techniques might be advantageous, and is recommended, but sometimes it is either impossible or unavailable. So this book seeks to support the people who are undertaking the task of caring for older people.

At the same time, the book takes a critical look at how older people are perceived within our society. Old age, like death, has become an issue that we do not like to discuss or delve into too deeply. 'Ageism', which surrounds so much of our thinking and practice with regard to older people, is discussed at length, both in terms of how it affects our attitudes to the ageing process, and in terms of the way it tends to structure the manner in which older people themselves function. Counselling can be a valuable technique for combating the power of debilitating ageist attitudes.

In my introduction to the first edition, I said that if carers of older people felt that by reading the book they had gained more knowledge of older people, their problems, and how these can benefit from counselling, and if they felt more confident discussing such issues with them, then the book would have achieved its principal objective. Many readers have been kind enough to say that it did just that. My hope is that this second edition will do likewise.

PART ONE

The need for counselling

Counselling and the older adult

Counselling . . .
. . . the older adult
. . . and their culture

Counselling . . .

Counselling is essentially an approach to human communication. Moreover, it is a human approach to communication. The subjects of counselling are troubled or unhappy people who, for whatever reason, are finding it difficult to live their lives in harmony with the world around them, or to lead their lives to their full potential. The problems they face – whatever their source – may be affecting their attitudes, their behaviour and their social relationships.

The primary objective of counselling is to involve people in a process whereby they can be helped to reflect on, and become more aware of, their current situation and the complexity of their personal needs. It seeks to allow them to express their feelings about their lives, without any attempt to impose the counsellor's own ideas and views. Thereafter, it seeks to enable people to initiate and develop new and appropriate responses to their situation. In doing this, the object of counselling is not to bring about change or to manipulate personality.

It is vital the counsellor does not believe that 'they' are the problem, and that 'we' are the solution.

Rather, counselling should seek to enable people to modify their own behaviour, and to review their own outlook on life, in ways that are acceptable to themselves, through the development of self-knowledge and self-understanding. Counselling is based on the idea that to talk about a problem is helpful – this is why counselling is sometimes referred to as a 'talking cure'. However, it is more than this. Counselling is based on the belief that all behaviour, however odd or irrational it might appear, has meaning. The meaning might be difficult for the outsider to decipher, but will usually be found to have something to do with the inner emotional life of the individual. Counselling seeks to discover this meaning.

At its simplest, counselling is no more (and no less) than the development of warm, empathetic and understanding relationships with those who are experiencing emotional and social stress, giving them time, listening to their troubles, and responding to them sympathetically. At this fundamental level, counselling is no more than a 'theoretical construction' of a basic human skill. As such, many older people receive 'counselling' every day quite spontaneously from people who would not necessarily elevate what they do by giving it that name. Yet sensitive and caring people who are good listeners, who like people enough to allow them to express their own feelings, and who are prepared to give depressed, confused, difficult and emotionally disturbed people sufficient time to express their feelings, are indeed practising counselling.

The problem with this 'simple' definition of counselling is that the development of 'warm, empathetic and understanding relationships', whilst common, is not a universal human skill or attribute. So whilst it is important to present counselling as a method that can be practised by any caring person, regardless of training and qualifications, it is also vital to stress that counselling is more than just 'being pleasant', more than befriending, and more than just 'talking to' people. Many people may believe that they are practising counselling when in fact their role within the relationship is too intrusive and too dominant to be any such thing.

This is a common problem. Too often we do not listen to people who tell us about their problems, especially when they are no longer able to look after themselves. We fail to find out what is on their minds. In the case of dependent people we are often too busy 'caring' for their physical needs to worry about their emotional life. We assume that we know, from the limited facts available to us, how they feel. We believe that we know best what they should do, and that our idea of 'right' and 'wrong' should determine the decisions and actions of other people.

The giving of advice (however good), the giving of directions (however correct) and the use of exhortations (however well intentioned) does not constitute counselling.

Such techniques are common in relationships based on dominance and submission, and they have no place within counselling relationships. Counselling is more than communication, giving useful advice, friendship, or influencing attitudes and behaviour. Counselling is the art of helping other people to come to terms with their problems and difficulties. It recognizes that it is not sufficient to care for other people, but that people should be helped to care for themselves. It is a process which seeks to support troubled people and to help them feel 'better' by discovering and utilizing their own inner strengths and resources. The counsellor also inquires into the causes of problem emotions and behaviour, something even good friends will often shy away from, perhaps feeling that they do not want to delve into 'difficult' areas. This means that to counsel effectively, a special relationship with very particular qualities is required.

Counselling is about facing pain and empathizing with it. This frightens some people. After all, what do you say when you face someone suffering personal grief? The best answer is to say just that – that you do not know what to say. It is better than saying nothing, or being frightened into absenting ourselves. There is an issue about whether carers can counsel the people they care for and love. They can provide them with many types of support, from tangible help, such as cleaning the house, to emotional support, such as offering a shoulder to rest on, to social support, through just being there, and providing them with safety, familiarity, routine and predictability. Why, then, can carers not talk to them in ways that are helpful?

The objective of counselling is to assist a person through a difficult or stressful period. The concept of social distress is important. People face many distressing situations. Some will be major difficulties, while others will be relatively minor. Some people will cope well with problems which others may find intolerably stressful. This does not make one problem more, or less, significant than another.

Distress is a personal matter, and is real to the individual who feels it. It is towards these feelings that counselling is directed.

Counselling seeks to take the individual on a journey which starts with self-assessment, progresses through self-awareness, and ends up with self-determination. The object is to help the person to live more happily, with less stress and in greater harmony with others.

Does it work? The effectiveness of counselling has been studied extensively, and the results have been conflicting and largely inconclusive (for a survey of this research, see O'Leary, 1996). Yet academic research, in conforming to 'scientific' principles, is almost inevitably concerned with highly controlled and regulated settings. Counselling, in contrast, is conducted within the confines of a dynamic relationship. The results of counselling concern how we feel before and afterwards, often in ways that are immeasurable. People, and especially older people, usually feel that it is 'good' to talk, regardless of any perceived benefits. My experience is that focusing on the problems of ageing is usually welcomed, and can often be beneficial. However, I am not sure that I could 'prove' this to the satisfaction of most academic researchers. Do we need to? The carers of older people will not usually look to academic research to decide when and if they should talk to those people, nor should they feel that they can do any harm by doing so.

. . . the older adult

Why is it that when a young person reaches adolescence, or has difficulties at home or school, then we assume that they require help, and we are anxious to provide it, but when older people reach old age the assumption is that they do not require help? The skills of counselling people in difficulty are well developed in schools, youth work, non-custodial work with young offenders, family therapy, marriage guidance, work with alcoholics and drug-abusers, potential suicides, and in many other spheres. As Halmos (1978) has stated, 'The counsellor's influence on his society is in a process of rapid growth'. In most areas this is supported by a considerable amount of literature. The reasons for the comparative neglect of older people are interesting to ponder.

- Is there an assumption that older people do not require 'theoretical constructs' such as counselling, and that their needs can be accurately assessed and readily satisfied?
- Do we assume that ageing brings with it an easy ability to express personal feelings and needs?
- Has the image of old age as a time of 'peace, tranquillity and serenity' obscured the real problems and insecurities felt by many older people?

Such ideas have no substance. People of all ages constantly juggle with conflict, trauma and contradiction in their social and emotional lives. They experience the joys and pain of life, often both at the same time. Just like any other age group, some older people cope better than others with the pressures. People who are in touch with their own feelings will tolerate their lives, cope better when faced with uncertainty, anxiety and loss, continue with their lives, and face death with greater equanimity. Other people will struggle with the realities of older age. Few will make the journey without the need to talk and come to terms with what is happening to them. Some will find the entire journey unacceptable. Meanwhile, facing this pain, younger people will often deny the unhappier realities of ageing, perhaps shielding themselves from the 'unpleasant' prospect of become 'old' themselves.

There may also be an assumption that counselling older people is essentially similar to counselling any other age group. Even a cursory examination of this would suggest that communication with older people is often not straightforward. Older people do not normally demand attention, and will not come forward readily to request counselling support. Yet even when the need is identified, there can be specific problems relating to older age. Poor hearing may impair the ability of older people to hold a serious conversation. Poor eyesight may restrict their use of body language and other means of non-verbal communication. Their health may be poor, and their morale may be low as a result of loneliness and grief. Their ability to look optimistically into the future may be seriously reduced.

Moreover, whilst counsellors of other age groups may have personally experienced the problems they discuss, it is unlikely that counsellors will have had first-hand experience of the problems of old age.

The counselling of older people is neglected for other reasons. The social neglect of older people can be witnessed in most areas of service provision. A BMA report stated that many doctors see 'geriatric medicine as a second-rate specialty, looking after third-rate patients in fourth-rate facilities' (British Medical Association, 1986). The quantity and quality of social work provision for older people, although taking up a high proportion of social services spending, has long been recognized as inadequate, and is often carried out by unqualified staff with limited resources (Barclay Report, 1982). The provision of sheltered accommodation remains inadequate, and access to public transport remains poor.

Yet the neglect of counselling older people may be found deeper within ourselves. The problem is that there are no answers to old age – no cures, and no reassurances that can halt or prevent the process of ageing. Consequently we feel powerless, and in order to ease our anxiety and discomfort we withdraw from older people. We choose not to confront their feelings of profound loss, loneliness, rejection and despair, or indeed the death and bereavement that are common in older age. Relating to older people can be a demanding task, especially for those who see in their experience a reflection of themselves and their future. Rather than engage with older people it is easier to deny their needs. We prefer to accept their (often false) reassurances, and we hide behind our defence mechanisms. Perhaps it is the easiest way for both parties to cope with loss and pain. Both parties deny reality by engaging in the activity of routine, task-oriented work, busying ourselves, rather than engaging with the wishes, feelings and difficulties of older people and their real human needs.

Thus it is not possible to understand fully the reason for the neglect of older people without reference to the widely held ideas and concepts about the nature of ageing and old age. The importance of counselling older people will only be accepted if we believe in the intrinsic worth of older people as 'people' in their own right.

. . . and their culture

Older people are complex, each individual having been moulded by the experiences of many decades. Their values, attitudes, behaviour and outlook on life were nurtured during a different time, and shaped through many circumstances and events. Over the years, older people will have witnessed massive social change, and some will have adapted to their changed environment better than others.

The tendency to consider older people as an amorphous group, with similar needs based on their chronological age, is a gross error. Despite – and perhaps even because of – their age, older people are individuals with a life history that is likely to have widened rather than narrowed differences over the years. There is no point and no age when someone becomes 'old'. Growing old involves a series of transitions through which each person travels in his or her own way and at his or her own speed. Each person is a product of their own life, their social relationships, working conditions and experiences. The transitions are not distinct or precise, and there is no set timetable, although there may be signals. These include:

• the loss of independence;
• an inability to cope unaided;
• increased frailty.

However, it is not possible to categorize an 'older' person, or their needs, by virtue of their age alone. An older person needs to be understood by reference to his or her background and experience.

In all counselling, the best starting point is always to ask the question *'What makes this person different?'*. With older people it is essential, and it is even more important for younger counsellors, who may find that they have much to learn about the factors which shaped the lives of older people, and their development and experience as youngsters, and then as mature adults. There are many elements to such an understanding, including:

- their social class origins;
- their experience of family life as a child;
- their education;
- their religious upbringing;
- their employment;
- their family and children;
- their recreational pursuits.

If the person comes from a minority ethnic community, all of these differences will be heightened further, not least by the difficulties they have experienced, and will continue to experience, while living within a dominant culture. Dein and Huline-Dickens (1997) stress that culture 'influences the development of personality, concept of self, consultation behaviours, what is perceived as stigma, options of adopting the sick role and the patients' own explanatory models for their illnesses'.

Therefore, for these reasons, it is important to realize that counselling older people is a complex process which is undertaken with complex people.

Ageism: the social creation of old age

Counselling should take an essentially optimistic view of an individual's ability to review and reconstruct their life. Yet is it possible that life in old age can be a time of hope? Can older people enjoy their lives – rich in expectation and high in fulfilment? Can their last years be personally satisfying and socially valuable, a culmination of a lifetime's experience? And can the 'younger' counsellor believe that all of this is possible?

Dominant social values and ageism

That such questions have to be asked would seem strange indeed to traditional societies where the status of 'elder' is one of prestige and distinction, and where age is valued for its wisdom and experience. Ever since Simmons (1945) described how traditional societies ascribe prestige and privilege to older people, anthropology has shown how concepts of 'old age' vary between different cultures. In many traditional cultures, old age definitions tend to be functional rather than chronological – that is, age is not considered to be as important as social performance and/or the ability to work. Philpot (1986) compared traditional and modern attitudes towards older people in Japan, and found that the roots of respect for older people were contained within Japanese culture and religion, and that despite the rapid development of industrialization and urbanization, and their rush for growth, efficiency and change, respect for elders has ensured that they have not fallen behind. Old age has still retained a certain authority and respect.

Thus the quality of life that older people experience is determined by social attitudes and values. If different societies define and react to old age differently, it becomes important to understand the social context in which old age is experienced, and the impact which this has on the lives of older people. Within a single society there are clearly different views and opinions. However, within each there exists a body of ideas which can be described as 'dominant'. This 'dominant ideology' consists of a complex set of values and attitudes that, to a large extent, determines how older people are perceived, how they perceive themselves, and how they function (or are allowed to function) within that wider social context. It is these dominant ideas that establish the structures which constrain the way that older people are expected to lead their lives. As Estes states:

> This requires an examination of society's treatment of the aged in the context of the national and world economy, the role of the state, conditions of the labour market, and class, race, gender and age divisions in society. At base, this requires examination of the relationship of capitalism to ageing. It also begins with the proposition that the status and resources of the elderly, and even the experience of old age itself, are conditioned by one's location in the social structure and the local to global economic and social factors that shape that location.
>
> (Estes, 1986)

Dominant ideology reflects the interests of the most powerful social groups. Laws are passed which not only work in their interest, but work against the interests of weaker or minority groups, including minority ethnic communities, the 'working' class, handicapped people, women and, of course, older people. From these dominant values and assumptions arise racism, classism, sexism and ageism, each comprising a set of negative attitudes, practices and values that forms a stereotype of the group, and that affects the way in which the group is treated and is able to function within the wider society.

Whilst it would be wrong to construct an idealistic stereotype of a former 'golden age', our 'advanced' western civilization has long abandoned positive perceptions of old age, or even those based on individual functionality. The impact of ageism on the way in which older people live can be devastating. It can be particularly difficult for people from minority ethnic communities, whose cultural background may harbour more positive ideas about ageing, and where elders are treated differently to the way in which they are treated within the dominant culture. Adjustment to this change can be very difficult.

Ageism: a definition

> Ageism creates and fosters prejudice about the nature and experience of old age. These ... project unpleasant images of older people which subtly undermine their personal value and worth. Commonly held

ideas restrict the social role and status of older people, structure their expectations of themselves, prevent them achieving their potential, and deny them equal opportunities.

(Scrutton, in McEwen, 1990)

Ageism is a powerful social force. It has developed a stereotype of 'older people' that has diminished and undermined their social status. It consists of several different myths, which have been outlined by Dixon and Gregory (1987).

1. *Myth of chronology* – the idea that older people are a homogeneous group by virtue of their age alone, i.e. once one's age reaches a 'magic number' one automatically becomes old and part of the group known as 'the elderly'.

2. *Myth of ill health* – that old age automatically involves physical deterioration and that illness in old age is part of normal ageing, not disease processes, and is therefore irreversible and untreatable.

3. *Myth of mental deterioration* – that older people automatically lose their mental faculties, slow down and become 'senile' (i.e. mad).

4. *Myth of inflexible personality* – that personality changes with age to become more intolerant, inflexible and conservative.

5. *Myth of misery* – that older people are unhappy because they are old.

6. *Myth of rejection and isolation* – that society rejects elderly people, and is uncaring towards them, preferring to believe that older people choose to 'disengage' from life, i.e. withdraw into themselves.

7. *Myth of unproductivity/dependence* – that older people are unproductive members of our society, because they are not engaged in paid employment and are therefore inevitably dependent upon others.

The social creation of ageism

Ageism is socially endemic and resides within all of us, regardless of our age. Indeed, it resides within the minds of those who have themselves become 'old', for older people will have learned that to be 'old' means that they should conform to ageist stereotypes and accept their ascribed role within the social order. They internalize the attitudes that they held about older people when they were younger. Perhaps they expected little of older people, and now they hope for little more from themselves.

Yet infants do not discriminate on the basis of age. Their judgement of people is based simply on the way in which they are treated. It is the process of socialization that transforms ageing into something to be avoided and feared. From birth onwards we are presented with unflattering images of old age. Children's books portray older people as clumsy, frail and pathetic – as people who need to be helped across roads. Younger people are given a more glamorous image. These early images make an impression which is confirmed in later school years, not least in classic literature.

> *. . . second childishness and mere oblivion,*
> *Sans teeth, sans eyes, sans taste, sans everything*
> (Shakespeare, *As You Like It*)

Generation by generation, ageism is intensified and perpetuated until it pervades the thinking, attitudes and expectations of young and old alike. The result is that both older people and their carers accept the socially constructed view of old age – not because it is true, or needs to be, but because the dominant ideology becomes self-fulfilling. Dominant ideology is concerned with the way in which things are seen to be, rather than what they might or should be. They are not natural, true and incontrovertible perceptions, but beliefs that have been developed by dominant social forces over the years.

> Society creates the framework of institutions and rules within which the general problems of the elderly emerge, and, indeed, are manufactured. Decisions are being taken every day, in the management and development of social institutions, which govern the position which older people occupy in national life, and these also contribute powerfully to the public consciousness of different meanings of ageing and old age.
> (Townsend, 1981)

Perhaps the paradigm of old age today is an individual, living alone, socially isolated, managing on inadequate income, suffering from poor health, poorly housed, dependent upon younger carers for support, and seen as a burden. Unhappy, withdrawn, but at the same time not interested in making new friends, they have lost their energy, enthusiasm and drive. They are no longer concerned with education or personal growth. In deteriorating physical and mental health, their only prospect is of further decline and, eventually, death.

This depressing but widely held view of life in old age provides the foundation upon which judgements are made about the status and value of older people. Thought of in this way, older people become dehumanized and vulnerable to oppression.

There is another popular and more amenable image of old age, associated with pensioners living in retirement on the south coast, or wintering in Spanish hotels. However, this is a reality that applies to only a few older people. It is also an alternative image which is used to deflect recognition of some of the more awful realities of life for most older people. Certainly, the fears about ageing, and life in old age, are concerned with the more ubiquitous and unhappier reality.

The origins of ageism

Ageism within western civilization has roots stretching back to ancient times. Minois (1989) describes how the Old Testament begins by attaching primary importance to Jewish elders, associating old age with divine favour. However, he traces how this declined through the centuries. Ancient Greece, the mother of western civilization, bequeathed a more consistently negative view of older people. Aristotle (384–322BC), in his book, entitled *Rhetoric*, accused older people of every conceivable fault, describing them as cowardly, hesitant, selfish, timorous, suspicious, parsimonious, miserly, smallminded, ill-humoured and avaricious. He traced the decline in respect once given to older people for their knowledge and experience to many developments, including the loss of an oral tradition, the decline in importance of custom, and the acceleration of change.

In contrast, youth is highly valued. It is associated with beauty, vigour, enthusiasm, energy, new ideas, innovation, change and progress – all highly valued attributes. By comparison, the old can only offer experience, competence, loyalty, continuity, security and reliability to a society that seems to have outgrown such values. The immaturity, rashness and naïveté of youth appear to be forgotten, together with the role that the experience of age can play in guiding it. It is the future, and the people of the future, that have become crucially important. To the extent that we have learned to regard most commodities as being 'disposable', and to the extent that we consider people to be commodities, with a value that can be bought and sold, once people have outlived their value then they, too, become disposable.

It is from the oldest of older people that this negative image of old age is drawn. One can distinguish between the 'young-old' and the 'old-old', and it is from the latter that the paradigm of a crumbling, decrepit old age springs. The young-old can – and should – have a more positive image. The aim should be to make the old-old stage of life as brief as possible.

Structural ageism

The most pernicious aspect of ageism is not that it is present in our minds and attitudes, but that it is confirmed and reinforced by the functions and rules of everyday social life. The structural analysis of ageing has been well documented (Townsend, 1981; Phillipson, 1982; Myles, 1984; Phillipson and Walker, 1987).

Productivity

The close association between productivity and social status within western capitalism is well known, and forms the basis of dominant social attitudes to old age. The value we place on people, and therefore their financial and status rewards, is in large measure based on what they produce. Older people have a 'non-productive' status, and are frequently seen as a social and financial burden. The projected rise in the proportion of older people within society – a frequent topic of discussion – serves as a constant reminder of their 'dependent' social status and the drain that they represent to public finances.

The concept of productivity, so important within capitalist societies, is central to the value we ascribe to older people. It explains and justifies the circumstances and conditions in which many are expected to live. Thus state pensions can be fixed at minimal levels, and the most significant effect of retirement for many pensioners is a drastic reduction in living standards.

Yet if older people are unproductive, it is the result of social policy. Compulsory retirement enforces non-productivity, depresses social status, and promotes the idea of older people as a burden. Most people retire from employment because they are expected or compelled to do so. This, we are told, is a consequence of social philanthropy. Older people have 'earned their retirement'. Such philanthropy forms the basis of age discrimination. Medical, educational and social service provision becomes a low priority given that there is only a marginal 'return' on such investment.

However, whilst this capitalist ethic (to the deserving, most, and to the undeserving, least) might explain why older people are treated in this way, it is not an adequate or suitable explanation for people who wish to perpetuate this situation, and need to justify the disparities of income, wealth and status that exist within society. There is a need to perpetuate the myths of conventional wisdom, namely that society does everything it can to value and revere its older citizens. Thus the link between productivity and poverty in old age is denied, and instead explanations which coincide more closely with our philanthropic ideology are developed. It is these explanations that form the basis of ageist social attitudes.

Religious belief

Ageism is firmly embedded in the values and beliefs of Christianity and most other major religions. Many religious attitudes can be traced back to ideas that linked old men with the image of sin, and old age as a curse and a punishment. The 'other-worldliness' of religion teaches us that the problems of this world are not as important as our place in the next, that suffering is part of our preparation for the next life, and that the imminence of death, and therefore the closeness to a 'better' world, is something to be welcomed rather than feared. Perhaps more sophisticated theology might argue that this is not the real religious message, yet the social message of most religious belief, especially for older people who are non-theologians, and whose beliefs are simpler and more traditional, is that they should forget their troubles in this life, for they are temporary. Happiness, contentment, fulfilment and all that is worthwhile will be available in abundance in the next life. It is therefore quite pointless for them to worry about their present condition.

The 'this-worldliness' of counselling is thus pitted against the 'other-worldliness' of religion. Religious attitudes can prevent older people from questioning their social status and situation, and stop them developing a level of dissatisfaction that might otherwise prove embarrassing to dominant ideology.

Psychology and ageing

Important elements in twentieth-century psychological theory have provided a deeply worrying ageist message. Nowhere can this be seen more clearly than in the work of the father of modern psychology, Sigmund Freud, who wrote that 'psychotherapy is not possible near or above the age of 50, the elasticity of the mental processes on which the treatment depends is as a rule lacking – old people are not educable' (Freud, 1905).

This view has had an ongoing effect on attitudes towards older people as rigid, less capable, less willing to adapt to new developments, and unable to change.

orthodox Freudian doctrine has long held the notion that basic personality characteristics are developed and set at a very early stage of development, well within the first decade of life. These basic characteristics, so this view goes, are little, if at all, amenable to modification. Consistent with this, then, is the conclusion that with advanced age the point of no return (with respect to behaviour or personality change) has long since passed.

(Schwartz, in Sargent, 1980)

Whitbourne and Hulicka (1990) examined psychology textbooks and found a condescending portrayal of older people, most such books stating that they suffer from personality deterioration, rigidity, inevitable biological decline, senility, loss of psychological functions and social losses. Yet research does not support such ageist views. Reviewing the literature, O'Leary (1996) concluded that 'older adults for the most part retain their intellectual ability as measured in intelligence tests'.

The idea of a fixed and unchanging ageing personality underlies the neglect of counselling older people. To the extent that counselling is associated with personal growth, such views discount the potential value of counselling, providing a 'scientific' explanation as to why older people tend to get into difficulties in the first place, and are then unable to resolve their problems.

Social class and achievement

The status of older people is closely correlated with social class, power, wealth and previous achievement. The more a person acquires these attributes during adulthood, and the more success they have in maintaining them in old age, the more likely they are to maintain their status in old age. Older politicians, composers, writers, industrialists and the like remain widely admired. Among the less notable, poorer classes the situation has always been more difficult. When older people are no longer able to fend for themselves, they become a 'burden' and are of no further value. Older people often sense a lack of interest in them as significant persons, both from professional groups and even from their own family.

Social disengagement

The theory of 'disengagement' (Cummings and Henry, 1961) suggests that older people voluntarily relinquish their social roles and responsibilities and withdraw from many aspects of social participation. The theory still enjoys widespread popular credibility, although it has been heavily criticized and largely discredited in academic circles. The suggestion that older people willingly withdraw from the pressures and responsibilities of everyday life serves to validate the social ageism that makes older people redundant and obsolete, and justifies their replacement with younger people with more up-to-date skills. Withdrawal then becomes acceptable. We can believe that older people do not withdraw because they feel undervalued, bereft of a social role, and unable to afford the financial costs of full social engagement, but because it is part of the 'natural' process of ageing.

In turn, this can affect the way in which we believe older people should be treated. What they require is time for reflection, rest and sleep, and the removal of unnecessary pressures and responsibilities. They neither need nor want an active and interesting life, so it is best that we do not disturb them too much, lest we upset them. This quiescent image helps to make the loneliness of old age more acceptable. Older people do not make new friends readily, and are likely to lose their long-standing friends through death, so it is reasonable to expect that they will increasingly spend time on their own. In this way, loneliness becomes understandable – an understandable and acceptable hazard of old age.

Allied to this is the idea that relationships in old age are less fulfilling, and that life is less enjoyable. For example, it is widely believed that sexual relationships are less important after a certain age. The massive Kinsey report devoted less than 1 per cent of its total length to people aged 60 years and over, and Renshaw (1991) stated that 'disbelief, condescending humour, silence and benign neglect have pervaded the topic of geriatric sexual expression through the centuries'. However, it is more likely that the social activities of older people are determined by social expectations, and whether dominant ideology considers them to be 'appropriate' at their age.

Medicalization of old age

Ageism closely associates old age with illness and pain. That older people become increasingly prone to sickness and ill-health is to some extent true, but ageism takes a 'tendency' and transforms it into an extreme and depressing inevitability.

- Arthritis will progressively rack the bodies of older people with pain.
- Their heart and other vital organs will decline in vigour and vitality.
- Their bodies will be subject to an inevitable process of wasting, the result of ailments for which there is little defence.
- They will lose control of their limbs, their muscles will weaken, and their sense of balance will diminish.

- Their sight and hearing will fail.
- The process of personal decline and ill health is pre-ordained and inevitable.

The medicalization of ageing is consistent with the image of old age as a process of inevitable physiological and biological decline. It suggests that the process can be temporarily halted, if only by skilled medical intervention. Such claims, alongside the fatalism of dominant attitudes about health in old age, require examination. It is certainly not the experience of fitter and more active older people, who can bear testimony to the fact that ageing does not *inevitably* lead to the dominant social perceptions of a pre-ordained decline. Rather, their experience suggests that with a sensible attitude towards the care and maintenance of the body (through good diet and sensible life-style) the ageing mind and body can be kept in good shape for far longer than conventional wisdom would have us believe.

The dominant assumption would be that it is older people who are 'fit' rather than older people who are 'sick', who are the exceptions to the otherwise general rule of nature. This is not necessarily so, but the consequence has been that the care of older people has become increasingly medicalized. If decline is inevitable, and if there is nothing that can be done to prevent older people becoming frail, sick and dependent, then they have to place their trust in medical experts. The medical profession has led us to believe that it alone can maintain the ageing body. The fact that people now live longer is regularly attributed to medical science. However, there is little evidence to support this claim. Illich (1977), Doyle (1983) and Thunhurst (1982) have argued persuasively that improved nutrition, public sanitation and better working conditions have been more influential than the medical profession in causing this trend. Indeed, there is evidence to suggest that when infant mortality is removed from the statistics, life expectancy now is not significantly greater than it was prior to the Industrial Revolution.

However, the medical view of ageing persists. When older people become ill (or face social problems, such as depression), it is often both easier and quicker to respond to them through the use of drugs. Yet it is palliatives rather than cures that are usually offered. Pain is controlled, but its source is rarely diagnosed. Depression is treated with antidepressants, but the cause is rarely considered. Fears and worries are tranquillized, but they are rarely discussed. In this way, medication is used to obscure underlying problems. It helps to avoid the time-consuming process of looking deeper into the causation of ill health in older people.

Medical provision that would be available to younger people is often considered to be inappropriate for older people. Assumptions are made about their quality of life, life expectancy, and the cost-benefits of such treatment. This classic form of ageism is informative about the value systems applied to older people. They are facing natural and unavoidable decline, and there is nothing that can usefully be done. Therefore the medical profession – quick to claim that it prolongs life – readily accepts the inevitability of decline and illness in old age, especially when it so regularly discovers that it has no adequate answer to the ailments associated with old age.

Indeed, the medicalization of old age is worse. Conventional medicine frequently offers treatments and drugs which are harmful. Polypharmacy – the prescription of multiple drugs for the same person (sometimes up to a dozen) with some given to overcome the side-effects of others – is common, and this professionally sanctioned drug abuse can often lead to problems far worse than the original condition. Drugs that are frequently prescribed for older people have regularly been found to be dangerous. The result is that older people receive the worst possible deal. Whilst their health problems have been progressively medicalized, medical science actually has little to offer them except palliatives. Our misplaced confidence in the efficacy of medicine shrouds what is becoming increasingly clear – that medicine has little time for and few answers to the production of good health in old age (Scrutton, 1992).

Counselling can assist in a better understanding of health in old age, but it is a time-consuming activity compared to the rapidity with which prescriptions can be written. Thus it is easier to allow older people to remain content in the belief that they are 'ill' because they are 'old', and that as illness is a medical problem, they must rely upon – and indeed be grateful for – medical intervention.

The mental processes of ageing

Old age is believed to lead to a natural diminution of mental abilities. Increasing numbers of older people become confused and suffer from dementia, and this has generally been interpreted as a 'natural' and irreversible process of deterioration in the ageing brain. However, young people also suffer from dementia, and the majority of older people remain entirely sensible, all of which suggests that the direct causal relationship between mental deterioration and increasing age is not so straightforward.

Here perhaps more than with physical ill health, counselling should question dominant attitudes and opinions. Studies comparing the brains of 'confused' and 'cogent' elderly people have not revealed significant differences (see Chapter 18). However, drug treatment has been found to be instrumental in creating confusion (again, medicine is shown to be potentially harmful to health in old age).

The experience of most people living to advanced old age would indicate that the human brain can function adequately for any natural life-span, given the right circumstances. Moreover, perhaps the right circumstances have as much to do with social, emotional and financial circumstances as with brain degeneration.

Dependence

Dependence is closely associated with old age, and it is widely assumed that older people will inevitably become a burden. It is a common fear that leads to many difficulties and misunderstandings. Older people do not want to be a burden, and they fight against becoming dependent. They will endure their circumstances and refuse to burden others. The link between old age and dependence can therefore actually reduce the opportunities that older people have to discuss their situation, especially with people who they know care deeply for them. This can be reinforced by younger carers if, for whatever reason, they are reluctant to take responsibility for their care. In situations where older people sense discomfort or denial, they may decide that it is better to suppress rather than express their problems.

For many, the worst aspects of dependence are the loss of human rights, the loss of freedom and choice, and the loss of dignity. Yet the emotional side of dependence often goes unrecognized. When dependence becomes self-evident, older people are offered practical help rather than emotional support. Moreover, the provision of routine and practical services can serve to reinforce and highlight their incapacity. People enter their homes to do their housework, to cook their meals, and to provide other personal services, yet what many older people want is not just practical support, but also an opportunity to discuss their strong feelings about being dependent on such support. Many of them feel deeply the loss of personal respect and dignity – an unintended consequence of care, but one that often remains unidentified because we fail to offer time to discuss their dependence.

Death and decline: purpose and meaning in old age

The expressed wish of many older people for a quick and early death becomes more understandable as the nature and impact of ageism are studied. These people are made to feel a burden, the future is expected to bring only inevitable decline, and death may seem to constitute a 'happy release' from the suffering of old age. Yet attitudes towards death are contradictory. On the one hand, discussion of death is avoided because it is felt to be an unpleasant and morbid subject (perhaps reminding us too much of our mortality). However, for older people death is clearly an issue, and they often find that they have no one with whom they can discuss their fears and anxieties about the next major stage of their lives.

The 'happy-release' attitude is widely prevalent among both young and old, even though euthanasia does not find widespread approval. Thus older people do not have the right to decide when and how they die, even when they no longer wish to continue living. Yet the desire for euthanasia is aroused by ageist attitudes which confirm that life in old age is both worthless and painful. Clearly, common attitudes about old age and death constitute a dilemma – an issue that will be dealt with fully in the final chapter.

Where ageism generates the absence of hope, it permits older people to live in poverty, loneliness and distress, and to die of neglect. If older people are merely waiting to die, then the value of providing time-consuming forms of care, such as counselling, can legitimately be questioned. Care becomes warehousing – making people comfortable for as long as they remain alive – and little more. Caring becomes a task devoid of hope, and the resources for counselling will not be forthcoming.

Ageism and the counsellor

It is not necessary to see old age as unproductive and futile, or for it to be so. If large sections of society do perceive it in this way, then it is legitimate to ask how we have arrived at such a judgement. The personal experience of many older people is that life, even when accompanied by declining powers, can remain full and meaningful. Dominant ideology describes old age as it exists within the current social milieu. It assumes that older people are set in their ways, rigid in their thinking, impervious to new ideas, immutably set in their life-style and incapable of change. They have become anachronisms – people who have lived beyond their time – and of no further value. Moreover, they have become so by virtue of the natural, predetermined and inevitable process of ageing.

Here we can recall an earlier submission, that the social purpose of ageism is to explain why older people are not entitled to a fair share of social resources. Ageism devalues older people, and does so in order to make it appear that what happens to them is the result of a 'natural' process rather than a socially constructed one.

Yet whilst ageism determines the attitudes that we hold about older people, and the attitudes which they hold about themselves, the counsellor needs to be aware of these attitudes, and to recognize that they will colour the views, attitudes and self-image of older people.

It is my contention that the counsellor has to tackle ageism within the counselling process.

However, it is important to stress the limitations of counselling in this respect. Whilst it can help people to overcome the impact of ageism in their lives, by itself it will do little to change the social structures which produce them. Many will say that time would be better spent on 'political' solutions which would have an impact on the lives of older people. They would question the wisdom and morality of helping people to adjust to living in an inherently ageist society. Such criticism is valid. Counselling is not a solution to ageism but, as Halmos says:

> there are two kinds of betterers, two kinds of righters of wrongs: those who would rectify the anomalies of society before giving a personal helping hand to the individual, and those who would consider the personal assistance of the individual as more urgent and potent than the bettering of society.
>
> (Halmos, 1978)

Thus it is important that the counsellor can draw attention to the injustices of ageism. One effect of ageism is that it can lead to negative caring practices.

Phillipson examined a number of features of professional practice towards older people and concluded:

> Apart from some limited areas of innovation, the overall impression is one of stagnation and conservatism in day-to-day work. Older people appear trapped within models of ageing which emphasise the deterioration and loss of function accompanying old age. Such models are, however, at last being challenged, not least by older people themselves in their own political organizations.
>
> (Phillipson, 1982)

The counselling process can play an important part in combating the impact of ageism. Living within the confines of ageism, older people will be unable to change and grow unless they are aware of the social factors which structure their lives. An understanding of ageist constraints can help people to break free, and allow them to reassess their lives. Counselling can help older people to challenge ageism, and enable them to find their own solution to the problems which they face. It can transform resignation into determination, and hopelessness into hope.

The danger of 'political' agendas

However, counselling is a person-to-person skill, in which the feelings and needs of the individual are centrally important. Otherwise, it is a 'neutral' activity, with no hidden social and political agendas. It should not seek to support the status quo by utilizing an overbearing approach which assumes that the counsellor knows best, and that 'their' need for 'our' support allows 'us' to override 'their' wishes. Counselling, with its ability to influence behaviour, can be a powerful technique when used to control behaviour for the benefit of personal, institutional, social or political agendas. Counselling should not be a means of modifying behaviour in the interests of social control nor, on the other hand, should it be an opportunity to 'politicize' people. Troubled behaviour is often the consequence of social inequity, and disaffected people can be natural recruits to specific social and political objectives. Counselling can be used to raise awareness, radicalize people's stance on social issues, and so become a means of social engineering.

The use of counselling for either social control or social engineering is morally suspect. Both taint counselling with hidden agendas, and fail to attribute dignity, respect and esteem to the individual. It is not that either the conservative or radical agenda can be abandoned entirely. Elements of both are present in any communication. When counselling older people, it becomes clear that many of the problems which they encounter are linked to social prejudice and injustice, so it is not possible to ignore these social dimensions. This means an understanding of the ageist social dimension is an important conceptual tool for the counsellor.

Combating personal pathology

Too often, a person's problems are seen as the result of personal failings and inadequacy. It is their fault that they are poor. It is their inadequacy that makes them depressed. Their loneliness is self-inflicted. Their pain is the result of a foolish life-style. The older individual is often seen as incapable of coping with the problems of ageing.

Personal pathology ignores the social context in which older people live, and the constraints imposed upon them by ageism. Counselling must recognize personal pathology because older people, in particular, are too ready to accept pathological explanations. They blame themselves for their problems rather than becoming aware of the social structures that underlie their difficulties, and which limit their ability to cope. They accept personal responsibility, their inadequacy and, above all, the 'natural' and 'inevitable' processes of ageing. These are easy to understand, but the fatalism they breed is often at the root of the powerlessness of older people, who too often accept their 'allotted' social role which, for many, is unrewarding and unfulfilling. Their acceptance of ageism does not arise from contentment, but is indicative of a sense of powerlessness and an inability to improve the quality of their lives (Scrutton, 1990). Their resignation becomes self-fulfilling. Many older people feel that such acceptance is expected of them, and that to respond otherwise might risk losing the support of their carers. Even those who do not accept their situation often strike out against those closest to them, rather than against the social forces which oppress them, leading to anger and bewilderment among their friends and carers, and to the withdrawal of care and support. This is a common but ultimately self-defeating strategy that leads to unhappy and discontented people placing themselves in further difficulties.

An anti-ageist perspective

An anti-ageist perspective is not contrary to the idea of 'client-centred' counselling, and an individual focus does not mean that ageist agendas must be abandoned. The counsellor needs to discuss the ageist agenda openly, but on the understanding that the individual can reject it without risk to the counselling relationship. Older people are often unaware of the social factors that make their lives an unsatisfactory experience. An understanding of ageism enables them to re-interpret their lives and reassess the circumstances which have led to their problems by introducing concepts which are often far outside their range of thinking and experience.

Above all, there is a need to distinguish between the factors of old age which are genuinely inevitable and irreversible (by the very nature of the ageing process), and those factors which result from an acceptance of ageist constraints on leading fuller lives.

Personal ageism

The counsellor needs to be aware of the existence of ageism, and to recognize its impact on the lives of older people so that he or she can present alternative ways of thinking and alternative explanations that can be liberating for older people. However, even more important is an ability to recognize the extent to which our own ideas and perceptions are influenced by ageism.

- What is our attitude to older people?
- Do we harbour negative images of old age?
- Do we believe that counselling older people will be a waste of time?

Ageism cannot be denied. It is not 'their' problem, it is ours. It is not 'your' problem, it is mine. So it is vital for the prospective counsellor to examine his or her own personal ageism. Given the paradigm of old age, who would want to work with older people? It must be depressing and unrewarding. Little research has been done in this area. O'Leary (1996), quoting research by Butler and Lewis (1988), lists six reasons for the negative attitudes of counsellors to working with older people.

1. Older people may stimulate fear of their own old age in some counsellors.

2. They may arouse conflicts concerning their relationships with their own parents.

3. Counsellors may believe that they have nothing useful to offer older people, because they regard their problems as arising from untreatable organic brain disease.

4. Counsellors may consider that their skills will be wasted if they work with older adults, who are near death and not really deserving of attention.

5. Older people might die while in treatment, which could challenge the counsellors' sense of importance.

6. Colleagues may be contemptuous of their efforts on behalf of older people.

To these alarmingly ageist reasons, O'Leary's summary of research evidence adds the fear that the counsellor might be overwhelmed by the presenting problems, and that they may lack empathy with them. Clearly, counselling older people is not something that should be embarked upon if these attitudes and beliefs are held.

3 Counselling agendas: old age

Coping with loss

Ageist attitudes and the experience of old age

Counselling seeks to offer help with the 'problem' emotions, namely depression, despair, anxiety, frustration, stress, low self-esteem and so on. Many factors in the ageing process can create troubled emotions. Indeed, the problems of living into old age should not be underestimated. Ageism shrouds these counselling agendas. Often we have not faced up to them because it is more comfortable to deny their existence.

The last 100 years have probably witnessed the most rapid process of social change experienced in human history. It is a useful exercise for counsellors to consider life as it was during the youth of an older person. It is during our younger years that we learn to comprehend and cope with our lives. These years become, for many, the 'good old days', treasured but gone, and it would be strange if the rapidity of change during this time period had not made it difficult for some older people to cope. Many of the old 'certainties' will have been lost, and new and puzzling realities will have taken their place.

Thus the experience of growing older will bring with it many emotional and social traumas. How older people react is a personal process dependent upon many factors. Most notably, they will have spent a lifetime dealing with problems and difficulties, and the way in which they face the problems of old age will depend to some extent on how successful they have been. This experience ensures that each person will bring a characteristic response to the process of ageing. When working with older people the counsellor is not working with fresh or unformed material, but with people who have considerable experience of life. They will have been shaped, and sometimes mis-shaped, by it. Some will bring wisdom, openness, flexibility, gentleness and kindness, while others will bring prejudice, dissatisfaction, rigidity, frustration and aggression.

Yet while the older personality is already well established, it is not as 'rigid' as many would have us believe. One objective of counselling is to assist people to adjust realistically to the problems and consequences of normal change in the ageing process, and to prevent them from becoming tyrannized by it. Even those who have dealt successfully with life in earlier years are likely to experience some difficulties in coping with ageing, but at least they will bring with them the skills and confidence gained over a lifetime.

Other people will not be so fortunate, bringing into old age an inadequate social base and many emotional scars. Some will have failed to make close and lasting relationships, and some will be reluctant to communicate their feelings. Such people are likely to be most vulnerable to the problems of ageing, as they will have fewer resources to help them cope. The counsellor should seek to determine whether they are dealing with someone whose difficulties are a recent experience, directly related to ageing, or whether they are part of more long-standing problems, with roots in earlier years.

This chapter will look at the 'age-specific' problems – that is, problems that all older people are likely to face regardless of their coping skills. In doing this we must recognize that, despite facing the common experience of ageing, each individual is unique and will respond differently. We shall examine the extent to which a person's social performance is constructed by ageism, and/or the extent to which these are genuinely the problems of old age. The following chapter will consider the counselling of 'unresolved' issues that date back to earlier stages in older people's lives, and how these can affect an older person's ability to cope with ageing.

Coping with loss

During childhood, youth and middle age, we develop roles and functions that create our social status and personal identity, and which give meaning to our lives. We form relationships with important people who become significant figures in our social and emotional lives. Many of these roles are shed in older age, and many good friends are lost. Hence the losses experienced in old age are many and varied. Bereavement is not restricted to death, and older people are particularly vulnerable to a broad range of losses.

> It is important to realise that the grief arising from a wide variety of physical, emotional and social losses closely resembles the grief associated with loss through death, both for those who suffer the loss, and those close to the bereaved individual.
>
> (Scrutton, 1995)

However, the losses that can be incurred in older age are neither an inevitable nor an exclusive consequence of ageing.

> Similar decline can occur at relatively early ages, whilst many older people can maintain a satisfactory level of physical performance through into late older age. . . . The loss of physical function will vary according to individual attitudes, personal relationships, the maintenance of health, and many other emotional and social factors.
>
> (Scrutton, 1992)

The loss of physical function

Older people cannot continue to function as they were once able to do. Sporting and recreational pursuits cannot be followed with the full vigour of youth. Reaction time, tiredness and pain intervene, and there may be some decline in vision and hearing. Some youthful dreams and ambitions may have to be relinquished. There may be some loss of sexual function. Each loss, perhaps small in itself, helps us to realize that we are no longer in our prime, and that life is limited.

As the process of physical decline accelerates, it is generally seen as a 'medical' problem, to be treated by doctors armed with their panoply of ameliorating drugs. The idea that physical decline may have an emotional side is less readily recognized. Yet a person who has been physically fit, dependent on no one and proud of their independence, will often find it difficult to cope emotionally with the increasing incapacity of old age. People who have never asked for help will need to do so, and for many this can be a humbling experience.

Moreover, people's hopes and expectations for the future will become increasingly prescribed by ageism. Their ability to fend for themselves is likely to decline, and they might eventually need to have assistance to accomplish even the most basic, personal daily tasks, such as bathing and toileting.

Both the contemplation and the reality of this scenario of decline can cause considerable emotional distress.

Losses through ill health

Older people can find that their health deteriorates. Loss through ill health can take many forms, and may affect people in many ways. Perhaps there is a loss of fitness, strength or mobility, or a general loss of well-being. Later on, matters may become worse. Diseases of the heart and lungs may severely weaken us, degenerative disease may cripple our ability to function nor-mally, or strokes and accidents may lead to a sudden loss of independence. Even the occasional memory lapse or forgetfulness might raise the spectre of dementia.

There are considerable social class differences relating to ill health and physical incapacity, particularly in older people. An Age Concern survey found that 35 per cent of people in the affluent 'AB' social groupings, but only 19 per cent of those doing unskilled or semi-skilled manual work, were considered to be 'very fit'. Similarly, of those in the highest group for incapacity, 9 per cent were from a professional or managerial background, and 22 per cent had semi-skilled or unskilled jobs (Bosanquet, 1978). Doyle (1983) argues this case more fully. The implication for counselling is that we are dealing with issues that arise as much from social structure as from the nature of old age and that, as a result, the social, emotional and economic realities of life need to be a normal part of the counselling agenda.

Losses through reduced social involvement

The 'disengagement' of older people from social life is only marginally a 'natural' process. Mostly it occurs because of the self-fulfilling nature of ageism. Yet the emotional and social welfare of older people depends crucially upon maintaining their engagement in social life, as it does in every generation. However, the ageing process does inevitably lead to the loss of two vital roles.

THE PARENTAL ROLE

The parental role disappears as children become independent and leave the family home. This can be an important loss, especially for women, and particularly for those who have not worked. The importance of the parent–child relationship can provide a deep and lasting meaning to life. As children reach adolescence, they can begin to establish social outlets which may be quite separate from the lives of their parents. When they leave home, parental investment in both time and energy is suddenly unnecessary, maybe even positively unwanted. When the last child leaves home a considerable gap can be left in the lives of the parents.

The rational response to this is that this process should be expected, and is not only natural, but that there should be joy in seeing children developing independent social roles. Yet many 'ex-parents' find the gap left in their life is difficult or even impossible to fill. They feel redundant. For those who have over-invested in their children and spent insufficient time developing their own lives, the feeling of emptiness can be immensely stressful.

PAID EMPLOYMENT

Paid, productive employment ends with retirement, and can constitute another significant loss. Questions about the meaning and value of life, and issues of self-worth, self-esteem and self-image may arise. Retirement can involve many losses:

- the daily routine of passing time in productive work is replaced by the passing of time with apparently little to do;
- the loss of companionship;
- the financial loss can involve a significant reduction in life-style and in quality of life.

Many retired people find it impossible to fill their increased leisure with worthwhile and satisfying pursuits, and this is particularly so for those who have not used their leisure time constructively in earlier life, or those who have invested their energy entirely in their work. The social class issues in this respect cannot be underestimated.

For many working-class groups ... there is a greater degree of dis-continuity between life in work and life in retirement. The factory environment itself encourages the development of a very limited range of skills, few of which have relevance beyond the factory gate. If work does have an influence on the non-work area of life, it may only be in a negative sense. People working different shifts from week to week may find it difficult to participate actively within the community; people doing assembly work may often be too tired to go out. The results of such practices may appear at their most acute in retirement, when individuals will require a far broader range of activities and relationships than their work environment may have allowed.

(Phillipson, 1982)

For current generations of older people, the concepts of 'leisure' and 'spare time' had little practical meaning. Life was concerned with struggle and work. Consequently, many older people are faced with spare time that they do not know how to fill constructively. Many will have spent their spare time in passive rather than active pursuits (e.g. watching television, or drinking at the local pub) and so are likely to experience more difficulty in coping with an enforced increase in leisure time.

The social difficulties experienced by older people from minority ethnic communities can be even greater. Their social role as an elder might be very different in their culture, and their experience of old age within a 'foreign' social setting may be alienating, especially if younger members of their family have, to some degree, adopted the dominant social attitudes towards older people.

The loss of relationships

Most people face the loss of significant friends and relatives regularly throughout life. We cannot anticipate such losses, and they are invariably painful. Perhaps by the time we reach our later years we should have become used to the process of grieving and loss, but this is rarely the case.

Indeed, as people grow older the loss of friends becomes more rather than less painful. The young are usually part of dynamic friendship groups which regularly gain and lose members. If loss is not painless, it is at least redeemable – there are other people to meet, other situations to enter, and other challenges to face. The young feel a strong and sometimes uncomfortable need to socialize. They are involved in both work and social groups. Life has an impetus of its own, and must go on. Grief must necessarily take its place. Yet even the young, with all of these apparent advantages, can find loss socially and emotionally intolerable. If this is so, some type of formal or informal counselling is often available to them.

Many older people find that their opportunities to engage in social life are reduced by factors such as ill health, declining physical and mental powers, and the financial costs of participation. They cannot readily find replacement relationships, and even when they do, they cannot entirely replace people to whom they have bonded over many decades.

Loneliness

Loneliness is the most common consequence of losing close friends. However, it is often the result of larger losses. It is the feeling of being apart – an inability to bridge a gap between where we are and where we want to be, or between what we desire and what we have. The morale and happiness of older people is more deeply affected by loneliness and related feelings, such as boredom, emptiness and exclusion, than by any other single factor. Some older people from minority ethnic backgrounds may feel particularly isolated, especially if their language skills do not allow them to socialize outside their immediate family.

Depression

Self-pity and depression will often follow losses of all kinds. Research has consistently found that the highest rate of symptoms of depression is in the 65+ age group (O'Leary, 1996). Depression is often associated with feelings of hopelessness and negative expectations about the future. In extreme situations, the loss of significant people can lead to loss of the will to live.

Suicide

When someone becomes depressed, when they feel that the future offers them nothing of value and when they question their own self-worth, thoughts of death and even suicide can become real. The rate of suicide increases with age. It is common to hear older people saying that they want to die.

The loss of financial and social status

Retirement brings a dramatic reduction in income and standard of living, especially for older people who have to rely mainly on the basic state pension. Tight budgeting is required, and any life-savings remain untouched in case of a 'rainy day'. The daily concerns of older people often revolve around the basic necessities of life, such as keeping warm and adequately clothed, and eating well. Such financial problems can lead to anxiety and despair.

Social status declines alongside financial status. Retired people are considered to be 'unproductive' in a society that ascribes status according to notions of a person's productivity. The growing proportion of older people within the population is frequently cited by the media as being a problem. Older people have become a financial burden, and this perception undoubtedly affects their feelings of self-worth. Some feel like scroungers, dependent upon benefits or charity – something many older people see as patronizing and hurtful.

The loss of independence

The ability to lead independent lives is an important cultural objective. When a person becomes dependent this can lead to hurt pride, anxiety and depression. When it happens suddenly, perhaps through illness or an accident, we are aware of the likely emotions that may accompany it. However, when disability arises through the gradual process of ageing, we often fail to recognize the equal significance given to that loss by the individual concerned.

There is no legitimate reason to believe that the onset of disability is easier to accept merely because of increasing age.

When older people have to rely upon others, more often than not it is their children who assume the role of carers. The former carer/dependency roles are thereby reversed, as the declining powers of 'ex-parents' make them increasingly dependent upon care provided by their children. Many older people feel this role reversal very deeply, and often with an intense sense of shame.

The spectre of residential or hospital care can then arise. The prospect of living in a residential home, however caring the staff may be, is always likely to be resisted in a society which values freedom and independence so highly. Where it becomes necessary, the process of preparing older people for institutional care is one that is often neglected. It is not necessarily regarded as a natural and unavoidable event that can be readily accepted. Rather, it is a crucial life event that, for many, can be deeply significant and even traumatic.

Counselling should be an integral element in preparing people to accept their need for care. It is essential to determine the personal wishes, desires and needs of the individual. If caring provision could more accurately reflect individual need, it would automatically be able to provide a more acceptable and more relevant service to dependent older people.

Older people from minority ethnic backgrounds

Older people from minority ethnic backgrounds are increasing in number. The 1991 census indicates that there were 164 306 people over the age of 65 years, and this figure is likely to double during the following decade. Although nationally the number of very old people from ethnic minorities remains small, their concentration in some parts of the country creates a particular need for local provision.

Many older people find that they are living away from their homeland, where the position of 'elder' has more social status, and their family members may be scattered around the world. For these reasons, it is often necessary to look back to their earlier lives, and to their diverse cultural, racial and social origins. On top of this, many will have suffered through racism, low income, poor housing, isolation and comparatively poor health. Indeed, minority ethnic elders can be at risk on three separate counts (Norman, 1985):

- they are old;
- they live in poor physical conditions, and meet with racial hostility;
- services are neither accessible nor ethnically sensitive.

Furthermore, their needs are often marginalized by assumptions (often mistaken) that they will be adequately looked after by their own communities (Social Services Inspectorate, 1998).

Loss of respect: the abuse of elders

Dependence makes people vulnerable. Older people can be as dependent as any other group, and equally vulnerable. Within any dependent–carer relationship, power rests with the care provider. Where the relationship is based upon love and respect, and an acceptance of the caring role, this presents few problems. However, when relationships are based upon uncertainty, annoyance and feelings of 'burden', older people can be abused, and the more dependent they become, the more vulnerable they are to abuse.

Abuse can assume many forms, some subtle and some more overt. Physical abuse may arise from neglect, rough handling or direct violence. Verbal abuse can take the form of implied threats, hurtful and derogatory comments, and strong insulting language. Emotional abuse can take many forms, leaving the dependent person feeling anxious and frightened.

Abuse is often difficult to detect. Older people who are dependent upon the care of their abusers are usually reluctant to speak out. In many cases they have no one to speak to. Often they feel that to say anything will worsen the situation, that they will be the loser, and that there will be no one else to care for them. Far from speaking out about the abuse, they will often praise the abuser to other people, particularly when their caring circle is small. Bruises are explained as accidents (older people bruise more easily), and depression is blamed on other factors.

In the same way as children, older people need to express their feelings and talk about their circumstances. Unlike children, however, they are adults who can determine what they want to do about the abuse (although older people with dementia are a special case, as they are unable to do so).

Death

In general, older people want to talk about their losses, their ill health, their incapacity and ultimately their death. Death can be a worrying, frightening prospect. They are not in control of what is going to happen to them, or when, and their very existence is uncertain. In reality, this was always so, but the young can – and often do – discount such thoughts. The old can no longer afford to do so, because death is imminent.

When death is close, there is a need to make sense of life. What has it been about? Have they wasted it? Has it had any real meaning or significance? Bland reassurance – too often the response that older people receive – is worthless, nor does it constitute counselling, which should seek to enable people to find meaning in their lives.

Then there is the question of what follows death. Religion and the religious precepts that we have been taught (whether accepted or rejected during the rest of our lifetime) may become more relevant or meaningful in this final part of our life. Is death just a return to ashes, or is there a better life hereafter? Whether we have believed in resurrection, reincarnation or nothing at all, old age raises such questions again.

What will become of those who are left behind? Will they be able to cope? The answers to these questions, whether positive or negative, can raise concerns. We might not like to think that our death will leave others unable to cope, but at the same time the prospect of our death having little or no impact on them may seem to be a judgement on our value.

Such concerns should be considered where appropriate in the counselling process. Often, however, we refuse to discuss such matters with older people. By so doing, we deny them the opportunity to come to terms with their mortality and their humanity. We also deny them the chance to look at their final years with an appropriate degree of optimism, for it is largely by discussing such concerns that they can be put to one side.

Ageist attitudes and the experience of old age

All of these agendas make counselling a vital technique for all those relatives, friends, doctors, social workers and others who have significant concern for older people. They are just some of the issues that might, or might not, be causing emotional and social distress. Even so, they are presented here with a 'health warning'. Ageist stereotyping creates a basis for the passive acceptance of the circumstances of old age. The stereotypical images of old age are not solely the result of natural life processes but, to a large extent, are socially constructed. If they do not create or determine the ageing process, they certainly enhance and accelerate it.

Older people can be taught to be helpless, with ageism acting as the teacher. Lubinski (1991) talks of a condition he describes as 'learned helplessness', and although he relates this specifically to people with dementia, it is something that can be observed in older people generally. It occurs when people no longer believe that they can or should control what is happening to them, and when other people have no expectation that the person concerned can make decisions for him- or herself.

Counselling should seek to overcome fatalistic and pessimistic models of ageing, which purport to be 'descriptive' but which become 'prescriptive' by limiting and confining the hopes and expectations of older people. Its task is not to reverse the ageing process, but to assist older people in rejecting stereotypes, to increase their knowledge of the ageing process, to develop an understanding of what old age is or can be, and to enhance their confidence in living life to the fullest possible extent for the longest possible time.

Ideally, counselling should be available to older people long before the ageing process reaches the 'pathological' stage. Perhaps the absence or inadequacy of counselling provision has contributed to the increasing levels of such pathology in older people. All counselling is concerned with helping people to come to terms with the paradoxes of life. Halmos (1978) says that 'psychological evidence is accumulating in support of the notion that sanity and an acceptance of dissonance may correlate with each other'. This is important when counselling older people, for it can create the most paradoxical of all paradoxes, namely *the belief in a happy and contented old age at a time of life when it is quite natural that decline and death are important concerns*.

The juxtaposition of the hope and expectation of life amidst the grief, pain and illness of old age, and the imminence of death, presents a counselling task of immense proportions.

Counselling agendas: the legacy of life history

A developmental psychology of ageing
The troubled emotions
Approaches to ageing
The unconscious world of meaning
Emotional repression
Professional assistance – the role of counselling
Self-image

It would be quite wrong to assume that the problems of older people are solely related to ageing. Older people are individuals, each of whom has survived a unique set of life experiences. We are each the product of our past. Our experience shapes us and forms our personality and character. Our history makes us what we are, and determines the nature of our social participation.

Understanding this is vital. It is difficult to understand other people, certainly older people, without being aware of their past. No one responds randomly to situations. We are all programmed by a complex system of learned responses and attitudes. Patterns of behaviour become discernible that can provide useful insight into how a person perceives life, takes up challenges and responds to difficult situations. They also provide some idea of how an individual is likely to respond to situations in the future. This makes individual responses more predictable. When faced with problems, each individual will respond in a particular way. In many respects this is the key to understanding a person's social performance.

- Some people seem to be dogged by misfortune and some by tragedy, while others regularly pass over opportunities.
- Some people always seem to be surrounded by friends who support them, while others appear to be let down regularly by people, and some seem to have few friends.

- Some people respond passively and some aggressively, while others sink into depression.
- Some people always appear to look optimistically to the future, while others remain permanently pessimistic.

This generality of individual behaviour highlights the importance to the counsellor of piecing together a full and accurate life history, almost as the first act of counselling. Many questions need to be asked.

- *When were they born, and where?* This gives the counsellor some general insight into the times and circumstances in which the individual was born, and during which they spent their most formative early years (this is particularly important when counselling people from minority ethnic backgrounds).
- *What was the composition of the family, and where did the person fit into it?* Much of their individual character was formed from the experiences, circumstances and quality of these early family relationships.
- *What were the dominant factors in family life?* These include the occupation and life-style of their parents, their social class allegiances, and their religious and other beliefs. Such factors are often crucial for our understanding of individual's social and emotional expectations of life.
- *What importance was attached by the family to education and social advancement?* What were their early hopes and desires for the future? How has the individual fared in comparison with these early life expectations?
- *What was their cultural background?* Older people from different social-class, cultural and ethnic backgrounds can have very different outlooks on life in older age, and it is important to know about these influences.
- *How important was, and is, religious belief?* Has religion been a means of making sense of existence and experience, and a way of shaping their morality and view of the world? In the youth of older people, religion was more important than it is now in helping people to come to terms with loss.
- *What were their main periods of employment?* Was work drudgery or a satisfying and fulfilling experience?
- *What was the nature of their life-style during successive stages of their life?* Were they affluent or poor? How did they spend their time? Do they feel that life has been rewarding?
- *How did marriage and family life affect them?* Or what were the reasons for them not marrying or not having children? How formative was this stage of their lives, and to what extent have they been able to relinquish these former roles happily?
- *How satisfactory are their current relationships?* These include relationships with life-long friends and relatives and, in particular, their relationships with their children.

All of these factors will have been crucial in the formation of personality and the personal qualities that older people bring with them to cope with their final years. The information which the counsellor gathers about these matters is vital. Within it lies a wealth of knowledge that will give important insights into the person concerned – a multitude of relationships (satisfactory and unsatisfactory, terminated and continuing), a variety of social attachments and commitments, limitless hopes, desires, wishes and impulses, an infinite number of insights into and beliefs about the nature of life and society, innumerable sources of conflict, despair and disappointment, and an equal number of methods of dealing with them. All these and more, over a considerable number of years, will have contributed to the make-up of the older individual.

To obtain this information may require many hours of careful conversation. The more different the individual's background is to the personal experience of the counsellor – and this can be particularly so when counselling older people from minority ethnic communities – the more necessary such information becomes. The effort will be worthwhile. It will elicit vital insights, and can assist in the formation of a good counselling relationship. The time taken by the counsellor can indicate that he or she is genuinely interested in them as 'a person' rather than just as an 'older person', or 'a problem'. The task is made easier by the fact that many older people find reviewing their life a pleasurable experience, but what specifically is the counsellor looking for?

A developmental psychology of ageing

Erikson (1965) developed the notion that unresolved issues from earlier stages of life influence the way in which people deal with problems in later life. He described eight such stages, in each of which one has to resolve specific psychosocial issues. Understanding how an older person has succeeded or failed at each of these stages can be important for gaining insight into how they will cope with old age.

1. *Early infancy (0 to 18 months), and the development of basic trust or a sense of mistrust.* Infants whose early life experience does not allow them to satisfy their emotional and physical needs will, according to Erikson, fail to develop a basic trust both in people and in life generally. The psychological problems this causes can prevent the formation of trusting relationships, and consequently reduce their ability to form such relationships at each subsequent stage of personal development.

2. *Early childhood (18 months to 3 years), in which the child develops either a sense of autonomy or a sense of shame or doubt.*

3. *Childhood (3 to 6 years), in which the child develops either a sense of initiative or a sense of guilt.* Children need to develop a sense of their own personal identity – separate from that of other people, even those closest to them – so that they are able to have a will of their own and initiate their own actions. Erikson describes these stages as being 'decisive for the ratio of love and hate, co-operation and wilfulness, freedom of self-expression, and its expression'. Failure to do so leads to feelings of personal weakness, incompetence, powerlessness and badness, leading to an

inhibited ability to act according to their own initiative or desire. Again, this can affect the individual for the rest of his or her life.

4. *Middle childhood (6 to 12 years), in which the child develops a sense of industry or, alternatively, a sense of inferiority.* The 'inner self', which consists of the confidence and belief we have developed in ourselves, has now been formed, and the child is now able to move out into the world in a competitive state with other people. This stage is about 'getting things done', and doing so by our own personal effort. Most children move into the wider world with some degree of inquisitiveness and optimism, but many will fail to live up to their own expectations, or to the expectations of others. This can lead to feelings of isolation, inferiority and despair, and a possible drift into mediocrity or inadequacy.

5. *Adolescence (12 to 20 years), in which the individual develops either a sense of ego identity or identity diffusion.* Adolescence, the transition to full adult life and its responsibilities, runs alongside major hormonal, emotional, social and sexual changes. It is a time when the issues of earlier stages, even when these have been successfully resolved, undergo a major reassessment. Do our own inner wishes and desires coincide or conflict with the wishes and desires of our social group? Where there is conflict between our inner desires and social realities, major doubts can arise about our personal identity, our sexuality and our social role.

6. *Early adulthood (20 to 35 years), and the development of intimacy or a sense of ego isolation.* Erikson associates this stage with the ability to commit ourselves to other people in new, mutually satisfying, fulfilling and long-lasting relationships. This requires an ability to share, and a willingness to give a degree of personal commitment and therefore to relinquish a degree of personal independence. Where this struggle is resolved in favour of isolation, people are in danger of becoming self-absorbed and developing a sense of being alone. Thereafter, they will tend to withdraw from intimate relationships with other people.

7. *Middle adulthood (35 to 60 years), and the development of generativity or a sense of stagnation.* Generativity is described as an interest and involvement in establishing and guiding future generations, mainly (but not totally) expressed through productive employment and child-rearing. Stagnation implies a general feeling of lack of personal involvement and fulfilment in life.

8. *Late adulthood/old age (60 years onwards), in which older people either develop a sense of ego identity or drift into feelings of despair commonly associated with old age.* This stage refers to the kind of issues and outcomes considered in the previous chapter.

Erikson's stages describe the main struggles encountered during each period of life. The end of one period does not indicate that particular crises have been resolved, or will remain unresolved for ever, but the degree to which they have been resolved – positively or negatively – will be important in later stages of life.

- *Those people whose life journey has been successful will be able to place their life in context and view their final years positively. They may feel that their losses are unfortunate, but they will tend to be more successful in finding responses which enable them to remain essentially optimistic.*
- *People who have been less successful will tend to view the ageing process as unfair and debilitating, and as a catastrophe that will restrict their ability to cope adequately with old age.*

Thus the past has implications for how a person is able to progress through life. Erikson's theory has taught us that people's passage through life, and their successful and unsuccessful adaptations, can have an important bearing on how they adapt to the problems of old age, and the counsellor needs to be aware of any 'unresolved' business.

- The non-trusting adult may have had difficulties from infancy onwards.
- Individuals who show an inability to act for themselves may well retain unresolved insecurities from their childhood.
- Individuals who are uncertain about their identity and role may well have been carrying those doubts since their adolescence.
- Individuals who are failing in their personal relationships may have been doing so since their early adult years.
- Individuals who feel isolated and detached from life around them may have had similar feelings dating from their middle years.

The troubled emotions

Failure at any stage of this developmental journey through life can result in an individual experiencing troubled emotions – the principal focus of counselling. The main emotions that cause problems in our lives are:

- depression and despair;
- anger;
- frustration;
- anxiety.

To some degree these emotions are experienced by every person at each stage of their life. Mostly we are able to cope. However, counselling is useful when such feelings become unbearably intense or indefinitely prolonged. Uncontrolled emotion can lead to attitudes and behaviour that restrict a person's ability to lead life to its fullest potential. They affect their outlook on life, cloud their judgement and cause them to act in ways that might otherwise be untypical.

Yet it is wrong to deny older people their right to these emotions. Their emotional capacity is not diminished by age, and they continue to experience all of these feelings. The idea that older people 'mellow' is a dangerous generalization. Some older people do become more sanguine, but others do not, while some older people who become dependent on care provided by others may curtail an honest and healthy expression of how they feel.

Approaches to ageing

The attitude that a person takes to ageing is therefore immensely varied. Reichard *et al.* (1962) identified five general responses.

1. *Constructive* – an approach taken by people who have a range of desirable personal and social attributes, including self-sufficiency, tolerance and optimism.

2. *Dependent* – again, an approach taken by people who are well adjusted and satisfied, but who have a largely passive, perhaps even lazy approach to life.

3. *Defensive* – an approach taken by people who make themselves busy so that they do not have to face up to the problem of ageing; often individuals who are obsessively hard-working and self-contained.

4. *Hostile* – an approach taken by people who have a history of poor social adjustment, who tend to react aggressively and suspiciously to problems, and who are afraid of growing old.

5. *Self-hating* – an approach taken by people who are socially inadequate, with low self-esteem, and who feel that they have little control over their lives.

The unconscious world of meaning

Older people do not adopt these approaches knowingly. In looking for patterns of behaviour the counsellor has to make a distinction between an individual's 'internal' and 'external' worlds, and the 'conscious' and 'subconscious' experiences that contribute to current problems. The belief that human motivation is straightforward, that we understand what we are doing and why we are doing it, and are fully aware of the likely outcome, is naïve. The idea that our behaviour is rational, and that we act according to known motivations and drives that are (or should be) under our own personal control, does not measure up to human experience. The belief that we always know how we think, feel and behave, and what motivates us, is false.

Ask older people how they feel about ageing, and most will be puzzled by the question. Ageing is an inevitable process, and it is not something most people have thought about, so they do not have any particular feelings about it.

Even those people who have some knowledge of psychology, and believe that they have taken into account significant or traumatic life events when explaining the difficulties they have experienced in their life, do not have a full self-picture. The situation is seldom so straightforward. Experience is continuous and cumulative, involving an enormous volume of daily interchange with people and things. Most of these seem to be trivial and inconsequential, consisting of the habits, beliefs and emotions of everyday life. However, it is often these repetitive and persistent minutiae of living that have a more lasting effect on how we lead our lives. We rarely question them, yet they determine how we respond to people and situations, probably to a greater extent than the more obvious tragedies and traumas, which are usually more occasional and isolated incidents in our lives.

Thus older people are a product of history at both a conscious and subconscious level. Decisions taken at one stage of life inevitably affect what happens at each subsequent stage. Counselling is usually most helpful when it is able to throw light upon the important life events and decisions that have been made in the past. This means that counselling older people often has to start with birth, rather than in old age.

Emotional repression

Many aspects of self-understanding are denied because we are encouraged, and perhaps even forced, to consign 'unwanted' and 'uncomfortable' aspects of our lives to the subconscious. Freud called this a 'seething cauldron' of all our wishes, impulses and desires that are considered to be socially unaccept-able, or which might be dangerous or anxiety-provoking. We do not admit them to our consciousness. The 'unconscious world of meaning' consists of those aspects of ourselves and our experience that have been disallowed, disqualified or made unacceptable by some external moral force.

The problem is that many feelings and desires that are repressed are natural. They have become social taboos. The individual cannot accept them because they are inhibited by some form of social, religious or moral imperative that is imposed during childhood and reinforced throughout life. Most people never evaluate and so never come to terms with their inhibi-tions. This can lead to conflict arising between our conscious desires and the unconscious restraints that we have been obliged to construct against them – a situation which can result in the development of a serious level of internal disharmony.

The younger counsellor needs to understand that older people have usually been subject to a greater number of 'moral imperatives', enforced more rigorously, than have successive younger generations. Traditional religion (often a powerful force in the lives of older people) and its teaching suggest that we should be able to deny or repress quite basic human motivations, particularly those surrounding sexual feelings and activity. 'Disqualified' feelings and desires and unwanted emotions are therefore consigned to the unconscious – necessary for our social survival but harmful to our emotional survival. Everyone has to do this to some degree.

This situation runs counter to Freudian analysis, which has shown that to repress feelings, desires and emotions in this way entails sacrificing part of reality – an important part of ourselves. The energy used to sustain denial and to load our subconscious with forbidden desires can lead to irrational, illogical and apparently senseless behaviour that can only be interpreted when we understand this part of our mind. Internal psychological dis-harmony often has tragic consequences when powerful and pressing forces operating from within the subconscious begin to dominate our conscious world. The origin of such inner disharmony is not attributable to old age, but is rooted in earlier times.

Professional assistance – the role of counselling

When troubled emotions appear there is a tendency to send for the expert – the doctor who provides drugs, the psychologist who offers therapy, or the social worker who assesses our social requirements. These professionals have become used to taking control or assuming responsibility, a tendency that is both unwise and, ultimately, self-defeating. At best, they can only provide palliatives, as they rarely investigate the origins of the troubled emotions.

Only the individual can both experience his or her emotions and come to terms with them. Counselling is based on the premise that everyone, even if they appear to have given up hope, have become totally prone to anxiety, or have lost themselves in the irrationality of their anger, possesses within themselves the only means of control available. Even the most damaged person can reassume control over his or her emotional life. The individual alone has the ability to reassert control, and to overcome his or her feelings.

Self-image

Self-image is the route through which troubled people can be helped to regain personal control. We all have a picture of ourselves as people who either possess or lack certain skills, abilities, aptitudes and qualities. We function within a social setting in which we see ourselves fulfilling, or failing to fulfil, particular roles. We construct a picture or image of ourselves throughout our lives that becomes a powerful motivating force. Self-image is what leads us to success and great achievements, and enables us to progress through life with a feeling of achievement and satisfaction. Alternatively, it can hold us back from achieving, and be the cause of ongoing failure, impotence and incompetence, constantly dragging us down to ever-deepening levels of self-criticism, depression and despair. Self-image consists of two factors.

The 'ideal' self and the 'actual' self

The 'ideal' self is composed of a set of images an individual harbours about the kind of person they should be, or would like to be, and by what standards of behaviour and achievement they judge themselves.

Set against this is the 'actual' self. This is the individual's assessment of their social performance. When there is a serious imbalance between the 'ideal' self and the 'actual' self, self-image is likely to be low, and this can have a major impact on the way in which people live their lives.

- Where the ideal self is unattainably perfect, or where assessment of one's social performance is unfairly harsh, the imbalance between the ideal and actual self will lead to low self-esteem. With older people, this can be important when they refuse to recognize their declining abilities and powers. Any inability to achieve an 'ideal' level of social performance can lead to despair, anger, depression, frustration and unnecessary anxiety about the future.
- If the ideal self is easily attained, self-esteem may be satisfied at a much lower level of social performance, but then the person fails to live fully or to reach their potential. Again this is important with older people, particularly when faced with ageist attitudes which persistently under-estimate the abilities of older people and the contributions that they can make to social life.

Thus whatever the combination of ideal and actual selves, imbalance will have a profound effect on self-image. Everyone needs to have a sense of personal worth, an identified social role, and to be realistically optimistic about the future. For older people, it can be difficult to maintain a positive self-image. Ageism would have us believe that it is impossible to be optimistic in older age, because there is little to be optimistic about.

An additional problem is that, although the counsellor can take an optimistic stance, this cannot be imposed upon older people. People need to genuinely feel or internalize it. Counselling has to focus on new ways of helping older people to look at the present, past and future, and to recondition the way in which they look at themselves, encouraging them to re-examine their supposed limitations and failings, and to view more optimistically what it is possible to achieve in old age. The value of counselling in facilitating this process can now be considered.

PART TWO

The process of counselling

The counselling relationship

> Client-centred counselling
>
> Power and the counselling relationship
>
> Resistance to counselling and counsellors

Two people are primarily concerned in the counselling process, namely the counsellor and the counsellee. The quality of counselling depends essentially on the quality of the relationship established between them. In this sense, the skills of counselling are secondary. As Rogers (1951a) said, 'In our experience, the counsellor who tries to use a method is doomed to be unsuccessful unless this method is genuinely in line with his own attitudes'.

This is important for any would-be counsellor. Counselling is not a complex body of skills that takes precedence over the more intangible interactions that take place between people. Technique is subservient to people.

In behaviourist approaches there is quite a different priority, where behaviour rather than the person is the central area of concern. The objective is change through a process of conditioning, rather than growth through a process of self-understanding. A set of scientifically established responses is applied to observed behaviour, and the method seeks to reinforce the 'required' behaviour. The 'human' factor, which is unquantifiable and therefore 'unscientific', is removed as far as possible.

Counselling is an 'art' rather than a science, relying heavily upon the unquantifiable impact of human relationships, first to determine the problems, then to develop self-awareness of those problems, and finally to enable the individual to decide what he or she is going to do. There are many different 'schools' of counselling, and it is not the intention here to consider them in any detail. The work of Carl Rogers has been particularly important in developing an understanding of the counselling relationship. His 'client-centred', 'non-directive' approach will be central to the approach adopted here, as it provides a sound basis upon which to build counselling skills. It is also relatively 'safe' for 'non-professional' people to use. In this approach, the type of relationship required has a number of important facets that are particularly important for those working with older people.

Client-centred counselling

Counselling is a 'client-centred' approach, with the needs and interests of the counsellee always central within the counselling relationship. There should be real concern about his or her well-being. If this concern is genuine, there should be no problem. Problems arise when the counsellor finds that the counsellee is difficult or awkward, or their behaviour is particularly hard to accept. Older people *can* be difficult. Not all older people are lovable, and many can be positively cantankerous, while others are apparently 'content' in their depression, and rigid in their thinking and life-style. In such circumstances, the counsellor may feel that it is difficult to develop the warmth which allows a close relationship to develop.

A non-directive approach

Counsellors cannot enter into a client-centred relationship with the intention of directing counsellees to alter their attitudes, change their behaviour or take control of their emotions. It may be that we believe this would be in their best interests, but it is often like telling a drowning man to swim when he does not know how to do so. It is likely that all counsellors will have their own agendas, including:

- a personal view of the best outcome for the individual;
- a professional objective or task to achieve.

To enhance the process of counselling, these agendas need to be harnessed and made secondary to the needs of the individual. The reason can perhaps best be understood by stating the case negatively. A 'directive' relationship has many implicit assumptions:

- that 'we' know best;
- that 'they' are not capable of reaching their own solutions to their problems.

Relationships based on these assumptions are unequal, with a dominant and a submissive party. They work only if the submissive party conforms, remains submissive to what they are told, and if there are no internal or external restraints preventing them from carrying through the directive. When directives are ignored or refused, the basis of the relationship crumbles. Moreover, if the solution to personal problems depends upon submission, it does not augur well for its continued effectiveness when the 'director' is no longer around.

Non-direction and respect for the other person are closely linked.

- Directiveness demeans individuality and dignity, and undermines feelings of self-worth.
- It removes personal responsibility in the belief that the counsellee is incapable of taking such responsibility.
- The director assumes a wisdom and importance that is justified only in the most extreme circumstances.

- The individual is denied the right to self-determination.
- We undermine the individual's ability to make sound decisions, and deny their potential for personal development and growth.
- We fail to treat them as people of worth, and by our own behaviour we subtly devalue them.

Non-judgemental attitudes

Another problem arises when the counsellor is faced with someone whose behaviour is, or has been, personally or morally unacceptable. There are numerous reasons for counsellors to make judgements about older people. Perhaps an old person has been caught shoplifting, or found to be abusing children, or has taken to practising regular masturbation, perhaps in public. Perhaps it is merely that they are rude or offensive in the way in which they treat other people.

The counsellor has to try to be 'morally neutral'. Counselling seeks to discover the causes of difficult or unacceptable behaviour, whether this be anger, frustration, sorrow or grief. The counselling objective is to understand the feelings and attitudes that underlie behaviour, not to make personal judgements about such things. Any hint of disapproval or condemnation by the counsellor can result in the erection of barriers that can prevent the formation of an adequate and dynamic counselling relationship.

Clearly there are limits to anyone's neutrality, but it is important that the counsellor accepts people as they are, rather than how they might want them to be. When a counsellor reaches his or her tolerance threshold, considerable care has to be taken. Troubled people will be used to disapproval, and the disapproval of the counsellor is unlikely to be effective, merely confirming that they are no different to anyone else who has tried to help in the past.

Unfortunately, this clearly fails to deal with the feelings of the counsellor. However, several techniques can be used that allow personal views to be expressed, but without alienating the counsellee.

- Our personal feelings can be presented as the 'general' social view of what they are doing.
- We can express concern about the impact that their attitudes and behaviour can have on other people, and the negative responses which they might illicit.
- We can present our views simply as personal feelings and opinions, that have no particular significance apart from the need to be frank and honest.

Unconditional positive regard

If counselling is to be helpful, counsellors must look positively at the counsellee. Rogers (1951b) talks of the need for 'unconditional positive regard', and Geldard has defined it as follows.

Unconditional positive regard involves accepting the client completely, in a non-judgemental way, as the person that he is, with all his frailties and weaknesses and with all his strengths and positive qualities. Having unconditional positive regard doesn't mean that I agree with or accept the values of the client for myself, but it does mean that I accept the client as he is now, value him as a person, am non-judgemental of his behaviour, and do not try to put my values onto him. I consequently enable him to feel free to be open in exploring his inner processes without censoring them for fear of criticism. This gives him the best opportunity for increased personal awareness and consequent growth.

(Geldard, 1989)

Counsellors cannot look upon older people as inferior or abnormal, despite all of the difficulties their social behaviour might present. The counsellee should be seen as an individual, perhaps in difficulty, but someone who is capable through their own inner resources of overcoming their problems and redirecting their lives. For the counsellor, this has several implications.

- They should believe that older people have inherent worth and dignity.
- They should respect their right to self-determination.
- They should accept that they are capable of adopting personal attitudes and values that are in their own self-interest.

Moreover, counsellors should continue to adopt this position, even if the counsellee proceeds to select behaviour and attitudes that we feel are wrong, inappropriate or harmful.

Empathy

The counsellor should try to view the world as the counsellee sees it. This involves trying to place oneself in the mind and the situation of the counsellee. Adopting this approach will make it more likely that we will understand some of the apparently illogical or self-damaging aspects of their social performance. Rogers (1951a) and Geldard (1989) describe what empathy means.

to assume, in so far as he is able, the internal frame of reference of the client, to perceive the world as the client sees it, to perceive the client himself as he is seen by himself, to lay aside all perceptions from the external frame of reference while doing so, and to communicate something of this empathetic understanding to the client.

(Rogers, 1951a)

I try to think and feel the way the client does, so that I can share with him what he is discovering about himself. I go on a journey with him, hand-in-hand, listening to everything he says, matching his every move, being right beside him. This is what is meant by empathy. Being empathetic means having a togetherness with the client, and as a consequence creating a trusting environment in which he feels cared for and safe. In such an environment the client can talk about his darkest secrets, his innermost feelings, and the things that seem to him to be so terrible or so personal that he does not dare to talk to others about them.

(Geldard, 1989)

It is vital that the counsellor avoids denying the problems of an individual, as they perceive them to be. Nothing is usefully served by denying the way a person feels about his or her problems and difficulties. It should be sufficient that they feel that way for us to take them seriously. To deny the way a person feels is to fail to respond appropriately. It can lead to the belief that we do not really care about how they feel. Our personal feelings and interpretations are of little value in this respect. Thus the ability of the counsellor to enter into the mind of the counsellee does not merely involve being sympathetic. Sympathy is often patronizing, and by its very nature is often unhelpful.

Empathy means that the therapist senses accurately the feelings of another person, and can communicate this understanding to them. It allows them to be so much inside the private world of the other person that they can clarify not only the meanings of which the other person is aware, but even those meanings just below the level of awareness.

Empathy enables the counsellor to form some tentative explanation or interpretation of what is happening to counsellees; what they are thinking, why, and linking this with their social performance. This is clearly an essential stage in the process of counselling. The counsellor will have some idea of the problems the counsellee faces, but until some ideas are formed about why such problems have arisen it is difficult to focus on the direction that counselling should take.

(Rogers 1951b)

However, there are also dangers in the concept of empathy. It is never possible to be certain that we know what is going on in the mind of another person, particularly if they are facing difficulties which we have not experienced. Nor can a counsellor assume that any particular insight holds true for any length of time. Consequently, there is a continual need to test and retest the assumptions that we make, in order to check that they are in fact accurate.

The counsellor can never be dogmatic. Certainty in a counselling relationship is a dangerous illusion, whilst doubt is a spur to the further clarification and updating of the counsellor's understanding – so vital to the counselling process.

Genuineness

Counselling is a two-way process. The counsellor should be able to relate honestly and genuinely to the counsellee, and should be capable where necessary of revealing his or her own feelings. 'The more the therapist is himself or herself in the relationship, putting up no professional front or personal façade, the greater is the likelihood that the client will change and grow in a constructive manner' (Rogers, 1951b).

Counsellors often have to share parts of themselves. People are more likely to share with those who are prepared to admit to their own feelings and weaknesses. Often we have to be prepared to talk openly and honestly, sharing those feelings and experiences that we have in common. Counselling cannot be conducted on the basis that 'they' must tell 'us' about their most intimate and guarded thoughts and feelings, whilst we are not prepared to talk about our own.

For troubled people there is no more depressing person than the paragon, the person with no personal difficulties, the person with all the answers.

Paragons highlight inadequacy rather than ameliorating distress. The helpful counsellor has to be a 'real' or genuine person. There is no room for false professional fronts, for the maintenance of 'social distance', for assumptions of superiority, or for similar aspects of so-called 'professional' relationships. It is important that counsellors present themselves as people, rather than as 'a doctor', 'a social worker' or 'a priest'. The counsellor should assume no special status or authority, but should take part in an open and honest relationship.

Trust and confidentiality

Trust is vital to an open and honest relationship, particularly when dealing with issues surrounding troubled personal emotions. No one reveals their innermost feelings to people they do not trust. If we believe that someone might be unsympathetic, or use information in ways we do not want, we remain guarded about what we reveal. The counsellor has to develop a sense of trust, and the counsellee has to be given firm grounds for believing in their trustworthiness.

Confidentiality is an essential basis for a trusting relationship. The sharing of intimate information, which might lead to embarrassment, guilt or anxiety if revealed, is not likely to take place if there is suspicion that it might be passed on or used to determine future plans that run counter to the personal wishes of the counsellee. Information given to the counsellor should be kept in strict confidence, but as Geldard (1989) points out, there may be circumstances in which this is not entirely possible, including:

- the need to keep records;
- the requirements of professional supervision;
- situations where other people may need to be protected;
- when one is working in conjunction with other professionals while participating in educational training programmes, conferences, workshops and seminars (but here, anonymity can be maintained);
- in cases where the law requires disclosure of information.

Where any of these situations apply, or in any other circumstances where information might need to be shared, this should take place with the knowledge and, where possible, the permission of the counsellee.

Power and the counselling relationship

The counselling relationship, as described, is an ideal to be striven towards rather than an attainable reality – but it is no less important for that. The closer we come to attaining the ideal, the more effective we will be as counsellors. Yet of all the factors that can skew the counselling relationship, power is the most important.

It is important that counsellors recognize personal and professional agendas, and can be open about what they are. The counsellor should ask him- or herself the following questions.

- Are we looking for change?
- Do we have a time limit?
- What do we expect for ourselves from our efforts?

Such agendas are usually unhelpful, and can place the counsellor in impossible positions. Some school counsellors have responsibility for discipline. Some young offenders are counselled by police officers. Some doctors try to counsel with a busy waiting-room outside. Some social workers, under pressure to place (or not to place) older people, try to seek their views. Some residential care staff try to talk to residents in the midst of a busy workload. In such situations, the agenda can not only become more important than the needs of the individual, but can lead to feelings that transfer blame or responsibility on to the counsellee.

- Why can't they be more reasonable?
- Why do they continue making demands on me?
- Why can't they just conform to my wishes?
- Why do they not realize that they are making my life difficult?
- And especially when I am being so reasonable and nice – it is ungrateful!

If these become the overriding concern of the counsellor, the seeds of counselling failure have been sown. The counselling relationship is not assisted by symbols of authority and status – it is not achieved on the psychiatrist's couch, or over the doctor's desk, or by fleeting social work visits.

This is important with regard to older people. Perhaps more than any other generation, they can respond badly to being manipulated or compelled into situations not of their choosing, no matter how well intentioned such actions may be. Yet when older people become frail or incapacitated it is all too easy for other people to assume rights and responsibilities over their lives. This is usually unjustified, and is often deeply resented. It is particularly true when older people become physically frail. Their declining self-caring abilities are often mistaken for an inability to think and make decisions. Carers might have to feed, dress, wash and toilet them, yet if we ignore their feelings and dignity, we risk transforming the caring task into a resented imposition.

Professional power

The power of the professional worker produces many problems, not least the power to assess individual need in order to provide or withhold service. These decisions can have a major impact on the lives of older people, and such power can 'skew' the relationship away from genuineness. The honesty within the relationship should ensure that there is no denial concerning the power of the counsellor, who should be aware of his or her power and should not use it within the counselling relationship. Counsellors of older people have to develop an ability to present themselves as safe, non-threatening people who, whilst they might possess certain powers, will not use them without the counsellee's willing and informed consent. This is not easily done. We can gain compliance with an explicit or implicit threat to withdraw our care or support. Even the possibility that we might do so (even if we have no such intention) can be a significant threat. People will be careful not to say or do anything that might upset us, or which is contrary to what they believe we want of them. Older people will speak frankly and honestly only if the relationship is one of mutual trust and confidence.

The task of forming power-free relationships is also affected by ageism. Ageist attitudes do not expect older people to make demands. Increasingly, it is older people rather than children who are expected to be 'seen, but not heard'. Many older people do have a more deferential attitude to professional carers than younger generations. As a generation, older people were brought up in times when more deference was both expected by and shown to professional people. Moreover, a high proportion of 'dependent' older people come from working-class backgrounds, where more deference was expected and shown to their 'betters'. The result is a tendency to defer, to hide their feelings, to accept their lives without complaint, and to be grateful for even the smallest act of kindness. Many older people feel that to complain is to appear ungrateful. Moreover, as the ageist paradigm is increasingly accepted, they feel that complaining serves no purpose.

Such attitudes can prevent genuineness within the counselling relationship. Indeed, they are features that distinguish counselling of older people from that of all other age groups. It is too easy to accept the non-complaining, accepting and even fatalistic façade that older people present. It is easier to walk away believing that there is no problem, no upset and no pain.

The carer-counsellor

The problems of the 'informal' carers – the carer-counsellor, the close friend or relative – who find themselves caring for an older person also have to be considered. Whilst having the benefit of knowing the person more intimately, problems can arise from too much intimacy. Personal emotions and feelings become involved, and this can mean that we are not sufficiently dispassionate to interpret all of the factors which contribute to the problems. It may also be that 'we' are part of 'the problem', but unable to see or admit this.

Although this does not make the task of the carer-counsellor impossible, as many suggest, it can cause difficulties. It is important that carer-counsellors are aware of the problem of closeness, that they challenge and re-investigate long-held assumptions, and that they carefully analyse their own feelings. If this is done, then the role of carer-counsellor is potentially a crucially helpful one.

Resistance to counselling and counsellors

Sometimes it may become clear that certain people are unable to counsel a particular individual, although the reason might not be immediately apparent.

- Some older people may be opposed to the very idea of counselling, and may associate it with psychological or mental illness. After all, counselling did not exist when older people were young.
- There may be cultural differences in accepting counselling (for example, O'Leary (1996) discussed Irish reticence).
- Some people, especially men, may associate counselling with personal weakness or inadequacy (Scher, 1981), and regard it as undermining self-sufficiency and personal autonomy.
- Insecure people (i.e. those who could benefit most) may be less willing to expose themselves to counselling.
- Some older people may fear change, or feel that change is not possible 'at their age'.
- Some people will prefer a counsellor of the same sex, whilst others will prefer to talk to someone of the opposite sex.
- Some people will trust younger rather than older counsellors, and vice versa.
- Some people will confide more readily in people of high status, whilst others might be put off by it.
- Sometimes a past incident might adversely colour a person's judgement of a prospective counsellor (especially a carer-counsellor), and this situation might be quite unknown to those concerned.

Such prejudices and preferences exist, but they are not common. What is more important is that the potential counsellor presents as a warm, caring and understanding person, with a genuine interest and concern for the counsellee.

6 The skills of counselling

However important, the counselling relationship is insufficient in itself. In order to counsel effectively, there are skills that need to be developed and understood. Counselling is the art of communication, but a very special kind of communication.

- It is communication with a troubled individual who is experiencing some kind of emotional or social stress.
- It seeks to allow the individual to explore, express and 'feel' their emotions.
- It seeks to assist the individual in developing self-awareness by enabling them to understand and define their own problems.
- It seeks to help the individual to measure their problems against social reality.
- It seeks to help the individual to make decisions about their life, and to find their own solution to their particular dilemmas.

Counselling skills enable this process. At its best, counselling involves a journey of healing and transformation which ends with a person who is more aware, and more able to cope with the pressures, strains and disappointments that their life entails. But how is such a process achieved? What is the nature of the journey through which the person passes?

Social distress

The counselling process starts with troubled people who have feelings of worthlessness, inadequacy, fear or vulnerability that are affecting their lives, sometimes in serious and possibly damaging ways, and whose relationships with other important people have become difficult or have even broken down completely. Their self-image, for a variety of reasons, may be extremely low. It is not that such people are 'inadequate' or 'worthless', but that they feel themselves to be so. These feelings are reinforced by dominant social explanations, usually based upon individual pathology, that if something is going wrong in their life it must be their own fault – the result of some personal inadequacy, corruption or laziness.

This view of the origins of social distress needs to be challenged, and a more adequate alternative found which emphasizes the social origins of personal distress. Sherman (1981) developed his *'social breakdown syndrome'* to provide a more comprehensive explanation which integrates many of the factors that can contribute to the social and emotional demoralization of older people. He describes a 'vicious circle of increasing incompetence' that demonstrates how a combination of factors can contribute towards the development of a troubled personality. Perhaps one criticism of Sherman's circle is that it does not emphasize sufficiently the impact which ageism has upon the experience of older people. If powerful social attitudes undermine old age, it is not surprising that older people do not experience a sense of personal fulfilment and well-being. If society has no use for older people, it is little wonder that older people feel that their lives are without meaning. Here this vital element has been added to Sherman's circle.

1. The impact of ageism on self-image and social functioning.

2. This works on some 'personal pre-condition' or susceptibility to psychological breakdown.

3. The individual begins to develop a social label as being 'deficient' or 'incompetent'.

4. The effect of the label in inducting the individual into a 'sick' or 'dependent' social role.

5. The gradual atrophy of the social skills and emotional resilience of the individual, which confirms the social label.

6. The self-identification and acceptance by the individual of the role of being 'sick' or 'inadequate'.

7. This acceptance is confirmed by the impact of ageism upon self-image and social functioning.

8. The cycle repeats itself.

It is into this cycle of social distress that counselling seeks to enter. The degree and the cause of social distress are not uniform. Feelings and situations which some people cope with adequately can become unbearable for others.

Social distress arises directly from self-image.

- Who do we believe ourselves to be?
- What is our role, our value and our usefulness?
- What is the meaning and purpose of our lives?

These enormous questions beset everyone at various stages of life, but they can be a particular problem for older people, whose self-image is closely linked with morale that may have sunk so low that, for many, they do not wish to continue living. It is important to stress that self-image is a powerful determinant of attitudes and social behaviour. Older people may have to accept many losses – in social role, status, and a declining ability to lead independent lives – and they have to adjust to this. Many fail, and it is when morale is low that people find it difficult to cope with life, and counselling can become vitally important.

The counselling process focuses upon self-image. The task of the counsellor is to help older people to modify their self-image so that it is both more positive and more in line with reality.

Skill: developing a relaxed, non-threatening atmosphere

The creation of a conducive atmosphere is important for facilitating work with distressed people. The counselling setting should be as relaxed as possible. The room should offer privacy and warmth. A cup of tea or something similar is a good relaxing agent. Sitting comfortably is also important, preferably fairly close together, although not too close, and facing each other. Signs of tension in the counsellor are easily transmitted, and can put people on edge.

Skill: presenting behaviour

First impressions are important. This can be particularly important when the counsellor has some authority or power, either to make important decisions in a person's life, or where they are dependent upon the support of a carer-counsellor. The counsellor should present as a supportive and caring person, and the initial conversation should be friendly and light.

The counsellor should be aware of potential worries that the person may feel and offer some words of reassurance about the purpose of their meeting. People talk more openly and freely when they feel at ease, safe and relaxed. If the counsellor is a doctor, priest, social worker, etc., or an important carer, this will not necessarily be an advantage, nor does it give us any right to intimate revelation. Status and position stand for little compared to patience, tolerance and a willing ear. Devoting our time, and paying attention to what the person is saying and how they feel are a crucially important part of the counselling process.

Skill: matching

The counsellor can 'match' the behaviour, the speed and tone of speaking, and the posture of the person in order to reflect and get 'in tune' with his or her mood and feelings. They can also seek to slow down or enliven the counselling process. Perhaps the counsellor feels that the person is too agitated or too depressed, and by altering the speed of their speech, or by relaxing, or sitting forward in their chair, they can subtly change the nature of the communication.

Skill: observation

The counsellor can learn a lot about a person through observation.

- How is the person presenting him- or herself?
- How are they standing or sitting?
- What clothes are they wearing?

These observations can inform us about how someone is feeling, and also how they feel about themselves.

Skill: getting started

Once a relaxed atmosphere has been established, and this need take only a few moments, it is important to start the counselling process. A brief, non-threatening outline of why the meeting is happening might be useful – perhaps some generalized précis of how you have become involved, and what you feel the issues or problems the person faces might be. Then it can be helpful to say little more, but to open up discussion by asking an 'open' question.

- *'How do you feel about this meeting?'*
- *'Tell me about how you feel about your situation at the present time.'*
- *'What is your biggest concern right now?'*

Self-expression

Counselling is often called *'a talking cure'*. This is misleading because counselling is more than this, but it is an invaluable underlying element of the process. Many people will have experienced the relief of being able to talk to someone about their feelings and difficulties. It is at the heart of the old saying, *'a trouble shared is a trouble halved'*. Older people usually relish any opportunity they are given to express their feelings. Many will feel that they have few opportunities to talk – they brighten up and become animated, grateful that someone is taking the time to listen to them. Often counsellors will see pressures and worries lift, almost visibly, from the counsellee's shoulders after a relatively short period.

Listening and self-expression are closely linked. It is unhelpful in the early stages to be judgemental about what is expressed – however wrong, misguided or unjust it might appear to be. Counselling should restrict itself to trying to understand, to expand and develop the counsellee's feelings.

It is usually the superficial emotions that are presented initially. They can be real, deeply affecting the way in which the person is leading their life. Normally, however, the 'angry' emotions have their origins in deeper and often more significant feelings. Soon the counsellor must try to move from the more superficial emotions of anger, hate and hostility to the deeper emotions of sadness and disappointment, inadequacy and grief – but not too soon.

Skill: listening

The most fundamental counselling skill, transcending all others, is listening. The ability to listen to another person's problems is not a universal human trait. Most people tend to relay rather than receive information. Politicians manipulate, entrepreneurs exploit, teachers disseminate information, priests sermonize, bosses (of all kinds) give orders, and even friends give advice. Everyone, to some degree and in their own way, is ready to lecture and opinionize. Too few bother to listen – to really listen. Professional groups are possibly slightly worse than the average. Mayer and Timms (1970) found that, when considering individual need, there was massive misunderstanding between client and social worker. Clients would arrive with specific problems, but would often be questioned on matters that were entirely irrelevant to the needs they were presenting. Although the concept of 'needs-led assessment' is now much in vogue in social-work circles, experience would suggest that matters have not improved significantly since the introduction of this approach.

Listening is the starting point of the counselling process, and to listen properly the counsellor has simply to stop talking.

Skill: assisting the listening process

To listen without saying or doing anything does not encourage self-expression. The counsellor needs to give continual reassurance of their interest and concern, and to confirm that they are actively listening. Several responses can achieve this, whilst at the same time clarifying important aspects of what is being said. They include:

- non-verbal communication, such as gestures of understanding and approval;
- good eye contact;

- facial expressions that mirror the expressed emotions of the person;
- reassuring touches of support and encouragement;
- simple verbal interjections such as, *'Yes, I see'*, *'I understand'*, *'that must have been awful'*, and so on.

Such interjections can relay responses, such as agreement or surprise, and can also be used to emphasize the importance of a particular statement, or to query its significance.

Reflecting back is a useful technique. By paraphrasing or asking a simple question about what has been said, the counsellor can elicit further responses and/or seek clarification. To paraphrase is to seek to capture the essential ingredients of what is being said, and this technique can be used at times when the counsellor wants to ensure that they understand what is being said. Simple questions or comments can encourage the individual to recap, elucidate or develop what they are saying, for example:

- *'I hear what you say'*;
- *'so you think that . . .'*;
- *'you mean that . . .'*;
- *'I'm not sure that I follow what you mean'*.

This confirms that you are interested in what they are saying, and that you are making an effort to understand their point of view. Keep the responses short. Long statements can interfere by distracting a train of thought.

Listening to people from minority ethnic communities requires special mention because most literature about communication skills and counselling is still 'Eurocentric', to the extent that Stewart (1992) felt that it was of limited value for work with people from other cultural backgrounds. He mentions that body language cues may be different, and that physical touch, or even giving comfort, may be perceived very differently.

Skill: reflecting back feelings

Other questions can take this a stage further by helping the person to describe their feelings, and by giving them permission to explore them further. Rather than talking about events, or general issues, people can be encouraged to talk about what is troubling them, and how they feel about their situation.

- *'Tell me about how this made you feel.'*
- *'Are you feeling angry about this?'*
- *'You have really been hurt by this.'*
- *'This seems to have affected you deeply.'*
- *'What did you do when you felt like that?'*

The encouragement offered by 'reflecting back' becomes increasingly necessary as more difficult areas are discussed, where feelings have become more important than thoughts. It can take the conversation from an intellectual to an emotional plane. The counsellor can assist the person to talk about the present rather than the past, and about themselves rather than other people. It gives them 'permission' to talk about difficult areas, and confirms that we are willing to listen, however difficult their feelings might be.

Skill: the choice of words

The counsellor must also be aware of the use of words, the possible impact they may have, and the possibility of misunderstanding arising from them. Tyler has outlined some of the problems:

> Still another difficulty has to do with the specific words the counsellor uses. The one thing he wishes not to do is to arouse defensive attitudes. Certain ways of putting things are more likely than others to affect people adversely. Words like coward, stupid or effeminate should probably never be used unless the client has used that very word himself. It is as feasible to say, 'You can't bring yourself to attempt it' as 'You haven't the courage to try'. Either is an expression of a painful emotional attitude, but the second is much more likely than the first to arouse defensiveness. Much the same rules apply here as in ordinary tactful conversation. This does not mean that reality should be watered down or glossed over. Counselling differs from most conversation in that problem areas and unpleasant facts are faced, not ignored or side-tracked. They need not, however, be presented brutally.
>
> (Tyler, 1969)

Conversely, if the counsellor is too conscious of saying the 'right' thing at the 'right' time, this can hamper the counselling process. Awkward silences might be considered preferable to choosing an incorrect word or phrase; however, this is nonsense. Even the 'wrong' word or phrase used in error can be rectified.

- *'Tell me why you have reacted so strongly to a word/phrase which I intended so innocently.'*
- *'Who has said this to you before? Does it hurt/offend you?'*

The existence of a good counselling relationship will overcome such mishaps, so long as they are not too frequent, or used insensitively.

Skill: the use of silence

There may be some points in the conversation when silence is appropriate – perhaps when someone has made an important statement or revelation, and seems to want time to reflect on what he or she has said. Certainly, the counsellor should not feel the need to fill every silence, as this might alter the direction of conversation and prevent an important point of clarification. Conversely, silences can be awkward, especially if they are too frequent or too long. As Geldard advises:

Match the client's silence whilst continuing to pay attention to him with appropriate eye contact. If you observe his eye movements carefully, you will be able to tell when he is thinking and needs to be left to think rather than to be interrupted. Whilst thinking, the client's eyes are likely to be focused steadily at a distance, and when he has stopped thinking his eyes will tell you.

(Geldard, 1989)

Identifying problems: interpreting what we hear

Listening does not just mean that we are aware of the words being spoken. From the words, the counsellor has to be able to elicit the feelings and meanings which often lie beneath the surface. Words are too often interpreted literally as signifying little more than their immediate, most rational meaning. When we are told that everything is 'OK' we prefer to believe this, although what people may actually be saying (by tone of voice or body language) can herald far deeper, more subtle emotion.

Older people will often use words that hide their emotions. They may express feelings of contentment or resignation which do not fully reflect their state of mind. This may be confusing. It would certainly be easier if we all said what we meant, but the fact is that we often do not do so. Disingenuousness has many functions:

- it says to others what we believe they want to hear;
- it stop us talking about the feelings that are difficult to discuss;
- it hides our pain;
- it avoids difficult subjects.

The rules of social politeness are based on the premise that we should not burden other people with our problems. Inquiries after our health are usually met with an automatic 'Very well, thank you', even when we are feeling downright miserable. These daily lies of politeness can often disguise major difficulties, and counselling has to seek to overcome this reticence.

- It encourages people to talk about worrying issues, as this might be helpful.
- It assures people that we are prepared to listen to their difficulties.
- It demonstrates that we are aware of their feelings and pain.
- It indicates that we are interested in talking to them about these matters.

Thus the counsellor has to be a mind-reader! Reading a person's real feelings is made easier by the relationship (people are prepared to talk openly to those who they feel are genuinely concerned, and who have both the time and the interest to understand), and by matching what is said to the person's known circumstances.

The art of good listening involves a degree of perceptive interpretation of what is being said, the reasons why it is being said, and how the words that are being spoken relate to reality.

Presenting problems

The process of counselling is not always smooth or straightforward. We cannot assume that people are going to be willing or able immediately to divulge the full nature of their feelings and difficulties. Time is often required to summon up the courage necessary to talk about their real problems and difficulties.

Even when people appear willing to talk about their difficulties, it is not always the core problems that they will present initially. Some people may find it easier in the early stages of counselling to raise subsidiary issues, as they may find these less difficult or embarrassing. Therefore the counsellor should be wary of accepting the earliest issues raised as necessarily the most important ones. Indeed, to focus too quickly on the presenting problem may prevent the more significant underlying problems from coming to the surface. They must be pursued when raised, but the counsellor should always give the person an opportunity to move on to other more crucial issues.

- *'Is this really what is troubling you, or is there something more?'*

How quickly the real issues will be brought into open discussion depends on a number of factors, including the difficulty or sensitivity of the issue, the ability of the person to express him- or herself, and the quality of the counselling relationship.

Skill: focusing on self and the here and now

Some people, when discussing their difficulties, will fix on other people, complaining about what they have done or not done, or what they should have done. Whatever their personal problems, they insist that they stem from the vagaries and shortcomings of other people somewhere 'out there'. Often it is the past that is dwelt upon to the exclusion of the present. People can be reluctant to talk about themselves, or about the here and now. It is safer and easier to blame other people for their discomfort. While listening to such complaints the counsellor may feel that these are the real issues, but invariably they are not.

The counsellor, whilst needing to understand how the person feels, must assist them to talk about the present and about themselves.

- *'How does (what happened) make you feel?'*
- *'How do you feel (about this person) now, after all this time?'*
- *'Tell me how you feel about (the situation) now, at this moment.'*
- *'I sense that you are still angry about . . .'*

Skill: clarification – open and closed questions

Although important information will arise from conversation, the counsellor can guide the discussion with well-formulated and well-aimed questions.

They can help to clarify particular points or feelings, or assist a person to be more specific. Open questions are preferable to closed questions. A closed question will usually elicit a brief factual answer, often 'yes' or 'no', and does little to enhance discussion. Conversely, open questions give scope for further exploration and clarification of feelings.

- *'Do you feel sad?'*
- *'How do you feel?'*
- *'Do you argue a lot?'*
- *'How do you get on with each other?'*
- *'Did you tell him how you felt?'*
- *'What did you do when you felt like that?'*
- *'Do you still love him?'*
- *'How do you feel about him?'*

Skill: summarizing

Counselling will cover considerable ground, and periodically it can be helpful if the counsellor can stop the process of disclosure to review the ground already covered. By summarizing, the counsellor seeks to draw together the salient points of the discussion, concentrating primarily on feelings rather than events. The summary can sometimes help a distressed person to organize the wealth of material they are struggling to cope with, and to focus on what is really important.

- *'Given all that you have told me, your feelings of depression seem to centre on the death of your husband, but the anger you feel has arisen mainly from the inadequate medical treatment you feel he received, and the lack of reaction or even concern by other members of your family, and their subsequent inability to talk to you about your feelings of loss.'*
- *'You have talked about many reasons why you do not want to involve yourself in social activities, or even with your own family. This seems to result from your feelings about your own value and worth, and not wanting to be a burden. Would it be true to say that you have felt like this ever since you were obliged to retire from your job?'*

Counsellors can usefully summarize the ideas, thoughts and feelings that have been expressed when it is appropriate, and particularly when either starting or bringing a counselling session to an end. They provide a valuable opportunity to ponder over the 'wholeness' of the problems, distinguishing the 'important' from the 'less important', and checking whether the summary accurately reflects and deals with the most significant issues.

The pain of the counselling process

Self-expression can be a threatening process, bringing to the surface many deep-rooted fears and anxieties, and uncovering many hitherto denied emotions. The skill of achieving this is closely connected to the counselling relationship, and to developing the mutual confidence and trust that are essential for real sharing. The counselling relationship enables the counsellor to explore feelings, especially the negative feelings of inadequacy, guilt and worthlessness, that people harbour about themselves. Within the safety of the relationship, the counsellor can help people to examine the emotional origin, meanings and purposes of their behaviour, and the reasons why they have had to deny the existence of their personal feelings.

However, this is the part of the counselling process which many people dislike, because it necessarily touches on stress and anxiety. People worry that it can open up all of the disturbing conflicts and inconsistencies that have been at the heart of personal problems, stirring up emotions and raking over apparently quiescent turmoil. As Rogers says:

> In the case of a radical re-organisation, the client may go through the most racking torment of pain, and a complete and chaotic confusion. This suffering may be associated with rapidly changing configurations of personality, being a new person one day, and sinking back into the old self on the next, only to find that some minor episode puts the new organisation of self again in a position of regency.
>
> (Rogers, 1951a)

This leads to accusations that counselling can create more problems than it resolves – and indeed that it can actually increase and exacerbate problems. As Rogers indicates, the accusation is based upon a measure of truth. Where counselling is effective, it will produce a degree of pain, as most processes of change are painful.

So why not leave the troubled individual alone?

The problem with such accusations lies in a kind of primitive logic that associates pain with whatever is closest to hand. When pain is seen to arise within the counselling process, counselling is thought to be 'the cause'. This is faulty logic.

- It is unlikely that counselling actually creates distress that is not already present within the person. Counselling may reveal turmoil, and bring it to the surface, but if it does so, that turmoil will have existed prior to counselling. Moreover, dormant and undiscussed feelings can produce a person who is troubled, unhappy and anxious, and whose behaviour is moving him or her inexorably towards despair.
- The process of increasing self-awareness is an essential prerequisite for emotional health. Emotionally troubled people cannot cope with their emotions until they understand what those emotions are, how they have arisen, and what can be done to overcome them.

Contradictions and dilemmas exist in most people's lives. They become a problem when we deny their existence or fail to recognize them. The exploration of painful feelings can help people to come to terms with troubled emotions, and to devise a realistic strategy for emotional and social survival and the recommencement of personal growth.

We should not avoid helping others because of some misguided sense of 'doing harm', but we do need to recognize that the counselling process might cause some temporary uncertainty and pain. If the quality of the counselling relationship is good it should prove more than sufficient to handle the outcome. If, in addition, it assists someone towards a resolution of emotional troubles, the short-term distress will have been worthwhile.

Skill: addressing difficult issues

The subject matter of counselling might be so difficult that both counsellor and counsellee might prefer to continue talking about inconsequential matters, and avoid the main issues. It is important that the counsellor finds the right time to outline the main areas of counselling concern openly and honestly. Once the initial ground has been thoroughly prepared, the counsellor should move to the 'difficult' areas, but should do so as gently as possible. Summarizing may be a crucial skill that enables the counsellor to focus upon the main concerns, interests and feelings of the person, whilst at the same time giving assurance that the primary purpose is to get to know how they feel, what they want to do, and what they wish to happen.

The counsellor is now doing more than listening. New concepts, new ideas and new connections are being introduced into the discussion, each presenting the individual with an alternative 'picture' of reality, many of which will prove to be challenging. The counsellor is also giving direction to the discussion, focusing on just some of the many areas of concern.

When the counsellor feels that particular problem areas need to be broached, and that the person is reluctant to enter them, the situation requires sensitive handling. The rules of 'social politeness' often run counter to what the counsellor wants to do. We are taught not to focus on difficult areas and not to dwell upon problem emotions. This is frowned upon as 'morbid curiosity', likely only to lead to highlighting and prolonging distress, and causing unnecessary pain. The reality is that the only pain spared by social politeness is our own. It is difficult to understand how personal problems can be resolved by refusing to discuss them. Problems that have been 'forgotten' are rarely out of mind, and bringing problems to the surface does not cause distress in itself, but merely uncovers distress which is already present within the individual.

Focusing on problems should be assisted by the genuineness of the counselling relationship. Certainly, counselling interest should arise from a genuine concern for the individual, and not from a prurient interest or inquisitiveness, and the counsellor should be able to focus on potentially distressing areas in a non-threatening way in order:

- to explain why we feel that it is such a crucial area;
- to confirm that the reason for doing so is to help them develop an understanding of their feelings about the situation;
- to enable them to come to terms with the issue.

Self-image: building a hypothesis

At this stage, the counsellor is interpreting what they are hearing, and seeking meaning and connection between a person's feelings and their social performance. Counselling is beginning to gain insight into another person, and this should take into account a wide variety of factors, including the following:

- the person's interests and aptitudes;
- their feelings;
- their relationships;
- their personal strengths and weaknesses;
- their medical condition;
- their past life, and the effect that significant life events have had on them;
- the way in which they view their future prospects.

Links and connections will begin to be made between the ways in which a person feels and behaves. Our emotions determine our social performance, and patterns of behaviour will emerge which might indicate that an individual reacts to similar situations in similar ways, and that this reaction reflects their feelings. Soon the counsellor can begin to build a comprehensive and coherent picture of the person.

This picture is a hypothesis. It exists only in the counsellor's understanding. It seeks to describe the whole person, recognizing and making sense of the interconnectedness of personal experience. It should not separate and isolate specific aspects of a person's life for special attention. Moreover, it should pay particular attention to the emotions, rather than to the 'facts' or the rationalizations and justifications that we tend to use in order to shroud our feelings, especially in times of stress.

> What the counsellor does is to concentrate on how the client feels about the incidents or facts he is reporting, rather than on the facts themselves, and then to respond to what appears to be the most significant part of each complex sequence. . . . Counselling is concerned with strain rather than with the facts.
>
> (Tyler, 1969)

Thus the 'fact' that someone is 'old', or suffers from illness or pain, or is dependent, whilst an important part of understanding that person, is less important than how he or she feels about such 'facts'.

It is how people 'feel', and how they see themselves, that determines their social performance. Understanding this self-image is an important part of counselling. Its origins, and the way it determines social functioning, particularly the debilitative consequences of low self-esteem, are central to social distress. Understanding self-image is therefore vital, and the counsellor should seek to build a picture of how a person's world has been shaped and developed throughout their lifetime.

Personal construct theory

In building a hypothesis, the counsellor may be assisted by the 'personal construct' theory of Kelly (1955), which suggests that social performance is determined not so much by external events as by self-erected mental structures through which the person views life, interprets it and decides how to respond. Depending upon their particular view of life, people always act in an orderly and predictable way. Understanding their viewpoint is therefore vital to understanding their behaviour. This explains why counselling is concerned primarily with listening, for it is vital that we understand the person's outlook on life – not because it is necessarily right or sensible, but because it determines their behaviour.

The 'personal construct' ensures that a person's reactions follow a predictable pattern. To understand why some older people do not respond to situations in more logical and less self-damaging ways, we must try to understand the system of prediction which the person is using. If older people see life through helpless, defeated eyes, and become resigned to disappointment and pain, loneliness and despair, their reaction to new situations and opportunities will be negative. Negative outcomes will, in turn, confirm the correctness of their viewpoint. The counsellor should understand that this is the way in which people predict and determine what happens in their lives, but that eventually counselling seeks *to help the person to develop a more positive set of expectations*. Where this can be done, it will enable less destructive and more positive responses to the problems that the person faces.

Skill: confirmation and clarification

The working hypothesis needs to be *tested and refined* through the process of discussion and questioning, requiring a continuous process of confirmation, clarification and reclarification in order to ensure that the hypothesis is accurate. Counsellors can never assume that what they believe to be the feelings and motivation of another person are accurate. By seeking confirmation and clarification, we examine the validity of our ideas.

- *'Does feeling (this way) make you respond (like this)?'*
- *'Can you see the similarity between the way you reacted in that situation and the way you reacted in this one?'*
- *'Can you think of other times when you have done this, or felt like this?'*
- *'Does the way you respond help the situation you face, or make it worse?'*

Through clarification and confirmation, the counsellor can test and refine their hypothesis so that it reflects more accurately the person's actual feelings, situation or state of mind.

Skill: reframing

Social distress colours our view of the world, often meaning that we interpret the events and circumstances that impinge on our lives negatively. This results from low self-esteem and depression. We can become paranoid, feeling that the entire world is against us. The counsellor has to listen and understand such perceptions, but it is sometimes necessary for him or her to 'reframe' an event, or to place it in a broader context.

- *'I know that you feel deeply that your son is avoiding you, and does not visit you often enough. But you have told me that he has a new child/new job. Do you think it might be that he is very busy? Perhaps he knows that you are angry, and he feels guilty about not seeing as much of you as before. Is there anything you can do to ease the situation for him?'*
- *'I know that you feel hurt by your partner, and feel unwanted. But you have also suggested that he/she has felt deeply your recent loss, and that you have not been able to talk about it together. Do you feel that these two factors could be connected? Is there any way you can talk about either or both? Would it be helpful to know how he/she feels about things at the moment?'*

Such reframing should be done tentatively. The purpose is to help to transform the negative interpretation of events or situations into a broader panorama that seeks more positive reasons, motives and intentions with regard to other people.

Blocks

Resistance, or blocks to communication, represent more than initial reticence. Some people may have used blocks to communication either consciously or unconsciously over a period of many years in order to hide the 'unpleasant' truth from other people, and perhaps even from themselves. Many older people hide behind the facade of being 'OK' – often a defence mechanism that is difficult to penetrate. Some older people might use stubbornness, anger and violence, depression and even confusion as blocks to communication.

All blocks to self-expression are linked with feelings of inadequacy and poor self-image. It is important to understand their nature and origin. In the earliest stages of life, people react more spontaneously. Babies have no knowledge of the social niceties that will later determine social behaviour. Thereafter, children are taught by parents, relatives, friends and teachers what is expected of them, and what is considered to be appropriate and inappropriate behaviour. Within this socialization process, people will learn that some emotions and feelings are unacceptable. This may cover such areas as masturbation and sexual activity, crying (especially in boys), and the expression of strong emotions such as anger and grief.

As a result, people learn that to gain rewards or avoid punishment, they must suppress quite normal and natural feelings, some of which are quite essential to the human condition. Where this is the case, people become unable to express their pain and grief (or their anger or fear), and they will learn to be ashamed of the various taboo feelings they harbour, which have to be suppressed or displaced because they are associated with 'wrong' or 'evil', or with pain and punishment.

Painful events and suppressed emotions throughout life can lead to the formation of blocks. Their identification is an important part of the counselling process and, when successfully tackled, blocks can reveal a wealth of information about the reason and meaning behind a person's social performance. When counselling older people, it is important to realize that blocks may not necessarily result from current attitudes, beliefs and taboos. They can be closely related to past sexual and religious mores which, because they are not as powerful in modern society, may not be so immediately apparent to the 'younger' counsellor. The ability to recognize such blocks is therefore an important skill, but like so many others in counselling, it is a perceptual rather than a concrete skill. The way that people react to particular restraints, and how this affects their general social behaviour and attitudes, is subject to no firm or clear rules.

Skill: challenging

Sometimes people use the counselling process as a social prop, and this can prevent it from leading to self-examination, change and growth. Lonely older people who enjoy the company offered by counselling, and who perhaps are not committed to the idea of personal change 'at their age', are a case in point. It can sometimes be too easy for people to gain comfort and reassurance from the warmth and acceptance of the counselling relationship without making any commitment to progress towards resolving their difficulties. Problems may even be recognized and identified, but without coming any closer to their resolution.

The counsellor needs to be aware of the person who is 'stuck', and to recognize when someone is more interested in the problem than in the solution. Geldard (1989) has outlined a number of situations in which confrontation is appropriate.

- The person is avoiding a basic issue which appears to be troubling him or her.
- The person is failing to recognize his or her own self-destructive or self-defeating behaviour.
- The person is failing to recognize the possible serious consequences of his or her behaviour.
- The person is out of touch with reality.
- The person is making self-contradictory statements.
- The person is excessively and inappropriately locked into talking about the past, and is unable to focus on the present.
- The person is going around in circles by repeating the same story over and over again.

- The person's non-verbal behaviour does not match his or her verbal behaviour.
- Attention needs to be given to what is going on in the counselling relationship, for example where dependency is developing, or where a person withdraws or shows anger or some other emotion towards the counsellor.

In such situations, the counselling process does not always remain a sympathetic process of listening, support and approval.

The variety and extent of 'the games people play' in their lives have been outlined in the classic work of Berne (1968). Such games can be played with the 'actor' entirely unaware that they are doing this. Where necessary, and when appropriate, the counsellor may need to embark upon a measured 'confrontation' in which they have to challenge the individual before further progress can be made. Several outcomes can be achieved.

- People who are playing emotional games, perhaps in the hope of gaining sympathy or confirming their particular viewpoint, can be drawn away from doing so.
- The roles attributed to, and accepted by, an individual can be challenged. People who have accepted ideas about their personal worth, impotence or badness may not be able to help themselves unless and until they are able to modify their self-image.
- Challenging may introduce an alternative understanding of an issue or situation – necessary, for example, when an individual has blamed some-one else for a problem, and has not looked at their own contribution.
- It may 'unlock' feelings that are adversely affecting the person's life, and help to resolve the difficulties which arise from them.
- It can stop repeating cycles within a person's behaviour or current relationships, which hitherto they have been unwilling or unable to break.

Challenges should not be made without counsellors first examining their own motivation – in particular, whether their agenda is to relieve their own impatience, or to put forward their own views and values – nor should people be challenged in a way that is destructive. Positive challenges do not put down the individual or damage their self-image further.

- *'I am concerned that you have raised (an issue) several times, but each time, you have not carried on to talk about it fully. Is it important? Do you feel uneasy talking about the subject? Do you feel we should try to talk about it?'*
- *'You seem so angry, and your anger is so focused on (an individual) that I worry that you might do something that would harm both him and you, and would not resolve the situation, but only make it worse. How can we avoid this happening?'*
- *'You seem to recognize your problem, but rather than concentrating on how you can come to terms with it, or resolve it, you appear to want to talk about what has happened in the past, which cannot be changed, and leaves you feeling bad. How do you feel we can change this?'*

- 'Our discussion seems to be going around in circles, and we are repeating ourselves. How do you think we can break this so that we do not arrive back at the same point again? Is there any way that the circle can be broken, and a new direction can be taken? Do you feel that you might have a reason for repeating yourself?'
- 'Although you deny that you have (a problem), you say this without conviction, and your general demeanour suggests that there is a problem. It leaves me feeling that perhaps there is a problem but you feel unable to recognize it or talk about it. Is there any way that we can talk about it?'

When a major challenge is anticipated, the counsellor should ensure that there is sufficient time to pursue the matter fully and return to some positive and mutual understanding by the end of the session. This can often happen when the counsellor challenges some form of self-destructive behaviour. Geldard (1989) says that these arise from 'should', 'must' or 'ought' beliefs, or from irrational beliefs. These are frequently powerful determinants of behaviour and feeling, and they commonly arise from a sense of duty that is often outdated or inappropriate. Such statements often express not only what they think they should do, but also what they do not want to do.

- 'I should do this, but I don't want to, and I resent having the responsibility.'

Often this can be dealt with by looking at what is actually happening, and then distinguishing between the person's sense of responsibility or duty, and how they actually feel about doing it, and then what they would prefer to do. This approach can assist the person in questioning where their 'duty' really lies.

Often people have the opposite problem, believing that other people 'should', 'must' or 'ought to' do something, and being disappointed when they do not. Their expectations might be irrational, unreasonable or inappropriate, but the anger that this can cause can be intense. Such feelings need to be challenged by asking whether they feel that their expectations are realistic or fair, and that if what they 'want' to happen is not going to happen, whether they might have to alter their expectations of other people.

Skill: dealing with transference

Transference occurs when a person projects his or her unresolved emotions on to another person, often someone who is close or who is attempting to help. The transference of irrational feelings and unrealistic demands, usually accompanied by anger and hurt, can come as a considerable surprise to the unwary, especially if they feel that 'they are only trying to help'. Many relationships can be damaged or even destroyed by transference.

Carers and counsellors are readily available for such transference. They are safe (because they are less likely to reject the person). They are prepared to discuss difficult situations (and so expose themselves to angry reactions). The counsellor needs to remain calm, and be prepared to listen without becoming defensive or reacting angrily to unreasonable allegations or demands. Whatever is thrown at them, counsellors should try to place responsibility calmly back where it belongs – with the individual.

- *'Why do you feel you are making (that comment)?'*
- *'Do you think that (what you are saying) is fair, or correct?'*
- *'Do you really believe that I am the problem?'*

Throughout, the counsellor should be firm and persistent but also calm and understanding – willing to listen, but unwilling to accept feelings that do not belong to them. People are able to recognize that they are transferring their feelings, and that their attitude is unreasonable. However, before this happens the counsellor sometimes has to exercise patience.

The actualizing or formative tendency

All behaviour, no matter how irrational or senseless it may appear to be, is logical and purposeful according to some particular viewpoint. The counsellor may not be able to identify that viewpoint readily, or may not like or agree with it. Nevertheless, the viewpoint will exist.

The counsellor's task is to find reason within the individual's emotional life. From within these emotional origins, counselling maintains that all human behaviour is modifiable, and that modification comes mainly through increased self-awareness. This confident outlook reflects the optimistic nature of the counselling process, which is perhaps best expressed through Rogers' concept of the 'actualizing' or 'formative' tendency: 'an underlying flow of movement towards constructive fulfilment of its inherent possibility, which resides in every organism' (Rogers, 1951b).

The actualizing tendency rejects explanations of individual pathology and of inherent badness, laziness or inadequacy, and replaces these with the belief that human problems arise from an interaction between individual experience and unfavourable social circumstances. The 'healthy' personality is one that is able to react appropriately to current circumstances, and is able to cope with fluctuating events and personalities. To achieve this requires a variety of social skills. When successful, people are able to maintain an equilibrium, whereas when unsuccessful they become fixed and unable to react appropriately to the people and circumstances around them.

The actualizing tendency intimates that even people who are failing are capable of change, growth and development. It is an essentially optimistic view of the human condition, and this is particularly important when working with older people. Rogers himself reflected on his own advancing years and, applying the actualizing tendency to the problems of ageing (in a chapter which asked the question 'Growing old – or older and growing?'), he concluded that 'I sense myself as older and growing' (Rogers, 1951b).

Such optimism about the human condition is very different from the dominant stereotype of old age. The most important element of this optimism is that growth is a continuous process during which our potential capacities can be drawn upon and developed at any period of life, including old age. This view is important to the counselling process for two reasons.

1. The lives and experiences of many older people prove it to be true.

2. It would be important, even necessary, both for the counsellor and for the older person, to believe that it is true – even if it were not!

Developing self-awareness

Whereas the objective of the counselling relationship is to enable self-expression, the objective of the counselling process is to promote self-understanding or self-awareness. *Self-expression* allows people to explain where they are at the present time. The picture drawn will utilize various materials gathered from the past, and it is an essentially static picture. It does not tell us why people act in they way they do, and it is unlikely to provide useful clues about their potential for future development. Self-expression is limited because it is a reflective rather than a contemplative process.

Self-awareness is a contemplative process. It provides people with the necessary knowledge and information to enable them to look at themselves and the lives they lead in a different way. Once the counsellor feels that he or she understands the person, and has developed a working hypothesis, the purpose of counselling is to pass that understanding on to the individual.

It is surprising how little most of us understand about our emotional lives, and the way in which this affects our social relationships and behaviour, including:

*   the way in which we present ourselves to other people;
*   how other people view us;
*   aspects of our personality that other people find attractive, and those aspects that are not so attractive.

If we could all step back and watch ourselves in our daily lives, we might learn a great deal and – with some effort – become nicer, more attractive people. Socially distressed people usually find that they are unable to focus clearly on their lives. They may be aware that something is wrong, but are uncertain about what is wrong or why, and confused about what they can do about it.

Counselling seeks to present people with a 'mirror' through which they can assess their social performance and the reasons behind their success and failure. When people develop self-awareness, they are in a better position to understand their problems, overcome past failings and develop new social skills.

Self-awareness involves the gaining of many insights.

1. The individual can learn to recognize the situations, events and people that provoke distress, and how they react to it.

2. The individual can learn to understand how they cope with distress, both positively and negatively.

3. The individual can learn new coping behaviour.

4. The individual can look closely at their emotions, and decide whether they are justified or merely an indulgence (e.g. some people enjoy the sympathy and concern that their distress can attract).

5. The individual can be more able to recognize their personal needs, and how they can best be fulfilled.

6. The individual can make connections between their unfulfilled needs, their emotions and their social performance.

7. The individual can become aware of repeating patterns of behaviour, particularly those that have led to unhappiness.

8. The individual can learn to recognize the part they have played in bringing about distressing situations.

9. The individual can look closely at their attitudes and beliefs, both about themselves and about other people, and the impact that these have on their own life and on the people close to them.

10. The individual can make connections between what has occurred in the past and how this affects what they are achieving, or failing to achieve, in the present.

11. The individual can understand how social factors (in particular, the impact of ageism) affect their ability to lead a fulfilling life.

12. Ultimately, the individual can examine their self-image and decide how this can be improved or modified, and what has to be done in order to achieve this.

However, just as self-expression is a 'static' position, so too is self-awareness. To 'be aware' is not the same as doing something about what is wrong and taking positive action to remedy the situation. For many people, social distress is a consequence of entrenched life positions that will not alter unless there is a positive commitment to change. Therefore when a person has to develop greater self-awareness, the counselling process needs to take a further step forward. Self-understanding is vital, but what the person decides to do with this information now becomes crucial.

Personal change: countering ageism

Helping people to make decisions is the ultimate goal of the counselling process. The skills of facilitating decision-making have been discussed by Tyler:

> There are times when, in order to proceed with his life, a person must make a decision. It may be one that is large and far-reaching, or it may appear relatively small and trivial but . . . (of) special significance for the person who makes it is that his choice will help to determine the

pattern of his unique development over time. Each life decision is to some extent irrevocable, since even if one goes back to the fork in the road and takes the other turning, he cannot eradicate the effects of the experience the first choice has brought him.

(Tyler, 1969)

Yet in order to contemplate personal change and development, there needs to be a recognition that it can only come from within an individual, and cannot be imposed from without. Imposed change is rarely effective in the long term. Giving advice is not only bad counselling, but is also ineffectual. Each person has to accept that the responsibility for doing something about their life is an entirely personal one, requiring important life decisions. Thus for change to take place the counsellor has to be an *enabler* rather than an *enforcer*.

Socially distressed people are often lacking in energy and determination. Self-awareness may help to mobilize their energy. Indeed, the individual might be able to introduce change immediately, and counselling may not be required beyond this point.

However, awareness can also be draining. An understanding of personal problems may make them appear to be even more overwhelming than was previously realized, and feelings of hopelessness may be temporarily increased. In these circumstances, the counselling task is to move the individual towards an acceptance of the need for change.

The ability of older people to develop and grow by making positive decisions can be restricted by ageism. Older people have to view the future in a way that allows them to believe that they can play an active and influential part in determining the course of their own lives. They must be able to believe that new attitudes, new approaches, new determinations, new behaviours, fresh outlooks and new challenges are possible. The counsellor may face many psychological barriers to achieving this.

- Have older people any right to choose?
- What influence can they expect to have over their own lives?
- Of what value are they to anyone?

These questions have to be treated sensitively and honestly. Ultimately, counselling outcomes are judged by the extent to which they facilitate personal decision-making, action and change. The most important factor that militates against this is personal doubt and lack of confidence. Many older people become defeatist about their depressed and unhappy status, and lack confidence in their ability to effect change and improve the quality of their lives. Many older people no longer have the energy or feel that they are incapable of change 'at their age'. They may lack conviction about their value and worth, they may feel that there is no future towards which to strive, and they may feel unwanted.

All this reduces activity. Against this, the counsellor has to try to convince older people of the need for making decisions and taking action.

Change has to be allied to a belief that change is both possible and worthwhile.

Moreover, change requires more than a momentary resolution. First, there must be a desire for personal change. Thereafter, there must be confidence that such change can happen. Ageism can make a massive contribution to despondency. We are led to believe that older people are too set in their ways and too old to change, and many will internalize these feelings, believing too readily that 'they are what they are' and that they are likely to remain so. Therefore, it is crucial that the counsellor addresses such questions as the following.

- *'Is change possible at my age?'*
- *'Is it possible to move out of loss and grief?'*
- *'Is it possible to lead fulfilling lives during our old age?'*

If the answer to such questions is 'no', then counselling has encountered a significant block that will have to be worked through. A person cannot be forced into action. The counsellor may need to help them become aware of the block to progress. Geldard (1989) outlines the possible reasons for blocks at this stage:

- an inability to deal with their own feelings;
- an inability to cope with the reactions of other people;
- fear of the consequences of change;
- fear of a repetition of past bad experiences;
- the intrusion of inappropriate 'shoulds', 'musts' and 'oughts';
- fear that something comfortable or rewarding will be lost;
- lack of skills to carry out the desired action.

All of these are legitimate and powerful determinants of behaviour in older people, and they will have to be tackled if progress is to be made.

Skill: examining all the options

If the answer is 'yes, change is possible', then the person has to make certain decisions about how to tackle their problems, and how they will cope more adequately. The counselling process may have moved the individual to make these decisions quite independently, but sometimes an individual may need assistance in embarking upon the process of change. There are several stages to this:

1. deciding upon the decisions that need to be made;
2. exploring the available options, and the possible consequences and outcomes of each option;
3. making a firm decision about what is to be done, and who is to carry out the tasks involved.

Some people may feel 'stuck' and unable to see a way forward, in which case the counsellor can assist by encouraging the person to discuss all of the possible options and outcomes. The options should be elicited by asking questions rather than by offering suggestions, as this encourages people to take personal responsibility and to consider what they might wish to do about resolving their problems. Some options may be discussed briefly and quickly discarded, while others might require a more lengthy consideration of the advantages and disadvantages. Throughout, the counsellor can play a useful role by summarizing the main options, and the potential benefits of each.

Decision-making should not be rushed. Hurried decisions are often found to be wrong, and should be avoided. Often such decisions can be crucial to a person's future life. Sometimes there are clearly 'right' and 'wrong' decisions, but there are always benefits and costs to be considered. There are benefits in allowing significant periods of time to mull over the possible options. The counsellor can encourage people to undertake a 'cost-benefit analysis' simply by listing the advantages and disadvantages of each decision on a piece of paper.

The counsellor can also discuss the difference between a 'logical' and an 'emotional' decision.

* *'I perhaps should do this, but I feel that I want to do this.'*

However, care needs to be taken when discussing the options for change. In some circumstances resistance to change may not constitute a block. Asking a person to make changes in their life can be likened to persuading someone to climb a mountain. Refusal does not necessarily indicate that someone is incapable of climbing to the top, but rather that he or she sees little value or purpose in doing so.

Some older people may be justified in refusing to change – indeed, it may be in their best interests to remain as they are.

People have to be realistic, and to balance the potential value of change with the personal costs that change might incur. Perhaps an individual quite genuinely does not have sufficient energy or interest in effecting change in his or her life. One option is always to maintain the status quo. Pushing people to make unwanted change is usually counter-productive – change cannot be enforced.

Skill: facilitating action

If decision-making can sometimes be an agonizing process, so too can taking action to implement decisions. The counselling process can assist people in moving towards action. Geldard (1989) has outlined how an individual can be taken through a series of gradual steps:

1. *psychological preparation* – taking the individual through all the potential feelings they might encounter that will facilitate against action;

2. *identifying the goal* – being absolutely clear what it is that the individual wishes to achieve through change;

3. *identifying the first step towards goal achievement* – most goals take time to achieve. The steps to be taken towards achieving a goal can be considered, and for those who are uncertain, taking the first step is often the most difficult:
    - what should the first step be?
    - how can the first step be achieved?
    - how can problems and obstacles to achieving it be overcome?
    - when is the right time to undertake what needs to be done?

    Often only a very small initial step might need to be identified in order to reduce the possibility of failure and maximize the confidence-building impact of success.

4. *Identifying the next step and subsequent steps* – reinforced and rewarded by achieving the first step, the person can move on more confidently to others. Counselling can be used as a means of rewarding progress and regularly reassessing the overall situation.

Skill: empowerment

To empower someone means to enable or permit them to take action in a way that provides them with the means to assume greater control over their life. It is deeply rooted in the concepts of personal rights and self-help. It seeks to identify the strengths and abilities that an individual has that will enable them to make up their mind to take action and to change their social situation.

Counselling is not concerned with 'doing things' for people, but with enabling people to do things and make choices for themselves. It can lead to positive change.

- Older people need to see themselves as individuals who have the capacity to make their own decisions.
- The counsellor needs to relinquish any idea that he or she can or should seek to exercise control over people's lives.

Many older people need to be empowered. Counselling needs to be a partnership of equals if it is to achieve this. Too many older people are too accepting of ageist stereotypes concerning what they can or should do 'at their age'. Too many older people are too accepting of the situation in which they find themselves, and the things that are done for them. Too rarely do older people insist that they want more from life, and feel empowered to go in search of it. Even when an older person has become dependent upon other people for his or her care, or when someone is losing control of his or her mental ability to make decisions for him- or herself (perhaps through dementia), older people can be assisted to master their own environment to the extent that remains possible.

The ultimate goal – successful ageing and personal growth

The aim of counselling is to achieve a significant improvement in an individual's social and interpersonal relationships. This is an optimistic view of the potential of older people that is not universally shared. Stuart-Hamilton (1994) has said that 'the best therapies can do is help the elderly cope with their problems'. Eweka (1994) felt that the purpose of counselling older people was not so much to 'cure' their existing conditions as to prevent those conditions from getting worse, and to stimulate realistic planning, realistic attitudes, education and other activities, and spiritual growth.

A more positive view is necessary. Five factors have been found to lead to older people feeling satisfied with their lives (Medley, 1976):

1. a sense of accomplishment;
2. a sense of independence;
3. satisfaction in interpersonal relationships;
4. interest in activity;
5. a flexibility and willingness to change.

Counselling can explore the presence or absence of these factors and through increasing self-awareness, can seek to assist people in attaining them. By recognizing their thoughts and feelings, and integrating them with their social performance and how they relate to other people, older people can more actively control the way in which they lead their lives. Above all, older people can be encouraged to participate in and to integrate themselves into life around them. To do so requires a positive outlook on life, an openness to experience (by touch, smell, sight, taste or hearing), a willingness to communicate (by listening and engaging with people at every opportunity) and a determination to overcome the physical and social restraints of old age.

A sense of mastery develops as older people become aware of their emotions and what elicits them. They come to realise that these are not fixed factors to be accepted, but rather dynamic and changing possibilities.

(O'Leary, 1996)

The counselling process may never achieve such an ideal but, none the less, setting positive goals for older people can be a counselling aim. The following goals seem to be appropriate for the older person:

- someone who is adaptable and flexible;
- someone who can live in and cope with the present world;
- someone who copes adequately with personal problems and difficulties;
- someone who is in touch with but realistic about their needs and personal objectives;
- someone who is able to strive for personal satisfaction and fulfilment;
- someone who is able to defend and protect him- or herself from setbacks and disappointments;

- someone who can accept responsibility both for him- or herself and for others;
- someone who can use their initiative to control events rather than drifting aimlessly;
- someone who feels reasonably content with their present life, although with some unfinished business to complete;
- someone who can remember the past with fondness but accept that it has passed;
- someone who can look to the future with a degree of optimism and hope.

Skill: never give advice – never problem-solve

At no stage in the counselling process should the counsellor either resort to giving advice or focus directly on problem-solving. It is often tempting to do so, especially when someone's attitudes and behaviour frustrate our attempts to achieve beneficial change. Counselling is concerned with helping people to sort out their own confusion and, by doing so, with enabling them to discover their own solutions to their own problems. Counselling ends when advice is given. To advise is to give an opinion about what another person should do, and this should be avoided. The counsellor might think that 'their' solutions are sensible and appropriate, but it is important for people to take decisions that are right for *them*. Self-determination enables people to take credit for the 'right' decisions and blame for the 'wrong' ones.

The 'wise' counsellor stays in the background.

The counsellor will sometimes discover that a person believes that counselling is about solving their problems, and that this can be achieved without their active involvement. In such situations, especially when the counselling relationship is good, the opinion of the counsellor is likely to be sought.

- *'What would you do, if you were in my position?'*
- *'Why don't you tell me what to do?'*

Although it may be tempting to answer such questions, this must be resisted. Change can only be brought about by the individual's own efforts. The role of the counsellor is to help people decide what is to be done, how and when – and should always be passed back to them.

- *'I am not you. I cannot decide what you should do. It is best that you decide what you want to do. What we can do is to talk about the options you have.'*

Referring the problem back to the person prevents the counsellor from falling into a common trap. Most people, ultimately, will do what they want to do, regardless of well-considered and best-intentioned advice. Troubled individuals will often take action, perhaps loosely based upon the counsellor's advice, and then return triumphantly to inform them that it was completely unsuccessful. This confirms that their situation really is hopeless, and that even the counsellor's support does not work. It proves that it is the hopelessness of their situation that defeats them, and that there is nothing that anyone can do about it.

Advice can also prevent people telling us what they want to do, in case this might mean disagreeing with us. It can also lead to the efficacy of our advice becoming the burning issue. Thus if the counsellor's personal agenda is focused on changing or manipulating the individual to make certain choices, it is best that they stop, go away and do something else, for they are interfering and certainly not counselling.

Thus counselling should avoid advice-giving altogether and allow the individual to assume responsibility for their own decisions, in their own time and in their own way. Ultimately this can add to their dignity and self-confidence, for when they make decisions which work, they can then take credit for their own success.

PART THREE

Related skills

Group counselling

7

Groups for recreational and social activity

Informal counselling groups

Formal counselling groups

Peer counselling

Self-help and self-action groups

Age-integrated groups

Counselling on a one-to-one basis can sometimes be a difficult process. It asks people to contemplate personal problems in isolation. For some depressed older people, counselling can sometimes appear to deepen feelings of loss, isolation and loneliness. If so, counselling on a one-to-one basis may be less successful, and groups can then become useful.

> Involvement in a group provides support during loss and an opportunity for developing new relationships. Group counselling gives older participants the opportunity to develop an awareness of some of the social, psychological, physical and environmental aspects of their lives. The group can provide support, increase self-awareness, develop alternative solutions to personal problems and provide an opportunity to learn new social roles.
>
> (O'Leary, 1996)

Whilst individual counselling recognizes the uniqueness of human problems, group-based counselling recognizes shared problems. Most of our lives are spent living in groups, whether based on the family, work or recreation. These are naturally formed groups, but groups can be formed in order to provide the 'social lubricant' that one-to-one situations may lack, opening up areas that people may otherwise be reluctant to discuss.

- Groups offer people a safe place in which to interact with other people.
- Within the process of group interaction, individual attitudes, opinions and needs are expressed and interactive behaviour is displayed.
- The group provides an audience for telling one's story, and an opportunity to listen to the stories other people have to tell.
- The group is a microcosm of life, enabling the exchange of information and ideas, and the compromise and shifting of position, that the formation of all new relationships requires.
- Conversely, the frustrations and antagonisms that arise in the interactions between people in groups can test their patience and their social skills.

For all of these reasons counsellors, through their observation and participation in a group, can gain valuable insights into the emotions and social
performance of another person. For a wider discussion of the theory and
value of group working, see Heap (1977). Work in groups is uncommon with
older people. Perhaps the reason for this is that the prospect of organizing
and/or controlling a group of people is more daunting than one-to-one
work. Goldsmith (1996) has outlined some work being done with people
with dementia, stresses its potential value, and concludes that it might
become an important area of future growth.

Groups can operate at several levels, all of which can provide useful social
outlets for older people, most notably social companionship, recreational
activity and intellectual stimulation. Counsellors can develop their confidence in working with groups by starting off with informal groups, and
subsequently moving on to groups with specific agendas as they feel able to
do so.

Groups for recreational and social activity

There are many informal groups whose purpose is to meet the recreational
needs of older people. Social clubs, luncheon clubs, day-care units and
church-based groups can help older people to maintain a sense of belonging,
and provide something for them to look forward to during the hours they
spend alone. Such groups can thereby be a valuable means of maintaining
the social and mental health of many older people.

However, informal groups are usually limited in their scope. Some are
organized by well-intentioned younger people whose expectation is that the
group's ageing members will be the passive recipients of organized activities,
and asked to play little part in the running of the group. Group objectives
may look little further than meeting the members' basic needs for companionship and recreation. At their worst, such groups are established and
function within an ageist agenda, eschewing the issues and agendas of older
people, assuming that they are incapable of playing a positive role in
deciding what they want to do, and paying insufficient attention to concepts
of choice, dignity, independence, fulfilment and self-expression.

At their best, activity is considered to be less important, members are
encouraged to integrate socially, and group interaction and involvement are
encouraged. Within such groups, older people can share many topics of
discussion:

- childhood memories, and the 'good old days';
- money and the cost of living;
- illness and physical ailments;
- hopes and expectations for the future;
- feelings of loneliness, loss and grief.

Whereas one-to-one counselling can lead older people to question socially
constructed ideas about old age, and encourage them to take a more direct

and active social role, the formation of groups can further the process, providing older people with an opportunity to share their problems with their peers. This can often help them to place their feelings within a different context. Groups can help older people to realize that they are not alone in their problems, a belief that depression and isolation can often encourage. The realization that they are not 'alone' can be worth several individual counselling sessions.

Social interaction in groups can frequently lead to new insights. Contact with other people can often help people to move out of their lonely, often closed world. They can begin to focus on other people, on the present and on problems that lie outside themselves. They can relate to what other people say about their situation, they can respond sympathetically to the needs of other people, and they can show care and concern for the situation in which other older people find themselves, perhaps becoming less self-centred. They may find that they can come up with solutions to other people's problems, and discover that these might be equally applicable to their own situation.

Informal counselling in groups

The introduction of an element of informal counselling can utilize and enhance the dynamic potential of groups. Informal counselling implies that group members are not seated, nor are they required to discuss particular topics or situations. They have the advantage that they are not directing their comments to the counsellor, but more spontaneously to each other. The group remains a vehicle that creates interaction, enabling older people to participate in and experience a variety of social situations, including:

- happiness and joy;
- sharing information and reminiscences;
- tensions and frustrations;
- friction and anger.

Informal counselling can be introduced into the group by positively encouraging and enabling self-expression and social interaction, where difficult subjects are not avoided and difficult situations are allowed to develop. Whilst it may be easier to stop squabbles and arguments in the interests of peace and harmony, to do so prevents the observation of significant behaviour and emotion that can provide valuable insights into how people feel about themselves, their personal situation and other people.

Group interaction can be used to initiate discussion on many topics, either in small groups, or on a one-to-one basis. These can help people to understand and come to terms with their own feelings, and give them an opportunity to change their coping behaviour within a real social situation. The group can provide an opportunity for actively raising and sharing problems and feelings with other people who may be experiencing similar difficulties. Groups can provide people with a safe environment in which to discuss their feelings and needs, and the mutual support provided can help them to develop new coping strategies for dealing with them.

Indeed, group involvement can sometimes be the only way to encourage more withdrawn people into a counselling situation, especially those who feel too awkward or vulnerable in a one-to-one situation. Concern about not burdening others with personal problems, and the idea that discussing such matters denotes personal weakness, are common among the older generations, especially when an individual has a strong sense of personal dignity and pride. Sometimes such defences can be almost impossible to break down on a one-to-one level. Sherman has outlined the value of group techniques of counselling.

> just hearing the problems of other group members is often very helpful. The member finds that his or her own problems are not unique. Also, by acting as auxiliary counsellors for others, members of the group learn how to combat their own self-defeating attitudes and behaviour. The fact that there are several persons in addition to the group leader who can reflect and provide feedback about such negative attitudes and behaviours makes it more likely that the individual member will take such information seriously and do something about it. The force of group approval can be an important incentive in this regard.
>
> (Sherman, 1981)

Formal counselling in groups

Counselling groups can be formed by bringing together two, three or more people, who perhaps share similar problems and difficulties, for the specific purpose of discussing those issues. Group size is important. More than two people constitute a group, but sharing and transference are often better facilitated with more people. Groups of between 3 and 8 people promote an atmosphere in which it is easier to share views and to ensure that members get to know each other. Groups of more than 8 to 10 people can be threatening, and not everyone will feel sufficiently relaxed to make a contribution.

Where the counsellor is involved in group formation, the aims and objectives of the group, and its mode of operation, should be carefully planned and shared with group members. All of the conditions that apply in one-to-one counselling apply equally to group counselling. Comfortable seating, in a circle so that all members can see each other, can be arranged. This ensures good eye contact, which is important for promoting mutual trust and confidence. The distance between seats should be arranged carefully so that the group sits close together, but not so close that personal space is invaded. It is always helpful to try to relax the group prior to commencing the session. Introductions are important, making each group member feel welcome, and saying a few encouraging words about each person. Thereafter, the use of names is important to make everyone feel part of the group.

The purpose of the group meeting should be made clear from the start, so that everyone knows what they are about and what is expected of them. A useful way of starting a group discussion is to ask each group member to give a short life history of him- or herself. Prior warning of this is important, however, and if someone lacks sufficient confidence to do so, they can be sensitively assisted by the counsellor. When the introductions are over, the reason for the meeting can be outlined, and any specific topic of discussion can be introduced. The agenda of meetings should arise from the interests and concerns of group members. No subject should be forbidden, and each person should be encouraged to raise issues of current concern or interest. Similarly, all feelings should be considered valid. Both the group as a whole and individual members of the group will go through many experiences that the counsellor can usefully follow up.

Observation of social interaction is important. As situations arise, the associated feelings can be discussed, enabling group members to share their sorrows, their grief and their loneliness with others who have experienced similar events. Even the anticipation of future loss, and the way in which it can be handled, can be the subject of discussion.

The role of the counsellor/group leader can eventually be reduced – certainly when a level of group sharing has been attained. Counsellors should try to limit their direct contributions, whilst ensuring that important issues are fully discussed and real feelings are expressed and not avoided. The counsellor becomes part of the group interaction, an involved and interested member, but at the same time he or she also has to be an observer. These are difficult, even contradictory tasks, but it is important to observe the group's dynamics. Certainly the group leader should be more concerned about what the group can do for itself, rather than what he or she can do for the group. The objective should be to enable group members to discover their own strengths and weaknesses. Group members should feel not only that they are contributing, but also that their participation is important. It has been suggested that group members should be encouraged to speak directly to each other, rather than through the counsellor (Corey and Corey, 1987). Encouraging self-help, self-motivation and self-action can lead to positive feelings of purpose, relevance and fulfilment. Therefore, during group sessions the counsellor should undertake several tasks.

1. *Give everyone an opportunity to contribute.* Some people will inevitably be shy whilst others will tend to dominate the discussions. The former may feel that they do not want to impose their views and problems on the others, while the latter may see their problems or viewpoint as essential. Encouraging some people to talk more, and others to talk less, has to be handled without putting down the extrovert or embarrassing the introvert.

2. *Develop mutual empathy within the group.* Group members should be encouraged to see the viewpoint of other people, whilst they in turn are

willing to talk about their problems. Some people put forward their own views without listening or sharing, and to prevent this several approaches are useful:

- the group can be asked to respond to what one person has said;
- the group can focus discussion on one person at a time;
- the counsellor can emphasize the importance of the group discussing general or shared problems;
- the counsellor can ensure that the group makes links and comparisons between the different problems faced by group members.

3. *The leadership role.* There can be a tendency for group leaders to interfere too much in the running of the group, and to be anxious that the group is not running well, or that they are not being sufficiently helpful. This should be avoided. The counsellor should leave the group to work out its own solutions, restricting his or her input to:

- occasional clarification of issues;
- keeping the group within the general areas of discussion;
- ensuring fairness;
- introducing an 'extra' thought or dimension to the topic;
- introducing a point of view which has not been considered.

If a group becomes too cosy, or is not moving forward, the counsellor can sometimes play 'devil's advocate' by introducing more controversial ideas into the discussion.

4. *Use games and exercises.* It is often helpful to group dynamics to introduce games and exercises in order to augment discussions. There are many books outlining group games and activities, often aimed at children and young people, but the activities described by Crosby and Traynor (1985) relate specifically to older people, and these authors explain how group exercises can be used to enhance group learning. Music, photographs and other memorabilia have also been successfully used to stimulate thought and discussion within groups, and activities such as painting can add to the group process.

5. *Life cycle group therapy.* Butler (1974) used groups of older people to develop individual life histories and share these in a therapeutic group setting. Certainly such an approach usefully combines the value of group work and reminiscence.

6. *Anti-ageism.* Group counselling can help older people to see what it is possible to achieve in old age, and how they can restrict themselves with negative or ageist thinking. This can help them to reassess their lives and strive towards achieving their maximum potential.

The objective of group counselling is to help people to feel confident enough to act on their own behalf and on their own initiative, pursuing objectives that match their own ideas about themselves and their lives. An agreed time for finishing each session is important, although this can be interpreted flexibly. It is important not to go on for too long, or to leave difficult business unfinished.

Peer counselling

Groups of older people unlock the potential of counselling *for* older people *by* older people. They can undermine the arrogant ageism of younger people who assume that only they can help older people. Just as children and adolescents have their secret understandings and life-styles, often intentionally separate from those of parents, teachers and other 'older' people, so older people have their own generational agendas. Many topics can arise in groups which can recall many shared formative memories.

- Members of the group can discuss and compare life during the Great War, or in the 1920s and 1930s.
- They may want to talk about changes that have occurred in expectations, duties, responsibilities and other social factors since their childhood.
- They may wish to discuss their present lives, comparing how they cope with the problems and difficulties of being old in a changed society.
- They may discuss their different ways of coping and finding solutions to shared problems.

Groups with special characteristics can be helpful. Bringing together groups of older people from minority ethnic communities can be particularly useful, especially when group members feel isolated in a predominantly foreign culture. Such groups can both provide the basis for valuable cultural reminiscences and help to establish new friendships.

Younger counsellors must bear in mind that the agendas and feelings of older people can be based on quite different values and assumptions from their own and, in recognizing this, accept that peer groups might provide something that one-to-one counselling can never offer, namely *solutions based on the values and ideas of their generation, rather than those which accord with the views and attitudes of the modern world.*

Peer counselling may have many specific advantages.

- Peers can share experiences and values, some of which may be unique to their generation, and cannot be fully shared by younger people.
- There is no 'generation gap'.
- There is less resistance to discussing their feelings than with 'youngsters'.

Self-help and self-action groups

There is evidence that some older people are becoming more assertive in demanding their independence and their social and political rights. The Gray Panthers in the USA started the process, but similar groups, consisting mainly of older people, now operate in many western countries with the aim of improving the condition, status and quality of life of older people. Their establishment recognizes that passively waiting for a change in public sympathy and political will is pointless. If attitudes towards, facilities for and the quality of life of older people are to be improved, this will only be achieved by older people actively engaging themselves in identifying the issues, organizing action and fighting for their own cause.

Self-help groups may have only a minor counselling role. However, when older people combine with the intention of involving, or reinvolving themselves in the wider social context, several benefits emerge.

- Participants are instrumental in raising their own self-esteem.
- The group can enhance the status of older people generally.
- Group activity can demonstrate to an ageist society that older people are full citizens whose needs have to be considered.
- The group can enable older people to be the 'givers' rather than the recipients of help.
- The group can enable older people to make provision for their needs as they – not other people – see them.
- Ethnic minority groups can determine to reach out to other isolated members of their community.

These are major counselling objectives, and encouraging older people to become part of such groups would constitute a major counselling success. Campaigning groups may be contrary to ageist social images of older people, running counter to dominant expectations of how they should behave. Self-help groups can move older people away from passive acceptance of their social circumstances. Involvement in self-action groups will mean that they are not taking life easily, accepting their situation, and enjoying their later years in peace. No one will need to feel responsible for them, or assume that they cannot or should not be responsible for themselves. They will no longer feel patronized.

Age-integrated groups

Not every older person wants to be in the company of other older people. Many prefer to include younger people among their circle of friends, and to become members of groups that emphasize their common experiences and interests, regardless of age. Age-integrated groups can lead to valuable exchanges of feelings and knowledge between the generations. However, there is an increasing trend towards age segregation, which subliminally teaches older people that they are different and separate to other age groups.

- Retirement differentiates 'pensioners' from the rest of the population.
- Special treatment for older people (travel permits, concessionary pricing, etc.) emphasizes that pensioners are, and need to be, treated differently.
- Sheltered housing schemes and residential homes for older people ensure that they are segregated from mainstream housing.

Membership of groups that focus on specific pursuits, interests or hobbies, and which often require no age differentiation, should be encouraged. Often when older people are no longer able to take part in more energetic pursuits, they can take a leading role in the running and organization of such groups.

Family counselling

8

Systems theory
Family construct theory
Maintaining the family group

The importance of family relationships tends to increase with age. For older people, their children can represent an important element of their legacy to the world and the family line. Family harmony, even where harmony has not existed before, can become important to peace of mind. Likewise, children can remain unaware of their debt to their parents until it is too late to acknowledge it, and then spend years regretting their ingratitude. For these reasons, family work can be an important element in the counselling process.

Whilst families spend a significant part of their lives together, and their needs can be closely linked, family members do not always share the same objectives. Indeed, they can often be mutually incompatible, and from this situation can arise the tensions and misunderstandings that lie at the root of many social and emotional problems experienced by older people. Where problems relate to the family, it is often crucial to involve key members in the counselling process.

Family counselling, or family therapy, began in the USA in the 1950s, underwent enormous expansion during the 1960s, and is now a well-developed technique with a sizeable literature devoted mainly to the issues of child development. However, the method is equally applicable to the problems experienced by older people within families (Benbow *et al.*, 1990). A justification for family work with older people has been given by O'Leary.

> Its underlying assumptions are that the family is the main source of social support; that its members influence and are influenced by one another; that difficulties emerge within the family context; and that resolution occurs within that framework. Problems experienced by older adults are considered to have less to do with the stresses of ageing than with difficulties in other areas of family life. These difficulties may arise from problems encountered by the family in adjusting and realigning itself as the members grow older.
>
> (O'Leary, 1996)

Systems theory

Systems theory developed in the 1940s as an explanation for human behaviour that took into account the dynamic impact which groups have on people. It focuses on 'systems', such as the family, and looks at them as an entity rather than just a collection of independent people. Indeed, each 'system' is considered to have an effect greater than the total of its constituent parts. Put another way, individual behaviour is seen to be strongly influenced by the systems in which the person operates, and in order to understand behaviour fully, it is necessary to understand the way in which systems function.

The family is an 'open' system which continually exchanges information and ideas with other similar 'systems'. Working with the family may involve bringing together several systems, including:

- the system formed by the older person;
- the systems formed by one or more of their children.

Within these complicated family networks, the wider, extended family unit will be found, consisting of any number of separate systems, all operating on and interacting with each other, adjusting to changing circumstances, and influencing (among other matters) the way in which care is provided for older relatives. The counsellor has to determine which family systems and which members of those systems are relevant to the problem, i.e. who to include and who to leave out.

Family construct theory

Family counselling is based on the premise that older people face problems that have their cause and effect within the family process. Kelly's construct theory (Kelly, 1955, see pp. 67) has been applied to the family by Proctor (1981), who proposed a model of family functioning based upon shared constructs. These 'constructs' constrain a person's view of the world. Whereas we all have the potential to make our own choices and decisions, we are restricted by the knowledge that by doing 'what we want' we will have an impact on other people. The complex family network, with its powerful expectations, acts to constrain the choices we make. Our understanding of family constructs, particularly how other family members are likely to react to what we decide to do, restricts our freedom of choice, but it also enables us to organize our lives with some degree of predictability and certainty.

It produces a state of homeostasis – a mechanism which enables a system to remain in a stable state through time.

Each interaction upsets homeostasis, but each part of the system is programmed to respond in such a way as to ensure a return to normality. Homeostasis is not necessarily a fixed and unchanging state, but rather it is one which allows change to occur in manageable stages, and preserves a measure of continuity and security.

Homeostasis can also be dysfunctional. Families can become stuck in patterns of behaviour that produce and reproduce failure, unhappiness and insecurity, where family members act in ways they know will be hurtful to others, who in turn reciprocate with actions that they know will cause further distress. It might be expected that dysfunctional families would break up, but usually they do not do so.

An example may be helpful. When ageing parents become dependent, a daughter may assume the main responsibility of care. Perhaps she resents the duty, feeling that other family members could do more, or that her parents do not show sufficient gratitude. By assuming the caring role the daughter ensures homeostasis – the family stays together. Yet the daughter is resentful, and she threatens to discontinue the caring tasks. The family now has a problem. Her parents demonstrate their distress by becoming ill. Other family members combine to make the daughter feel guilty. Threatened by family hostility, and in danger of exclusion, the daughter reassumes her caring role, albeit with increased resentment. The parents, chastened by the incident, feel unhappy about being a burden, and feel unloved and deprived of the respect they had expected as a right. They become resentful, constantly describing everything they have done for their daughter in the past. A pattern of guilt and resentment, frustration and anger emerges. A network of family duties and expectations has arisen that causes unhappiness and stress. Yet within this system, a homeostatic mechanism ensures continuity. The family remains together, however painfully.

This family construct can create considerable unhappiness. The real issues are never discussed, and do not have to be, for established patterns of behaviour will ensure that the status quo is maintained. Yet even within such negative systems each family member has an allocated role that provides an unpalatable security based on an uncomfortable certainty and predictability.

Family care of the older relative

There is a popular perception that the modern family has increasingly renounced its former caring role for older people. It is argued that there has been a trend from family-centred care towards state-provided care, and that this has happened throughout the western world, and even in the more traditional oriental societies. This is not a new idea. Gray and Wilcocks (1981) trace the attitude back to a Royal Commission on the Poor Law in 1909, but it is no doubt much older than this.

It is important to place this trend in perspective. Contrary to this perception, the family remains the major source of care for older people (Means, 1986), and it is wrong to assume that there has been a widespread decline in family care. Indeed, the perspective should not be accepted just as an expression of social concern, but should be examined for its wider social purpose, for it is a perception that usefully obscures the inadequacy of social provision available to support the army of family carers, usually female, who are expected to carry the caring burden, often at considerable personal cost. Blaming the family for the plight in which some older people find themselves distracts attention from the real problems that structural social change has placed upon family care. These include:

- the rise of the small nuclear family unit;
- the construction of smaller housing units, with limited accommodation;
- earlier marriages, and younger births;
- the rise in female employment as an economic necessity;
- increased population mobility.

The structure of modern social life exacerbates family problems, and these trends have been encouraged by a variety of social, fiscal and economic policies which have conspired to increase the number of families who find it difficult to meet the care needs of older relatives, and so have increased the incidence of unfulfilled need picked up by state provision. Some carers feel imprisoned by the demands made on them. They are often torn between their wish to care for older relatives and their need to lead independent and fulfilling lives. The balance between these conflicting objectives has no doubt always been difficult, but perhaps no more so than within the modern family. The need for family work has therefore increased.

There is sometimes an assumption that minority ethnic families are more cohesive, and offer more support to their elders, often leading to the mistaken assumption that they do not require outside support and assistance (Social Services Inspectorate, 1998). Yet their families face the same social and economic conditions as indigenous families, and have the added difficulty of existing within a dominant culture. The social and cultural values of the family can vary considerably between generations, often leaving older people feeling sad and angry that traditional values have been abandoned (Neuberger, 1987).

The origin of family difficulties

The problems that arise between older people and their adult children will be based upon the relationships and patterns of interaction that have developed over many years. Their origin will be the unresolved issues that arose whilst the children were growing up and perhaps moved away from the parental home. After many years, the family dynamics will have moved on. New issues will have arisen, and perhaps old ones will have deteriorated. This will be so regardless of whether the 'children' live independently or remain within the family home. In either case, an almost complete role reversal will have taken place.

Former carers now require care.
The 'cared for' will be needed as carers.

It is easy to underestimate the immense process of adjustment involved in this process. Children who were formerly dependent and subservient can find it difficult to come to terms with the responsibilities of caring. Parents who were formerly dominant and independent will find dependency difficult, and probably also demeaning. The caring task will be daunting, particularly if mental confusion and incontinence arise. The lives of carers will be disrupted as they will be unable to make personal decisions without considering the needs of their parents. They may often have to forgo social events and holidays in favour of their caring task. Even the sexual lives of carers can be handicapped, especially if the older relative lives in the carer's home.

In addition to this major change in role, Sterns *et al.* (1984) identified four types of family dysfunction relating to older family members.

1. They may be used as scapegoats for family problems.

2. They may find it difficult to allow their children to function independently.

3. They may face powerful new sibling alliances which overwhelm them within the family group.

4. They may insist on an over-dependent attitude with regard to their children.

Such problems often remain undiscussed within families, and before anyone is aware of the situation, they can escalate towards family breakdown, elder abuse, and reception into residential care.

Family issues

Counselling older people in a family context can often focus on fundamental changes in power and status roles, although it can involve issues dealt with elsewhere, such as retirement, health, loneliness and bereavement. The counsellor needs to ask key questions about family roles, duties, responsibilities and expectations, for when these are uncertain, confused or mutually incompatible, problems can arise.

*   What is the nature and quality of inter-generational family relationships?
*   How does the existing pattern of relationships and interaction within the family match the needs and expectations of the different generations?
*   What rights, duties and debts do various family members feel towards each other?
*   How do these expectations match, and to what extent do people feel that family and personal expectations are being fulfilled?
*   What are the patterns of dependence and independence within the family, and to what extent are these accepted or resisted by each family member?
*   Are there issues of unresolved stress and conflict within the family?

- What was the nature of the former parental–child relationship, and what impact does this have on current relationships?

No counsellor can assume that 'good' relationships are, or have been, the family norm. Idealistic images of family life being reciprocally supportive and loving should be abandoned. Family construct theory suggests that it is wrong to assume that 'good' family relationships exist, or even that they are wanted within families that are held together by conflict and disharmony.

Change and development within families can also be affected by ageism, especially when younger members assume that as their parents are growing older they and the problems related to their care can only get worse. Such fatalism can be a reason for failing to discuss the problems relating to care, for there is no point in discussion if there is no prospect of resolution.

Developing self-awareness within the family

The starting point of family counselling is to bring together key family members, and to embark upon discussion that seeks to define and highlight problems. The initial task is for each person to discuss their particular viewpoint. The aim is to enable family members to examine their needs and expectations, to compare them with the needs and expectations of others, and to establish how differences and misunderstandings can create stress within family relationships.

Greater awareness within the family makes it possible to tackle the existing conflicts and incompatibilities. The object is to help the family to negotiate mutually acceptable expectations, with each family member being aware of what is expected of them and how much they can reasonably expect from others. This can be a demanding counselling task, relying on many skills, including:

- an ability to referee and control the expression of different and conflicting attitudes;
- giving equal time and importance to everyone's point of view;
- encouraging family members to explain their own feelings and to listen to the feelings of others.

The counsellor needs to be aware of the wishes and expectations of the givers and receivers of care, and the role of each family member, old and young alike. No assumptions should be made.

- Some older people may want to be cared for by their children, whilst others most definitely do not.
- Some people see state support, in all its guises, as a benefit, while others regard it as an intrusion or an indication of failure.
- Some older people will see their need for care as a matter of fact, while others will regard it as a matter for shame and a cause of guilt.

The possible permutations of such feelings between any two family members are endless, giving rise to complex and perplexing interactions from which a variety of emotions can arise, including:

- guilt and despair;
- sorrow and disappointment;
- anger and frustration;
- depression and hopelessness.

The generality of behaviour

When interpreting this complex situation, the counsellor is helped by the generality of behaviour within families. Apparently small and isolated family incidents that are observed by the counsellor are often examples of typical family interactions. Walrund-Skinner (1977) describes family therapy sessions as 'a slice of real life', providing the counsellor with a 're-enactment of the ongoing patterns of behaviour', a 'microcosmic expression of the family's continuous drama, enacted during the other 23 hours of the day, when the therapist is not with them'. To extract this generality from observed family behaviour is important. People do not alter their feelings, behaviour or interactions because of a particular situation, not even the presence of a counsellor. Apparently isolated incidents can vividly illustrate more generalized patterns of family life.

Impartiality

Family counselling can subtly change an individual counselling relationship. It is no longer a one-to-one relationship in which the counsellor can concentrate exclusively on the feelings and needs of a single person. Other people must now be considered. This inevitably alters the relationship, and can often cause difficulty if the individual feels that his or her problems are being ignored, and that 'their' counsellor is no longer 'on their side'. Preparing the older person for family meetings by outlining the purpose of the meeting, and explaining the stance that the counsellor plans to take during family meetings, can help to avoid potential misunderstanding.

Counsellors have to be impartial. Often the family will focus blame on one person, perhaps a dependent ageing parent or a struggling main carer. Jealousies and conflicts may abound, and the counsellor cannot afford to become embroiled. To be seen as partial can lead to a lack of family trust and the possible withdrawal of key people. Even if an older family member is the primary focus of counselling, the counsellor cannot take sides. The family dynamic has to be considered in its entirety, with the aim of helping the whole family to consider, face up to and develop a wiser, more considered understanding of the problems.

Family power structures

There is one important exception to the rule of impartiality. All families have their power structures, and family work often has to concern itself with balancing the power of the strong with the rights of the weak. The very young, and dependent older people, are usually the least powerful (they have least to offer the family in return for the support and care they may need), but there may be other power and status differences within the family, based not on age, but on gender and on the control of money and resources. The counsellor cannot always deal impartially with existing power relationships, as to do so is likely only to preserve the status quo, with the needs of dependent older people continuing to receive inadequate attention.

These family power structures cannot be ignored when it is clear that the power of one party is being used to the detriment of another.

The usual outcome is that the shortcomings of weaker individuals are blamed for each and every family problem. The counsellor's task is to enable weaker family members to present their needs and feelings as coherently and forcefully as possible, perhaps by clarifying, expanding and focusing on what they say. The object should be to achieve a more equitable balance in the discussion and, where possible, to highlight the negative role of more powerful individuals within the family dynamic.

However, if the counsellor compromises impartiality by supporting weaker family members, care has to be taken. Neutrality, which is so necessary to develop mutual trust and confidence, should be breached in such a way that powerful individuals are not annoyed or upset by this. If powerful family members begin to see the counsellor as partisan, developing awareness of the needs of weaker individuals can become difficult. Failure will occur if the counsellor no longer has any impact on family dynamics. He or she has to be sensitive to the needs of all family members, so that he or she can maintain the confidence to tackle family issues diplomatically.

How these paradoxical objectives are achieved will depend upon individual style. Family therapy is not a precise skill, with 'correct' and 'incorrect' approaches. Different methods can be used in similar situations with equal success. Counselling responses often have to be rapid, based on personal judgement rather than on precise theoretical principles. The counsellor has to enter the family dynamic unintrusively, not demanding compliance to the wishes of specific family members, but to ensure that the feelings and needs of each member of the family, even the weakest, are heard. The development of family therapy has been pragmatic, more involved with solving problems than with adhering to particular dogmas.

Maintaining the family group

Once family sessions have begun, the counsellor has to ensure that the group is maintained while many potentially explosive family problems are discussed. There are many ways in which open and honest discussion of problems can be harmonized with maintenance needs, whilst ensuring that family members are not damaged in the process. The counsellor will meet resistance, and maintaining attendance at family meetings can be a problem, particularly if progress is slow or the problems are particularly intractable. This is a normal reaction to discussing painful and difficult issues. Refusal to attend meetings is one way in which key individuals, or those who feel they have most to fear from change, can undermine the process. There is usually no way of enforcing attendance, so when someone threatens not to attend, the threat should be taken seriously, with the counsellor working through the person's feelings and paying special attention to their particular needs.

Family history

The initial focus of family discussion is important. Rather than starting with the current difficulties, it is often possible to begin with the family history. To do this can be helpful when there has been a genuine basis of care and love within family relationships in previous times. It can remind the family that they have experienced better times, and raise the prospect that such times can exist again. From these more harmonious beginnings the counsellor can seek to move on to consider when family relationships began to falter, what the circumstances were, and how people felt about the issues at the time. By adopting an 'historical' approach, old misunderstandings can be traced to their origins, linked together and brought up to date. Recalling better times can lead to a mutual reaffirmation of care and affection between the warring parties. Thereafter, when the family is discussing more difficult issues, and the discussion becomes heated and acrimonious, they can be reminded of their commitment to each other.

The present

Some families, however, will want to talk about the present, feeling that what has occurred in the past is of little consequence. In this situation, family work can start immediately. An observant counsellor can gain an understanding of the existing pattern of family alliances and tensions by the way family members choose to seat themselves. Looks and body language can also provide useful clues about the current state of family relationships.

Openness and honesty

However contentious and divisive the family problems may be, and whatever the difficulties involved in persuading the family to engage in discussion, issues should be tackled rather than avoided. In considering how the counsellor can encourage openness and honesty, it will be helpful to look at a generalized example.

Family hostility often arises when the expectations of older family members make unrealistic demands upon younger relatives. The usual if not inevitable result is that their expectations are disappointed, with all the hurt and anger that can accompany this. Similarly, younger carers might need to be given an opportunity to express their feelings – to say, perhaps, that nothing they do is sufficient, and that they have begun to assume that they can do nothing right.

Whilst it might cause short-term distress to discuss these feelings, failure to tackle the underlying issues is trading short-term distress for long-term relationship breakdown.

When both sides are able to talk frankly about their feelings and expectations, the other party has to consider them and respond accordingly. This can be mutually beneficial. If young carers do eventually withdraw their help and support, their older relative will feel abandoned, and they will often feel guilty about doing so. Whilst they may be able to rationalize what they have done, there is usually a strong element of mutual disappointment about the broken relationship and the abandonment of older relatives to domicilliary or residential care.

Disclosure of personal feelings within the family group is important. In manipulative family situations it is better for people to talk directly to each other. Some people find face-to-face honesty difficult, especially if they feel weak or threatened within the family group. To avoid direct communication, devious messages are often sent, transferring their feelings to mysterious 'others'. One way of overcoming this is to encourage family members to use 'positioning' (Bowen, 1978), in which people are expected to use 'I' statements when expressing attitudes and feelings.

Dealing with anger

During family sessions, feelings can arise so quickly that very damaging statements can be made, which may be frank and honest, but which have a destructive meaning or impact that might not have been intended in calmer, more reasonable moments.

- *'I don't give a damn about you.'*
- *'You can go to hell.'*
- *'You were the worst father/mother/daughter/son that anyone could wish to have.'*

If such comments are left entirely unqualified, they can do considerable long-term damage to family relationships. A closer inspection of the statement, rather than trying to pass it off, or pretending that it was not said, can be helpful. The counsellor can:

- seek to analyse and ascertain exactly what is being said;
- seek to ascertain why it was said;
- seek to ascertain what the real message might be.

*In doing so, it is important that the counsellor tries to distinguish between the **feeling** and **emotion** contained within the statement (which was probably real and should not be ignored) and the **literal meaning** of the words (which were probably used in anger, and may not have been meant).*

This highlights one of the main differences between normal communication within the family, and the counselling process. It is usually the literal meaning of words which is heard. In counselling, it is the emotions behind the words that need to be pursued. It is important that people understand why someone feels strongly enough to say 'go to hell', and that they do not merely believe that this is an accurate statement of their position. Violent and damaging words are used to express feelings, not intentions. There may be no wish to damage or end the relationship, although this can be the outcome. It is often through anger and frustration, perhaps by someone who feels unwanted or neglected, or who is struggling with guilt or frustration, or who feels imposed upon and taken for granted, that such words can be used. It is the counsellor's task to move the discussion to these underlying emotional meanings.

Noble intentions

Another technique is to ascribe 'noble intentions' to words and actions that have caused friction and animosity between family members. This involves developing explanations for actions or behaviours that are expressed in more positive and acceptable terms which both parties can understand and recognize. For example, it is often possible to explain hostile behaviour in terms of the love and concern someone feels for another person. Not all angry behaviour is a straightforward expression of hostility or hatred, and *noble intentions* reinterprets behaviour in a way that can bring together two or more people after serious conflict. Clearly, a *noble intention* has to exist. The skill is in recognizing rather than inventing it.

If the atmosphere becomes particularly strained, the counsellor can attempt to move the discussion on to a more harmonious subject. Whatever the need for honesty, there is little point, and usually no advantage, in allowing discussions to continue on the basis of anger or mutual recrimination.

Setting family tasks

Another typical resistance to family work occurs when key people adhere rigidly to old patterns of interaction and behaviour, often despite what is being achieved in terms of family understanding and awareness. Recent developments in family therapy have suggested that seeking merely to increase self-, and family awareness may be insufficient to bring about effective change within such families, and they stress the importance of structural change through the use of family tasks. These give the counsellor a more active role within the family, and are based on the idea that change in such situations is brought about more effectively through action rather than self-awareness. Family tasks can achieve several objectives.

- They can focus the family's attention on the need for change.
- They can highlight the importance of personal action, showing how family members can undertake small, practical tasks which can help to change the family dynamic.
- They can provide an opportunity to pursue positive and helpful activity within the family setting between family sessions.
- They can help the family to define in precise and concrete terms what can be done to improve their situation.
- They can enable powerful family members to modify their impact.
- They can enable weaker family members to point out what is happening to them whilst it is happening.

How the tasks have been performed, and what family members feel about the 'new' way of doing things, can then become the starting point of the next meeting. Tasks are most appropriate for families that have become 'stuck' in hurtful and damaging interactions, and who seem to be resistant to or incapable of change. Their aim is to provoke change rather than to enhance awareness. Discussion can lead to new understandings, and to more important and complex tasks being developed. Examples of such tasks might include the following:

- the exchange of pleasantries, and spending some 'quality' time together (perhaps relaxing, or playing a game);
- reaching an agreement at the start of the day as to what needs to be done, and who is to do what;
- other members of the family agreeing to give the main carer some respite.

Paradoxical tasks

Where there is resistance to positive ideas, change can be effected by suggesting 'paradoxical' tasks. These can recommend that family members continue or even intensify the difficult interactions at the root of family problems. This technique can place the family in a 'double-bind'. They can either accept the task, tacitly admitting that they are in control of what they do and the situations which they create, or they can protest that to do so will worsen the situation. An example might be when a daughter who is caring for her dependent father is continually met with ingratitude and unkindness, making her feel guilty that she is not doing enough. If all attempts to change this pattern are resisted, the task might be that she tries to increase the level of care she gives him and that, in return, her father should increase the unkindness and unpleasantness of his response.

Reminiscence and the life review

9

Reminiscence
The reminiscence group
The life review – making sense of a lifetime

We are all the product of our history and the multitudinous influences of events, circumstances and people that impinge upon us. People reminisce at all ages, but in older age looking back at life and reviewing our triumphs and failures, joys and sorrows, pleasures and regrets is particularly important. Yet whilst older people have many memories, some will have few friends of the same age with whom to share them (Gillies and James, 1994). When older people recall the past, it can be both spontaneous and therapeutic. Some need little encouragement, while others may require help, support and encouragement. Reminiscence can facilitate communication and companionship, especially among isolated and lonely people. In a world of shrinking human contacts, it can provide an instant means of rapport with other people of their generation.

Reminiscence

Reminiscence has not always been considered helpful. Aristotle, in his 'Treatise on Rhetoric', said that older people 'live by memory rather than by hope, for what is left to them of life is but little compared to the long past'. The ancient world presented this melancholy view, describing older people as irresolute, without positive opinion, pessimistic, small-minded and cowardly. This view dominated our perception of older age and reminiscence until relatively recent times (Coleman, 1994). Some consider reminiscence to be a mixed blessing, particularly for people whose past life experience seems to lack purpose or fulfilment. In the 1950s and 1960s reminiscence was regarded as a symptom of mental deterioration, a failure to maintain contact with present-day reality, and a potentially harmful process. The idea that older people should not live in the past or dwell on the 'good old days' was common, devaluing reminiscence as the aimless meandering of a decrepit mind. This attitude can inhibit discussion of the past.

Reminiscence work became popular during the late 1960s, when the benefits to older people of reviewing their life and validating their life experience were recognized. Klein *et al.* (1965) found that many older people needed help and encouragement to reminisce, and they often hesitated to talk about the past because they feared rejection. For older people this is a common experience, perhaps reflecting the dominant social preoccupation with the future, and the dismissal of the past as uninteresting, irrelevant or unimportant. Tobin (1991) illustrated how the capacity of sympathetic listeners to make the past vivid can be an important element in helping very old people to maintain their psychological health, and showed that people often turn to their memories in order to find comfort, and to boost their sense of self-worth in the eyes of others.

Reminiscence is now regarded as a normal, if not essential, element of successful old age – an opportunity to enjoy pleasant memories from the past, or to revisit unresolved conflicts and make sense of them. Norris (1986) points to five reasons for its importance.

1. Reminiscence highlights older people's assets rather than their disabilities.

2. It can enhance their feelings of self-worth and self-esteem.

3. It can help older people to recognize their individuality and identity.

4. It can aid the process of life review.

5. It is an enjoyable and stimulating experience.

The benefits of reminiscence to older people have also been observed. They become less restless and less anxious about their present situation, they show a reduction in confusion and forgetfulness, they become calmer and more attentive, their mood lightens, and there is a greater willingness to share their feelings about the present with their families and carers. They are able to talk vividly and humorously about the past. Many older people gain great pleasure from reminiscence, especially those who have lost close friends.

Reminiscence can be a valuable counselling aid, although it is important to place its value in perspective. In a review of research, Coleman (1986) concluded that generalization about the value of reminiscence therapy should be avoided. People were either 'reminiscers' or 'non-reminiscers', and that even amongst reminiscers, some found the process unhelpful. Amongst non-reminiscers, many felt that there was little purpose in looking back, while others did not reminisce because they found it too depressing.

The counsellor's problem in deciding whether to use reminiscence is to determine its value to a specific individual. The counselling relationship will assist in this. With 'reminiscers', even those who find it difficult, counsellors can utilize the process confidently. With 'non-reminiscers' there might be less reason to dwell on the past, and with some it might be useful to avoid it altogether. Overall, it is important to consider its potential value to the counsellor.

Empathy between generations

Early formative experiences are powerful factors in establishing personality. For older people, these experiences took place in a very different world. The current generation of older people was born when the motor car was uncommon, aeroplanes were a rarity, the telephone was a recent invention, and radio and television were unknown. Ethnic minority elders may have been born in a different country and a different culture. This fundamental change in social life has altered their perceptions about the nature of life – its problems, pleasures, responsibilities and duties.

When younger counsellors share experiences with older people, both are doing more than 'recalling the past'. They can share a common heritage that has been formative for both young and old alike, as well as trying to understand their different experiences of and outlook on life. This can be helpful to younger counsellors, who may become more aware of generational differences, and attain greater empathy. Certainly the counsellor needs to have some knowledge of and interest in the world and culture in which older people grew up. This will help them to understand:

- the complaints and uncertainties older people have about the 'modern' world;
- their sadness about change;
- their cynicism about 'progress';
- their regret for the passing of former values, traditions and customs.

Living history

Biography plays an important part in historical understanding. Most biography centres on the lives of the rich, famous and influential – the people we believe to have moulded history and shaped the society in which we live. Yet more recent historical study has seen a shift in focus towards the lives and experiences of 'ordinary' people.

- How did 'ordinary' people live?
- What were their main concerns, difficulties and problems?
- How did dominant social, economic and cultural forces affect them?

To cite an important example, it is the difference between looking at the Great War as an event centring on the policies and machinations of politicians and generals, or as one that impinged upon the lives of soldiers and ordinary people. Lloyd George and Kitchener have their biographies. Yet those who directly experienced the disruption, turmoil and loss of the war have this information locked within their memory. Historians now realize that if this experience is not sought we shall lose a unique insight into the times and events they report – an insight that will die unless it is recorded (Thompson, 1978).

Both viewpoints are historically important, but the latter is more important in counselling. Counsellors will have learned about the war from books, films and documentaries, all largely based on a political viewpoint. Older people will have experienced the war in personal terms. Their experience is not only an invaluable source of history, but it is also an essential element of counselling. By concentrating on personal experience, counsellors will not only learn important social insights, particularly if a record is kept, but will gain an understanding of how the war affected the individual. To achieve this, counsellors may have to 'unlearn' some conventional understandings about the nature and significance of historical events. The counsellor as 'historian' is perhaps an unusual view, but by travelling through a person's life history, especially if one is making a physical record through family scrapbooks, albums, memorabilia and genealogies, the counsellor is producing an important autobiography that serves a dual function.

Reminiscence can provide an initial point of contact. Taking time to talk about the past, and focusing on personal experience in all its detail and complexity, can help to forge the counselling relationship. It can also reverse the power balance, with the counsellee becoming the teacher and expert, and the counsellor the pupil. It can help to emphasize the value and significance of the counsellee's life, and the part they have played in the history of their times.

Life history as insight

In order to understand an individual fully, the importance of a lifetime perspective – especially in older age – is important. Personal history – what we have done, who we have been, what has been important to us – is what makes a person come alive. This is important with regard to older people, who in many cases are 'no longer what they have been'. It helps an individual emerge from 'elderly', 'infirm' or 'dependent' stereotypes. Understanding a person in the context of his or her past can be essential for understanding the present person. Reminiscence can provide the counsellor with invaluable insight into the nature of a person's formative years, which in turn can be informative about many current issues. For example:

- how they decided on their personal aims and objectives;
- how they developed strategies for fulfilling their needs and desires;
- how they constructed their social attitudes and moral values;
- how they face up to and deal with problems;
- how they cope with disappointments;
- how they form relationships.

These have been called 'life scripts' , general personality traits, and regular ways in which people tend to respond to all new situations and circumstances. Reminiscence can provide information that indicates not only how someone has arrived at their present position, but the way in which they are likely to respond to it. Although life scripts can be modified, more commonly they remain essentially intact throughout a lifetime. Examples of life scripts include:

- a tendency to cope with life optimistically or pessimistically;
- a tendency to react with hope or to become depressed;
- a tendency to tackle issues or to leave them unattended;
- a tendency to be extrovert or introvert;
- an ability to make and maintain new relationships.

Locating the origins of current problems

Some older people find it easier to talk about their childhood and early years than their current problems. As reminiscence naturally proceeds from past to present, it can often give an indication of where, and in what period, problems have arisen. There is often a point when reminiscence is blocked – when there is resistance to proceeding further. Such blocks frequently correspond to times of particular stress or social change. This can often coincide with the onset of depression or confusion, suggesting that this is the time, or these are the events, that require counselling attention. The counsellor can frequently obtain invaluable information from relatives and friends who were aware of the individual's personal circumstances at the time, although they are perhaps unaware of their full significance.

The counsellor should recognize that there will be regrets and disappointments, as well as joys and successes, associated with the past. Reminiscence can lead to painful and unresolved conflicts. Bender (1997) suggests that older people rarely discuss traumatic experiences, and the emotional distress caused by the World Wars, because too much psychological damage was done in the first half of the twentieth century for them to handle. People were killed or maimed, marriages were ended and whole life-styles terminated. Other older people may be preoccupied with negative aspects, or the sheer ordinariness of their lives, particularly when there has been a lack of life satisfaction and fulfilment, failed relationships, unfulfilled hopes, and events that elicit feelings of disgrace and shame. Bender (1997) reminds us that the 1920s and 1930s were decades of massive social dislocation and change, mass unemployment and hardship. Thus counsellors face the problem of whether to delve into the past, or to leave it alone. The balance lies between two possibilities.

1. Reminiscence can provide a means of re-examining such matters which, if successfully addressed, can enable people to come to terms with what has happened in their lives, and to forgive themselves for past failures. Many older people are proud of their life struggles, and reminiscence can lead to greater happiness during their remaining years.

2. One is risking the possibility that reminiscence will take people back through stressful and disturbing memories, and that they will fail to come to terms with what is disturbing them.

Such a decision should not be taken lightly. Reminiscence can play an important part in ameliorating personal distress. The view that upsetting issues should be avoided has already been discussed. People will talk about what they feel is important and/or acceptable – what is not will be self-censored by those who are overwhelmed with grief. Some older people may have lost so much that they cannot bear to consider the past and how happy they have been. If appropriate, the counsellor can concentrate on positive memories to the exclusion of negative ones, but Bender (1997), for example, believes that there was collusion after the war to deny its most unpleasant and painful aspects at an individual, family and societal level. However, provided that people can be coaxed and not coerced into exploring sensitive areas, and the counsellor has time to cope with any distress that results, the outcome can be positive, especially with older people who are facing crises such as retirement, dependence, depression, ill health, bereavement and death.

Buchanan and Middleton (1994) pointed out that there has always been confusion about whether reminiscence is a recreational activity or a therapeutic technique. The two are not mutually exclusive. Reminiscence can be either helpful or unhelpful. It can be fun or it can be traumatic. The counsellor should venture into the past, but he or she should venture carefully.

However, there are good reasons for confronting painful memories. Surveys of older people have highlighted the negative influence of regrets and self-blame about the past, and Coleman (1994) reminds us that loss and grief are essential parts of the experience of ageing, and that older people are well equipped to handle grief.

Supporting good mental health

The sensitive use of memories can help older people to retain a positive sense of self, and provide a framework for serene old age. Many older people suffer from what can be described as mental health problems, ranging from depression, anxiety disorders, drug and alcohol dependence to phobic and paranoiac illnesses. Some will bring mental health problems with them from earlier years, while others will develop such disorders as a result of ageing. When supporting older people with such difficulties, certain skills and resources are required, although there is probably still no substitute for personal relationships (Gillies and James, 1994).

Mental health problems can result in altered social and emotional behaviour, and may eventually lead to personal suffering and collapse. The sadness generated by the loss of a long-standing partnership can often be a trigger, but whatever the cause, it can be helpful or even necessary to talk about the past and the reason for their feelings, and come to terms with what they have lost.

The reminiscence group

Groups can be rewarding and exciting, but they can also be daunting (see Chapter 7). Many of the experiences of older people will be unique events that have shaped their personal circumstances and attitudes. However, people born in a particular period will have been influenced by the historical, cultural and social events through which they all lived. Each generation will have shared experiences, and it can be beneficial to bring groups of older people together to participate in sharing these memories.

The same can be said of minority ethnic groups, who have had a very specific experience of life within a foreign cultural setting. Many will be first-generation immigrants who will recall their origins in quite different settings. The difficulties they experienced in settling, and the racism they encountered, will be shared experiences. Reminiscence might be painful for such a group, but it can also prove to be of considerable value.

The life review – making sense of a lifetime

Young people live with an eye to the future, and with a sense of their potential for further work or achievement. Nothing is yet complete or whole. Only in old age (whenever that is supposed to start) can we experience and reflect upon an (almost) entire life cycle. An important objective in counselling older people is to help them to live for today rather than for an uncertain tomorrow. Counselling should encourage reflection and use the life review as an important element for growing old positively.

When a person thinks of the past they are not just taking stock of their life, but deciding what to do with the rest of it. By doing so, they can make sense of their life. Butler (1963) showed that preparing a life history can be a genuine comfort to older people, especially those close to death. It is a healing process. It demonstrates our interest, concern and respect, and they are checking on the legacy they want to leave. This can be seen in relation to the characteristics of an 'ideal' old age outlined by Erikson (1965) (see p. 36), which is concerned with identity and generativity. The life review can help to address the problems surrounding the social role of older people. As their social network and known physical landmarks diminish, and their role and integration in society decline, older people experience an increasing sense of alienation. Current and past life experience become progressively more different.

The life review can provide a means of re-establishing and confirming personal involvement, linking their past work and influence with the social changes that have occurred, and recognizing that in a variety of subtle ways they will themselves have been part of the changes they are witnessing. It is possible in this way to help older people to face death with an understanding that they have played a role in the continuity of people and events. When discussing the achievements of children or grandchildren, it is often possible to trace elements of their own qualities, and their own contribution to their success. Doing so can improve their quality of life, provide a pleasurable experience and enhance their sense of self-worth.

PART FOUR

Employing counselling skills

There is no solution to ageing. It happens, it is unavoidable and it is generally unwanted and unwelcome. It is neither right to resist it, for then we find it hard to come to terms with the inevitable, nor to accept it, for then we are often unnecessarily accepting ageist perceptions. Counselling should seek to open up the discussion and to look openly and honestly, but questioningly, at the issues.

The remaining chapters will look at the issues that counselling older people needs to address. The subject matter is artificially separated into chapters, although the counsellor cannot deal exclusively with any one area of life, which is a whole and needs to be considered and treated as such. Nor is it likely that older people will experience problems in just one area, as these difficulties will be likely to lead to problems in other areas. Similarly, solutions in one area will help to resolve those in others.

The order of the chapters is sequential in that they begin with the problems of earlier old age and move forward to those which are likely to arise later. Each chapter considers the nature of the problems (on the basis that the more we understand, the more likely we are to be able to help people cope with them), whilst also dispelling some of the myths that surround them. Consideration is then given to the role of the counsellor in addressing the issues that are likely to be involved.

Whatever the problems, it is important to deal with them as early as possible. Although it is too idealistic to hope that the process of ageing could be dealt with during childhood, it is certainly true that ageism takes root during those years. The reality is that counsellors will have to work with people whose lives have already been deeply affected by the problems of ageing, and this will require all the skills and insight outlined earlier. Social distress, when ignored, becomes worse over time, and takes longer and requires more patience to resolve.

Counselling older people is concerned with maintaining their quality of life for as long as possible, and looking optimistically at the ageing process. It does not deny the ageing process, or seek to change natural physical laws – only to delay them.

For carer-counsellors it is important to recognize the limits of their competence, and to realize that specialist help should be called for whenever necessary. However, it is important to emphasize that professional competence is not something that can or should be taken for granted, and that the intimate knowledge of the carer-counsellor can often be as useful as the most vaunted professional skills.

Preparation for retirement

10

Economic policy and retirement

Social attitudes and individual need

The social impact of retirement

Post-retirement counselling

In the perception of many people old age begins with retirement. Productivity – the ability to contribute to the national wealth – is a powerful element of social status. We place considerable value on work. For many, it is the largest single social contribution that they make. Thus retirement constitutes the end of an important aspect of life. Old age, as defined by retirement, prevents people from remaining in a productive role. For these reasons, Parsons (1949) considered that the loss of employment was a central feature of growing old, significant for its impact on self-esteem, social interaction and identity. Hazan (1994) linked retirement with the loss of power, respect and social rewards.

This has not always been so. Prior to the inauguration of state pensions at the turn of the twentieth century, working people did not retire. They might be forced, through declining health and strength, to take lower-paid or unskilled work, but for most people the idea of ending their work role was impossible, short of a desire to risk starvation or enter the workhouse. Thus retirement is a comparatively new concept, particularly among the poor. In the UK it has been estimated that 73 per cent of the male population over 65 years of age were occupied in 1881, but by 1981 this figure was only 11 per cent (Johnson, 1985). The International Labour Office has found this to be an international trend (Townsend, 1981).

The reason for this trend is interesting. It is popularly attributed to social philanthropy and successful campaigns to relieve people from the need to work in old age. In this sense, retirement is seen to have been earned – a period of peace and dignity, a right, recognized in law and social provision. However, there are less philanthropic reasons for the growth in retirement.

Economic policy and retirement

When considering retirement, it is important that counsellors look beyond the apparent social compassion for ageing workers. There is a more cynical view of retirement that looks upon it as a form of compulsory unemployment – using older people as a 'reserve of labour' – made necessary by an economy which can no longer offer full employment (Phillipson, 1982). Laczko and Phillipson (cited in McEwen, 1990) described the two conflicting views on retirement in the 1980s.

> In the early and middle part of the decade they [older people] were being urged to leave the workforce as soon as possible, as a way of coping with high unemployment and large numbers of school leavers. By the end of the 1980s, however, the position had been reversed, with calls on older workers to remain in employment for as long as possible.
>
> (McEwen, 1990)

For many older people, the problem of retirement is that they are caught between these conflicting social views of their working status.

- If older people continue working, especially in times of high unemployment such as the 1930s and early 1980s, scarce employment leads to the view that older people should give up their jobs, with demands to lower retirement age. Older people who continue working are seen as selfish, depriving younger people of work opportunities. They are described as being 'too slow', 'too set in old work practices', or 'possessing skills which have become redundant'.
- Alongside this, retired older people are considered to be an increasing social and economic burden, a major consumer of resources, never likely to have future productive value and, increasingly, they are seen as an economic liability.

Older people will view retirement as either a positive or a negative feature in their life, and disparate social attitudes towards retirement will certainly be reflected in ambivalent feelings. Whilst some people will welcome retirement (especially those who are unable to retire or who are locked in tedious work), others will see it as an unwanted imposition and a period of personal crisis, depriving them of income, status and role. Either way, older people will be confronted with damaging social attitudes. Either:

- they are doing the work that younger people could, and perhaps should, be doing, or
- they are part of a growing population of retired people whose idleness is creating social and financial difficulties for a declining productive workforce.

To work is wrong. To retire is wrong.

The result is that older people can be attacked from both directions. Pressure to work and pressure to retire are exerted in proportions that can be both confusing and callous. It is these 'non-philanthropic' social attitudes that can cause older people distress. Counselling can play a vital part in helping retired older people to cope with the many dilemmas and pressures placed on them. Retirement brings with it not only the loss of the largest single activity in which they have engaged, but also a massive drop in income, standard of living and social status. Whilst this may appear to be a pessimistic view, it is the reality for many retired people.

There are more palatable visions of retirement – armies of retired couples peacefully spending their time in retirement homes by the sea, or in the warmer climes of Mediterranean hotels – yet these are opportunities available only to the more privileged few. For most people, retirement does not offer such a prospect, and for many it represents poverty, monotony, and lack of purpose and fulfilment in life.

Social attitudes and individual need

Whilst retirement counselling is more readily available, these wider aspects are too rarely considered. Retirement counselling should do more than encourage people to take up useful and interesting hobbies to fill their leisure hours. It should recognize that social attitudes can cause problems for retired people, bringing into question their personal value and worth, and placing them under considerable stress. The effect of retirement can only be understood on an individual basis. Its significance will depend upon the value and importance a person has placed on work, and what they want and expect from retirement. Counselling must focus on individual need, personal situations and feelings.

It is a subjective evaluation that determines whether retirement leads to personal satisfaction or emotional distress.

Atchley (1976) proposed that retired people have a 'hierarchy of goals' which lead to personal expectations, behaviour and a sense of well-being. When these goals are frustrated, for whatever reason, people have to make one of two positive choices:

- they can maintain their expectations, and seek new ways of meeting them; or
- they can modify or substitute new goals which are more readily obtainable.

The third outcome is that they fail to reconcile the discrepancy between goals and achievement, and it is this failure that leads to problems in retirement. The role of the counsellor is to help people to resolve this discrepancy by:

1. helping them to understand and determine their particular goals, making sure they are realistic, and, indeed, sufficiently ambitious;
2. helping them to decide how best this can be achieved;
3. helping them to come to terms with retirement and play a more active part in its outcome.

If this is achieved, older people will be able to make appropriate choices and decisions about their retirement which they can justify both to themselves and to their social critics.

The social impact of retirement

Retirement counselling should consider the wider implications of dominant social attitudes. Its development in recent years has arisen from the experience of many retired people, even those who have had a positive attitude towards retirement. The losses involved are often either unforeseen or not recognized as a problem, frequently leading to depression and serious illness. Indeed, many people die shortly after retiring.

However, it is important that the problems of retirement are kept in perspective. After reviewing the literature, Braithwaite and Gibson (1987) concluded that the belief that retirement was a major crisis of old age was not substantiated. Thus while many older people will not experience problems as a result of retirement, some will. Here counselling can play an important role in making people aware of the potential hazards of retirement, and in helping them to understand and interpret those hazards in terms of their own feelings and priorities.

The loss of activity

Work usually occupies a considerable portion of life prior to retirement. Despite the need to work for a living being widely recognized, the necessity of doing so can be bitterly resented, particularly by those involved in repetitive, unskilled manual labour. Evenings, weekends and holidays may have become the 'highlights' of life – much treasured, but all too brief. Retirement appears to offer these 'highlights' on a permanent and ongoing basis, and from a distance this can seem very alluring.

Yet even people who have seen work purely as an economic activity may discover that the workplace and/or work itself has become a central feature of their life. Even the most monotonous work occupies the mind and body for long periods. Travel to and from work may have been combined with other activities, or with a knowledge of other activities going on around them.

The problem can be worse for people who have not used their spare, non-work time for 'constructive' purposes (perhaps best defined as activity that provides people with an interest, and usually has a particular purpose and a planned outcome); it has not been activity that has led to a sense of personal fulfilment. Often, people may have devoted little time or energy to developing fulfilling interests or hobbies, instead engaging in more passive, less constructive activities such as watching television or having a pint at the local pub. Such activity has little end result, and whilst such pursuits might be sufficient for short periods, by their very nature they are an inadequate basis for full-time retirement.

The result is that retired people often become bored, dissatisfied and unfulfilled. They begin to look back rather than construct a new future. Perhaps work was not so bad after all. Instead of seeking to replace work with constructive leisure, its loss becomes the subject of grief, made worse when they then come into contact with the social attitude that equates retirement with idleness. Alternative activity is an important factor in successfully adapting to retirement, and whilst counselling does not have a direct role in its provision, it can encourage people to seek it.

The loss of social companionship

The workplace also provides us with a base for social interaction. People spend more time in the company of their work colleagues than with their marriage partners, and almost certainly more time than with other friends and relatives. Work provides people with a social network that is often taken for granted and only missed after retirement.

For many people, companionship at work can be the most important single source of new friendships. This becomes more important with age, when people can start to lose long-standing friends with increasing rapidity. Retirement combines these two aspects of companionship, namely an increasing loss of friendships, and a reduction in social opportunity to replace them through new work-based friendships.

Loss of income

Whereas the counsellor can hope to point retired people towards new activities and new sources of friendship, the loss of income associated with retirement is a matter over which counselling has little direct influence. Old age and retirement have always been associated with poverty. Despite the political rhetoric of the modern welfare state, which has sought to create contrary images, the reality is that the basic state retirement pension provides an income that represents between one-third and one-half of average earnings. The rates are fixed according to officially designated subsistence needs which are much lower than net earnings during the period of paid employment. The result is that poverty and retirement are close allies. Townsend (1979) found that the risks of poverty were highest among older people over 75 years of age. Whilst social provision allows retired people to exist, there is little scope for them to grow or to make full use of their later years.

The reality which many pensioners face involves basic life choices – for example, deciding whether to spend money on food or heating. The inability to do more than survive can be deeply depressing. People on basic pensions have little spare cash for continuing old leisure activities and social contacts or commencing new ones. The income of most pensioners excludes any social involvement that requires significant expenditure.

Health

Good health in old age is not just a matter of avoiding bugs and reducing wear and tear on the body. Many other factors within the control of the individual are at play (Scrutton, 1992). Unemployment causes unhappiness for many older people, and this can have a serious impact on both mental and physical health. Argyle (1987) found that the health effects of retirement are worst for people who are committed to the work ethic. The failure to adjust to retirement can form the background to future poor health and many other age-related problems. This suggests that if the hazards of retirement are not adequately discussed, the seeds of depression, ill health and other problems can be sown.

On the other hand, good adjustment to retirement is likely to ensure good health. Braithwaite and Gibson (1987) found that good health shows a strong correlation with good adjustment to retirement, and with an ability to take advantage of the opportunities that retirement provides.

Social participation

The counsellor should avoid the simplistic but convenient notion that older people withdraw from social activities and friendships because they no longer want them, or because withdrawal is an inherent part of old age. Often withdrawal is a straightforward but tragic response of older people to an inability to finance social integration. Moreover, enforced withdrawal from social integration can quickly cause demoralization, which is so often associated with old age. The fact is that restricted social participation and loneliness have more to do with the economic difficulties which older people face than with the ageing process.

Gender

There is a popular assumption that it is men rather than women who feel the full impact of retirement. Even Simone de Beauvoir suggested this:

> the elderly woman adapts herself to her stage better than her husband. She is the person who runs the home, and in this her position is the same as that of the peasants and craftsmen of former times – for her, too, work and life merge into one another. No decree from without suddenly cuts her activity short. It does grow less from the time her grown-up children leave the home and this crisis, which often happens quite early in life, often disturbs her very badly; but still she does not see herself thrown into total idleness, and her role of grandmother brings her fresh possibilities.
>
> (de Beauvoir, 1972)

If such an assessment of the impact of retirement on women can be made by an eminent female writer, it is perhaps not surprising that the idea is firmly integrated in our social attitudes. Yet women have been part of the world of paid employment for many years. Indeed, poorer women have never been able to leave it. The increase in female employment, and women's liberation from a life centred entirely around the home and the family, make such an assessment increasingly outdated. It is wrong to assume that older women should experience retirement as any more or less significant than do older men.

Social class

The differential access that people from different social classes have to resources is a major determinant of who can and who cannot provide for themselves in retirement. Professional, managerial and skilled workers have many advantages over semi-skilled and manual workers. As mentioned earlier, it is likely that their life-style will involve more constructive and fulfilling leisure activities. They are also likely to have more savings, better pensions and additional insurance income that will enable them to maintain their life-style and social status, and to pursue their main interests without too much regard to cost. They are also likely to be healthier in old age, and to have better access to a good diet and medical assistance.

Race

Many older people from minority ethnic groups find that they have retired in – and are likely to lead the rest of their lives in – a 'foreign' country. It may have never been their intention to stay permanently. Many may have intended to earn sufficient money to be able to return to their homeland, and this may be a matter of considerable disappointment. They may not want to die and be buried separated from their parents and forebears. Often their children, born in this country and fully integrated here, may not realize the full extent of their disappointment.

Post-retirement counselling

The counsellor will meet problems associated with retirement at many different stages. Clearly it is better if consideration can be given to the potential hazards of retirement prior to the event. Pre-retirement courses are now more common, organised by such bodies as the Pre-Retirement Association and the Workers Educational Association in conjunction with employers. Phased retirement schemes are also making a small but important contribution. People approaching retirement should be aware of the need to pressure their employers to provide suitable courses for their staff.

However, many people will retire without formal support, and the counsellor is likely to be involved with people facing post-retirement problems. The task at this stage is to ascertain the person's feelings and problems, and to discuss them at an individual level. This may involve dealing with related problems of depression and ill health that have arisen since retirement. It may also be necessary to ask people to look at alternative ways of approaching and coping with their work-free circumstances, perhaps by trying to start the process all over again, but with an increased awareness of the problems and difficulties that are involved.

Counsellors should seek to present a positive view of retirement, but also one which stresses the need for personal commitment and effort. Too often retired people say that retirement has not turned out as they had expected. This may arise from the absence of a realistic concept of the practical implications of retirement. Many people may recognize the negatives that retirement represents, including:

- the end of work;
- the end of paid employment;
- the end of having to rise early from bed.

People may even expect to slow down after retirement, and may anticipate that their health will deteriorate. In fact, their expectations may be so low that they do little to make their lives fuller and more interesting.

Retirement should be viewed positively as the start of a new phase of life, not just the end of an old one. The opportunities available to retired people should be stressed, particularly in the context of the need to maintain personal commitment, involvement and activity. Retirement can be seen as a time when:

- there is no further need to engage in work;
- they are free of the need to be in paid employment;
- they can either stay in bed or get up, according to their own desires;
- they can maintain their energy and enthusiasm for whatever they want to do;
- they can determine to maintain their health for as long as possible.

Weir (cited in Phillipson *et al.*, 1986) distinguishes between *reassurance*, warning against 'the bland, cosy suggestion that our troubles are all illusory and will melt away with little or no intervention on our part', and *encouragement* in dealing with retired people. Counselling has to be rooted in reality, with the dangers and opportunities of retirement being presented side by side, and with the understanding that the outcome will be largely determined by personal decisions and action.

Social engagement

Human life is gregarious. Our quality of life depends to no small degree upon our relationships with other people. Social relationships which are close, confiding and supportive are a major source of happiness. No one has the ability to live in isolation. Solitary confinement is recognized as a punishment which causes severe psychological damage and if, like Robinson Crusoe, we are subjected to enforced exile, whilst some people will undoubtedly cope better than others, few individuals willingly choose isolation or loneliness as a favoured way of life.

Attachment behaviour

The need to make strong social and emotional attachments is a deep one. Attachment theory (Bowlby, 1980) describes 'attachment behaviour' as that which seeks to maintain strong affectional bonds. This behaviour arises from strong biological needs, such as the need for food, sex, security and safety. Attachment behaviour starts in childhood and endures throughout life. Each person directs this behaviour towards a few specific people whose continuing presence is considered vital to their emotional and social survival. When such attachments are threatened or removed, this can lead to intense reactions such as clinging, crying, grief and other forms of distressed behaviour.

Old age is closely associated with an increased experience of isolation. Everywhere older people can be seen living alone and, in many cases, suffering the recognizable effects of 'solitary confinement', namely apathy, depression and ultimately self-neglect. Only at specific times, such as during periods of festivity or spells of excessively cold weather is this recognized as a problem. Too often it is accepted as 'the norm' – something that older people have to expect, and part of the process of growing old. Moreover, current social policy seeks to move away from institutionalized forms of care (e.g. residential homes, long-stay hospital accommodation), and to concentrate instead on maintaining people in their own homes. Whilst community care policies are soundly based on principles that seek to maintain people's independence, they can also lead to social isolation.

Social change has contributed to the increasing isolation of older people.

- The decline of extended family networks and their replacement by smaller 'nuclear' family groups have meant that valuable support networks have been eroded. Traditional family networks offered older people not only a place, but also an important and respected role within the family group.
- The nuclear family has arisen from and created a desire for independence and privacy by younger family members. Some live quite separate from family ties, with little capacity to care for older relatives.
- These changes have been structurally confirmed by the size and design of modern housing. Homes are now small, compact and designed principally for two adults and their children. There is little provision for elderly relatives without causing inconvenience, and this predisposes young and old alike to decline the offer and acceptance of joint occupation.
- Increased social mobility adds to the isolation of older people. Children not only live in separate houses, but often move away from their families in order to pursue their career. The mutual support they could formerly provide has diminished accordingly.

However, whilst it is important to recognize these trends, we should not forget that the family still performs most caring functions for the majority of older people. There was no 'Golden Age', but undeniably family trends since the Industrial Revolution have led to the increasing isolation of older people. This has been accompanied by younger relatives feeling guilty, and older people feeling abandoned. Consequently, there has been a need to develop alternative explanations to explain and justify such trends.

Disengagement theory

The loneliness of older people has been given respectability by social theories that either seek to give, or are interpreted as giving, an explanation for their isolation. The theory of 'disengagement' (Cummings and Henry, 1961) describes a process in which older people gradually and voluntarily relinquish their social roles and activity. It arose from observations of older people who appeared to initiate their isolation as a means of releasing themselves from the problems, pressures and difficulties of life. They interpreted this as a 'natural' process, arising from a loss of skill, energy and determination in coping with the pressures of mainstream social life. Through disengagement, older people were believed to transfer their time and energy to more congenial matters – to reflection, reminiscence and rest.

Disengagement can be viewed positively, and is chosen by some older people. It is associated with freedom from pressure, e.g. from work or other unwanted sources of stress. However, disengagement is often unwanted, and is forced on older people by social factors that disqualify them from remaining involved.

In this latter sense, disengagement justifies the loneliness and isolation of older people. Rather than seeing declining social involvement as 'a problem', it becomes a natural social and psychological mechanism. Disengagement is not to be avoided, but is an integral part of the process of ageing, to be accepted, without the need for guilt or expensive social intervention. It is a comfortable view of the nature of old age, explained by the diminishing needs and lower expectations of older people, who are 'content' with their loneliness.

The problem with disengagement theory is that it fails to ask whether the observed characteristics are attributable, at least in part, to cultural expectations.

- Do older people initiate withdrawal?
- Or do social structures and institutions (retirement, poverty, expectations about ill health and disability, etc.) suggest that this is what older people are expected to do?

Certainly, older people learn to 'play the game' according to the social rules.

- They do not make demands.
- They do not complain.
- They do not put pressure on younger relatives who, after all, have their own lives to lead.

Disengagement is socially enforced. Older people are obliged to retire from work even if they do not wish to do so. However, more subtle factors are at work. Dominant social attitudes suggest to older people that 'disengagement' is expected of them, and they learn to respond to these expectations, even when they do not correspond to their own feelings and needs. Whilst some people may desire a degree of social disengagement, it is far from being a 'natural' or inevitable process.

Disengagement is just one of many social theories that Phillipson and Walker (1987) called 'acquiescent functionalism'. This is a body of thought which attributes the problems of older people to the natural consequences of physical decline, mental inflexibility and the failure of people to adjust to ageing, as opposed to explanations which focus on contemporary social developments (e.g. the economy, social inequality). These factors are either dismissed as inevitable or unalterable, or not considered at all.

The counsellor's task is to try to unravel the part played by cultural norms, social theory and individual need. We need to discover the real needs and feelings of the individual. The counsellor should not be beguiled by the comforting reactions that older people might initially present, but instead he or she should question the assumptions that they and others have made about their withdrawal.

If ageing is a period of social withdrawal, the logic would be to leave older people alone, and not seek to improve their quality of life through continued social engagement.

Activity theory and the loss of social roles

Activity theory sees older people as active and involved, even when their work role has finished. Proposed by Havighurst (1972), it states that older people should maintain their work activities for as long as possible, and then replace them with others. It assumes that active, productive people are happier, and that continued productivity and social interaction are essential for a sense of well-being and fulfilment. This is a sensible basis for counselling older people. Clearly, not just any activity will do. It must be purposeful, and it must arise from the interests of the individual. Counselling should focus on encouraging social engagement, and in particular the loss of crucial social roles. One of these, namely the loss of employment, has already been considered.

The parental role

The loss of the parental role is vital to understanding the problems of many older people. The crisis often faced by married couples when their last child leaves home is well known. Much of the previous 20 to 30 years of their lives will have been associated with child-rearing, and the developing independence of children can be a matter of concern rather than joy, especially for people who have been over-committed to their children, or who have over-identified with the parenting role. When the children leave home, and no longer require support, how is the time to be filled?

- What meaning and importance are left in the marital relationship?
- Where are the opportunities for a new life and new relationships which can make this new stage of personal development more meaningful and less empty?

The end of parenting is often the first important social loss. If a new direction in life can be found at this time, many difficulties of later role losses can be more successfully faced, as this transition will demonstrate the importance of a periodic reassessment of the purpose and meaning of life. It can help people to become more aware of their personal needs, and the importance of dealing with them when former roles and responsibilities are shed. However, many people fail to make the transition, becoming embittered by their 'abandonment'. Marital relationships can also fail at this time, often because the difficulties of being 'non-parents' are insufficiently understood. Counselling can perform two vital functions which assist people in facing up to their lives as non-parents.

1.   It helps them to come to terms with their new situation.
2.   It encourages them to fill their lives with new interests and pursuits.

The opportunity to do this is often missed. The end of parenting rarely corresponds to what we consider to be 'old age'. Unlike retirement, the loss of the parental role is not widely discussed as a social issue, and certainly not as a problem, and it often passes without notice. Parents may feel some emptiness, but other people are as likely to assume (and even joke about it) that they are lucky to have so much spare time now that their children have left home.

Indeed, this is the positive way to view this loss. Perhaps the trite remark 'life begins at 40' (or even 50) is true because it recognizes the opportunities available to people after their parenting responsibilities have ceased. However, people have to be willing and prepared to take advantage of those opportunities. If they are not, then not only will those chances be missed, but advancing years can be synonymous with increasing loss, boredom and isolation. Often this is the attitude adopted by older people. They see their lives as becoming progressively more empty and meaningless, and this pessimistic outlook is reflected in all that they do, or perhaps, more accurately, in all that they fail to do.

The loss of social networks

Many people facing the loss of their work and parenting roles will have failed to maintain an adequate network of friends and social activity. The origins of this failure may go back to early parenthood, when children have to be looked after, and opportunities to participate in the wider social circle are reduced. Visits to social venues and to friends decline at this time. Friends also have children, and contact can be lost. The value of social groups can be undervalued, and they can be discarded. Social life now revolves around child-minding, in all its many forms, and this normally takes place within the family home. There is nothing intrinsically wrong with this situation, but with people's lives centred exclusively around their children, the potential for later isolation exists.

The 'disengagement' may not have been intentional. It will certainly not have been brought about by the process of ageing. The failure is to maintain an adequate level of social life beyond parenting. When children become independent, many parents may find that their lives are no longer fulfilling. They may have forgotten what makes life enjoyable as non-parents, and other factors confirm this.

- Dominant social attitudes stress the importance of parenting, particularly for women.
- People's adult children can highlight their increasing age, and release the ageist pessimisms and fears of growing old.

Older people from minority ethnic communities may also face a language difficulty. Some may not have learned the language of the host nation, or have a poor grasp of it, and this can severely restrict the number of people with whom they can engage in meaningful communication.

Too often the result is that people become social non-participants, cut off from what is happening around them. The counsellor has to determine to what extent these factors exist, and at what point they arose. The task is to encourage people to reconsider their real needs for social engagement.

The marital relationship

Marital relationships undergo considerable stress with the arrival of children. A once exclusive partnership has to be shared, and this sharing can unbalance even the closest relationships. Marriages increasingly break up at or soon after this point. Partners can begin to move in opposite directions, with the husband feeling abandoned, and devoting his time and energy to work. It is common for men to assume that the 'breadwinning' role is their main, perhaps only, contribution to family life. However, this can seem to the mother like rejection, or an abandonment of the parenting role. Now that she has another role to occupy, she can content herself with it and throw herself completely into motherhood. Partners can often be depressed by the disinterest that each shows in the other. Couples can forget to give time to themselves, and their relationship can be damaged as a result.

When the children leave, the marital relationship can be very empty, extending little further than sharing the family home. The problems of readjustment are considerable, and it is common for counsellors to find long-standing relationships that are little more than empty shells, incapable of providing significant mutual support or even meeting the need for mutual companionship.

Sexual relationships

Many myths surround sexual needs and potency in older age. There are changes in sexual capacity and in the sensory and emotional experience of sexuality with ageing, but older people are not sexless, and they can and do participate fully and joyfully in sexual activity. Research shows that older people remain sexually active, and that age does not undermine either the need or the capacity for sexual activity. There appears to be no age limit to sexual potential. Kaye (1993) showed that sexual activity, interest and desire can continue into the nineties. (For a wider discussion, see Thienhaus *et al.*, 1986; Butler and Lewis, 1988; Greengross and Greengross, 1989; Gibson, 1992; Brecher, 1993).

When there is a reduced sexual response in older age, this has more to do with social factors such as:

- the absence of a partner;
- hostile, derisory and ageist social attitudes;
- health problems, particularly those relating to cardiovascular disease, diabetes, multiple sclerosis and prostrate difficulties;
- drug side-effects (many prescribed drugs can have adverse effects on sexual functioning, especially in older people).

There is no age limit to the enjoyment of and participation in sexual activity, and counselling can play an important role in dispelling some of the myths that surround sexuality. Several tasks can be undertaken. The first is to ascertain whether the person wishes to talk about sex. Hostile, anti-sex attitudes can lead older people to believe that it is inappropriate to discuss their sexual feelings and needs. Although attitudes towards sexual matters have become more liberal, older people can be reluctant to talk about these issues.

Conversely, it should be remembered that older generations were not as innocent as they are sometimes portrayed. There were illicit affairs and pre-marital sexual relationships. Indeed, many older people take pleasure in reporting their sexual escapades. However, the uncertainty about whether to raise the issue of sexuality can leave the counsellor with problems.

- Failure to talk about sexual matters may mean that the person does not consider the subject to be an issue.
- Alternatively, it might be that the person finds the subject embarrassing to discuss.

If people do not want to discuss sexual matters, their feelings should be respected. Some older people may never have experienced a satisfactory sexual relationship, and may feel that there is no reason to believe that this situation is likely to change in older age. Other people may feel too embarrassed or even morally outraged to discuss the subject, especially with a younger person. If so, the subject is best left alone unless there are good reasons to pursue it (for example, on one occasion I had to interview a man who had been accused of abusing young girls).

When sexual issues are discussed, it is important to develop an under-standing of the person's sexual needs, as they can be central to their problems. Many older people may need to understand the changes in their sexuality if they are to continue to be sexually active and come to terms with other aspects of life in old age.

Sex is a taboo subject for both young and old, and many restrictive and repressive attitudes may have to be overcome. Small-group counselling can be useful, enabling older people to realize that their sexual needs are shared by others. It can also put them in contact with people who have the same or corresponding needs. Certainly the counsellor should be able to discuss sensitively sexual feelings and needs whenever it is either relevant or necessary to do so.

Women and the menopause

Although Masters and Johnson (1966) found that women showed no significant loss in their capacity to enjoy sexual intercourse, the menopause did cause them anxiety because they did not understand or could not control the physical changes in their bodies. This anxiety is often reinforced by descriptions of the menopause as a 'deficiency disease', indicated by low oestrogen levels. An extreme and distressing form of this attitude described post-menopausal women as 'castrates' (Wilson and Wilson, 1963). A more sensible view now prevails which sees the menopause as a natural life event, the effects of which can be controlled.

Older men and potency

Men associate their virility with their ability to have sexual intercourse. Impotence, the inability to obtain and maintain an erection, is a fear experienced by males of every generation, but it is particularly important for older men. Masters and Johnson (1966) investigated the causes of impotence in older men, and found that anxiety about physiological change and the ageist expectation of impotence were as important as the ageing process itself in bringing it about. Impotence can be so damaging to male pride that affected individuals may eschew sexual activity altogether rather than risk repeated failure.

Sexual attractiveness – the ageing body

It is easy for older people to assume that sex is just for the young. Older women, in particular, suffer from anxieties about the 'sexual attractiveness' of the ageing body, arising particularly from male-centred ideas that associate sexual attractiveness with the bodies of youthful 'pin-ups'. Older people can feel that they lose their sexual attractiveness with ageing, believing that whilst youth is concerned with vigour, grace and beauty, old age is associated with ugliness and degeneration. They believe that sexual activity, and even love, concern young people, and that when older people indulge, this is somehow undesirable or even a cause of mild amusement.

Sexuality and morality

The dissociation of sexuality and old age, despite more 'liberated' sexual attitudes, remains strong. Social attitudes, reinforced by religious ideas, assume that sex is primarily for procreation not recreation. This places sex beyond the moral boundaries of many older people, who make a strong connection between sex and immorality, believing that sex is wrong or indecent. There may be a need to talk about feelings such as shame and guilt, or what is 'normal' and 'abnormal' sexual behaviour in older couples, or for people living alone.

Sexual partners

Sex can remain a strong personal need, and should be recognized as such. However, fulfilling that need can remain difficult if an individual has no sexual partner. This is especially so when people have internalized ageist attitudes concerning the unacceptability of sex in old age.

However, even without a sexual partner other forms of sexual fulfilment are available, although rarely discussed. Masturbation can be a source of pleasure, once it is removed from traditional ideas about immorality and its adverse effects on health. It can help to relieve sexual tension when there is no other way of doing so.

Joining local groups in order to meet new people is possible, and advertisements in local papers are becoming increasingly common and socially acceptable.

Painful sexual intercourse

Older people can give up sexual intercourse because it becomes painful. Vaginal lubrication does decrease with age and where this is the case, counselling can suggest simple solutions, such as the use of lubricating jellies.

Sexuality and physical contact

Sexuality is more than just the act of penetration and intercourse, as it also involves close physical contact – touching, stroking and caressing – with another individual. This fulfils the basic human need for closeness and contact. Even physical disability (caused by illness, such as strokes and arthritis) does not need to signal the end of sexual activity. Indeed, it has been found that depression in older age, which is at the root of much illness, can be caused by the lack of this physical contact.

Conclusion

The maintenance of social engagement is crucial. If older people can maintain a reasonable level of social involvement, including satisfying relationships with other people, their quality of life can remain as fulfilling as at any other stage of their lives.

12 Health

The medicalization of health
Health and ageism
Health and mental attitude
Health, exercise and fitness
The importance of good diet
Monitoring medical practice
Alternative medical practice
Counselling sick people

The concept of health used in this chapter is not the narrow medicalized term meaning merely the absence of disease. Good health is as much to do with being in good spirits, being happy and content, coping with the problems and difficulties of life, but enjoying life to the fullest extent possible. The World Health Organization has called this 'complete physical, mental and social well-being, and not merely the absence of disease or infirmity'.

Old age is not an illness. It does bring with it an increased susceptibility to illness and disease, and because old people are seen to be more ill more often than other age groups, illness and old age have become closely associated in our minds. This has led to the belief that old people must expect to experience physical ill health.

This can lead to doctors, relatives and older people themselves accepting levels of pain and discomfort greater than would be tolerated by younger people. This is entirely wrong.

The medicalization of health

Alongside income and social relationships, health is one of the most important issues for older people. Yet health in old age has become highly medicalized.

Medical propaganda influences all age-groups, but is especially persuasive with older generations, who have lived through the years when medical breakthroughs in the treatment of illness have appeared to be most striking. Older people are aware of their increased susceptibility to illness, and are generally too grateful for medical care, accepting without question the value of what they receive. Indeed, more than any other generation, they are made aware of their dependence upon medical assistance, and they have increasingly handed over personal responsibility for their health, accepting too willingly their dependence on medical help, and harbouring instead a debilitating pessimism about the nature of old age.

(Scrutton, 1992)

The process of medicalization leaves people increasingly unaware of their role in maintaining their own health. Conventional medicine concentrates heavily on the treatment of chronic and acute illness, and even now the role of preventive medicine suffers comparative neglect.

Older people probably represent the largest consumer group of health provision, yet they are generally less informed about matters relating to their own health, and more deferential to medical authorities, than any other group. Gray indicated that programmes of health education among older people 'can make a significant contribution to the promotion of a healthy life' (Gray, 1982). A Pensioners Link initiative in Barnet (Meade, 1986) to promote health activity for and with older people reached four main conclusions:

1.   that health education sessions with older people have a significant impact;

2.   the importance of active participation by older people in course planning;

3.   the need for critical preventive work to be recognized as a priority;

4.   the need to challenge traditional patterns of health education, with one-off talks on broad topics to groups of older people.

These findings indicate a role for counselling in health issues. If older people were given more accurate and relevant information about the factors that maintain good health in older age, this could lead to the prevention of ill health, and even to better treatment.

Health and ageism

The health of older people might be improved if they were freed from the many ageist attitudes that surround the issue and, above all, if they were able to feel more positive about their health prospects. The platitude 'you must expect to be ill at your age' is too often heard. It is based on a popular image of health in old age:

one associated with an increase in pain, discomfort, illness, disease and dependence; loss of energy and personal drive; significantly greater need for rest; long and increasing periods of sickness; permanent experience of pain and discomfort; increasing immobility; the gradual loss of personal control and responsibility; the onset of incontinence, with resulting loss of dignity and self-respect; increasing confusion; and, ultimately, the most feared condition of all, senility.

(Scrutton, 1992)

Counselling should challenge this stereotype whenever it appears, by encouraging older people to examine the myths about the inevitability of ill health. Most older people enjoy a healthy life, untroubled by the incontinence, dementia and other 'elderly' disorders that receive so much publicity. Moreover, there is no reason why we should assume that illness in old age is untreatable. Illness can be treated at any age, right up to the very end of life.

Ageist medical practice often fails to connect ill health with the living circumstances of many older people, such as extreme isolation, social withdrawal and self-neglect, all of which are important causal factors in illness.

The difficulty in differentiating between illness and natural ageing processes is another, more subtle excuse for ageism. It is simpler to assume that 'the problem' is old age rather than a treatable medical condition. There are significant differences. 'Illness', or a decline in function and energy, usually has a distinct starting date, whereas old age does not. Declining function arising from ageing is usually imperceptible, only being noted when present ability is compared with that of many years past.

Counsellors cannot pretend to be doctors, but they can question whether ill health is more concerned with social/emotional factors than with ageing. Moreover, health could be maintained if older people had access to more relevant information, and felt more positive about the potential for good health in old age.

Health and mental attitude

There is a strong connection between health and mental attitude, demonstrated within conventional medical circles by the study of psychosomatic illness and the placebo effect, and in many alternative medical practices, such as faith-healing and yoga. Argyle (1987) concluded that health is linked with happiness by preserving the immune system and encouraging good health habits. Martin (1987) suggests a link between psychology and the immune system, based on the idea 'that the brain influences the immune system and, therefore, our resistance to disease'. He outlined how studies had found a small but statistically significant correlation between life events which had forced people to alter their life-style (e.g. bereavement, loss of job, etc.), and the frequency, severity and duration of illness.

This indicates that a positive mental attitude is as important to good health as a negative or resigned attitude is to illness and disease. The links between the mind and health are not fully understood, but there is sufficient evidence to suggest that physical illness is not simply a matter of bodily components 'breaking down' or 'wearing out'.

If we expect to be ill, the likelihood is that we will be.

However, to acknowledge this is to recognize that our health is under our own personal control, and to an extent far greater than is currently accepted. Given the ageism inherent in our highly medicalized attitudes, it is crucially important to understand this. It suggests that health should not be left entirely in the hands of the medical profession, particularly if they continue to perpetuate the belief that good health is a 'mechanical' matter, to be remedied by drugs and surgery. Counselling can clearly play an important part in challenging ageist medical assumptions, and in promoting more positive (but realistic) states of mind which counter the belief that pain and illness are the natural and unavoidable consequences of ageing.

Older people can become dispirited and depressed by chronic illness. When they can see no end to suffering they begin to assume that their condition is immutable, and this serves only to confirm and reinforce the illness. It is important that older people look more positively at their physical condition. Whilst accepting reality, they should be encouraged to resist feelings about the 'hopelessness of recovery' or the 'inevitability of further decline'. It is too easy to become resigned to 'the inevitable'. Even stroke victims usually retain some mobility, so the message to all older people should be not to give up, but to use what they have, to exercise it, to find new and interesting things to do, and to insist on living life to the full as much as possible.

Good health is a combination of many factors, most of which reside within us. Helping older people to deal with health issues is therefore within the competence of counselling. Social factors, such as the experience of loss, bereavement, depression, isolation, lack of exercise and poor diet, can determine the way in which people think about themselves, their life expectations and ultimately their health. Counselling can discuss these feelings and, by doing so, make a more positive impact on health than the tranquillizers and sedatives which are too readily and too frequently dispensed for older people who are ill.

Health, exercise and fitness

Lack of fitness results from the failure to keep our muscles, organs and joints working. Disease and lack of fitness are closely related. Disease causes lack of exercise, but more importantly, lack of exercise increases susceptibility to disease. Moreover, as joints become stiffer, muscles become weaker and organs become progressively less efficient, a vicious cycle can develop.

Fitness arises from regular exercise. This does not mean embarking on extremely vigorous pursuits, although people in their seventies and eighties still run marathons! Walking, swimming, gardening and even general housework are all good forms of exercise.

It is sufficient to exercise little, but often.

What is important is to become breathless and raise the heartrate, to bear weight, and to stretch all parts of the body. Such exercise corresponds to the following three aspects of fitness:

- *stamina* – which relates to the efficiency of the heart and lungs and their ability to sustain effort without becoming tired and breathless;
- *strength* – which is concerned with the muscles and their ability to lift, move and carry;
- *suppleness* – which is concerned with the muscles, ligaments and tendons and their capacity to allow freedom and ease of movement.

All of these aspects are important elements in maintaining good health. Yet older people often avoid taking exercise because of the ageist assumption that it is dangerous. Light exercise is rarely dangerous, but if one is uncertain it may be wise to consult a doctor. However, it is important to stress that ill health in old age is not the result of physical and mental wear and tear and that the only effective action is to call for a doctor. Unlike machinery, we do not deteriorate with use. Indeed, the body maintains itself through continued activity.

The importance of good diet

Good nutrition is a vital factor in health, but is often neglected by older people, especially those who live alone on low incomes. It is a common but ageist assumption that older people do not need as much food. The food requirements of older people are more closely associated with their level of activity than with their chronological age. What is certain is that an inadequate diet can lead to ill health.

There is now a high level of agreement about what constitutes a 'good diet', arising from many years of research evidence (Rogers, 1986; Tudge, 1986). Foods to be avoided or reduced are:

- those which are high in fat, e.g. fatty meats, sausages, pies, polyunsaturated margarines and oils;
- those which are high in sugar, e.g. many processed snacks, soft drinks and sweets;
- those which have added salt and other additives used extensively in processed foods.

A healthier diet is composed of natural foods, such as vegetables and fruit, lean meat and fish, low-fat dairy products such as skimmed or semi-skimmed milk, and foods which are high in fibre, such as wholemeal bread, brown rice and pasta, and potatoes.

Many factors in older age can facilitate against good diet.

Poverty

Poverty can lead to an inadequate diet, arising from the inability to purchase the foods that constitute an adequate or balanced diet. Older people who have fewer than eight main meals each week, or who go for long periods each day without food, are especially at risk.

Self-neglect

Self-neglect can arise from isolation, loneliness or depression. Some older people cannot be bothered to prepare food, relying on quick, easy foods, often resulting in an inadequate or unbalanced diet.

Knowledge of good diet

Inadequate information about what constitutes a 'good diet' can also contribute to nutritional problems. Diets often consist of foods favoured in our younger days, but which may now be known to be inadequate or harmful to health. Eating the wrong food, drinking insufficient milk, and the absence of fresh fruit and vegetables are common problems.

Appetite and illness

Illness is a major cause of loss of appetite, often compounding existing health problems. The circularity here is often confused. Poor health does lead to a loss of appetite, but more important is the fact that poor eating habits play a major part in causing ill health.

Physical disability

Both physical disability and mental disturbance can lead to difficulties in shopping for, preparing and cooking food.

Poor dentition

Poor dentition and the absence of teeth can affect what is eaten, and how well it is masticated and absorbed by the body.

Drugs and diet

Alcoholism, smoking and the side-effects of drugs can all affect the eating of food and the absorption of vital nutrients. For example, smoking reduces the absorption of vitamin C.

Nutritional elements

Poor diet is closely associated with most of the main illnesses linked with old age, and attention to detail may be very important. If dietary deficiency seems to be a factor, the counsellor should be able to obtain assistance (from nutritionists or dietitians) to ascertain the dietary factors that might be contributing to poor health. The deficiency can then be remedied, and thereafter eating habits can be improved through careful discussion and support.

The dietary intake of nutrients declines markedly in old age, and whilst it is difficult to determine to what extent this is either caused by or is the cause of increased physical illness, the connection with health is significant. A fuller consideration of the relationship between nutritional factors and the health of older people can be found in Davies (1981). What follows is a consideration of a few vital food elements, outlining their importance to the health of older people, and looking at the effect that dietary deficiency might have on conditions hitherto considered to be 'normal' factors in the ageing process.

1. *Vitamin C* deficiency can lead to scurvy, but in less extreme forms can be the cause of listlessness, weakness and a general lack of energy. The body becomes more subject to bruising, sometimes spontaneously, wounds heal slowly, and there is greater vulnerability to infection. All of these symptoms arise from simple dietary deficiency, but often are mistaken for normal ageing processes. Many older people have been found to have inadequate levels of vitamin C, and by increasing their dietary intake many problems can be overcome. Oranges and other citrus fruits and fresh vegetables are a ready source of vitamin C, although the vitamin is easily lost in the process of preparation and cooking. Vitamin tablets are also available.

2. *Vitamin D* assists in transporting calcium to the bones, and a deficiency can cause muscle weakness and bone disorders. Vitamin D deficiency can cause a loss of bone density and strength. Again, such disorders can be mistaken for normal ageing processes, but can be readily rectified by eating liver, eggs and 'fatty' fish, although perhaps the best source is exposure to normal sunlight.

3. *Potassium* deficiency can also cause muscle weakness, but is perhaps more significantly associated with its effect on the mind, and particularly with depression and mental confusion. Although most foods contain potassium, especially potatoes and green vegetables, it is known that a high proportion of older people select a diet low in potassium (Davies, 1981). An additional problem is that some drugs commonly used by older people, notably diuretics, cause potassium deficiency.

4. *Calcium* deficiency can lead to osteoporosis, namely the loss of bone density that appears to be a universal phenomenon among older people (Exton-Smith, 1971). Calcium is found in abundance in milk.

Monitoring medical practice

Conventional medical practice is held in high social esteem. The medical profession is one of the most powerful, high-status groups in society. Most older people and their carers will look to their doctors in times of poor health, yet conventional medical wisdom need not, and perhaps should not, be accepted at face value. Indeed, in my experience many doctors welcome (and the accuracy of their diagnosis and treatment can benefit from) the interest and advice that informed counsellors can give about their patients. They can also help by noting the more subtle effects – both beneficial and adverse – of the treatment.

Prevention rather than treatment

Modern medical practice has many shortcomings. It is wrong to assume that older people are 'safe' in the hands of medical professionals. There are many reasons for this, merely outlined here but explained in greater detail elsewhere (Illich, 1977; Thunhurst, 1982; Doyle, 1983). Conventional medicine has been concerned more with treatment than with prevention. The obsession with organ transplantation takes precedence over discovering the causes of organ disease. The effects of stress, the impact of pollution, the benefits of dietary guidelines and the importance of exercise all take second place to 'heroic' surgical techniques and 'miracle' drugs.

Medical ageism

Many doctors reflect the ageism of society, believing that the medical problems of older people represent a low priority. Consequently, diagnosis is often hurried, more likely to deal with symptoms than with underlying causes, and resorting to palliatives rather than cures. In extreme cases, certain forms of treatment might be refused purely on the grounds of age, based on a cost-benefit analysis which concludes that treatment would be 'wasted' on people with a low life expectancy.

Iatrogenic illness

The iatrogenic (or drug-induced) effects of modern medical treatment are now better known, but are still largely discounted by the general public. Drugs often produce effects that are far worse than the original problem. The side-effects of drugs regularly used by older people can lead to mental confusion, incontinence, diabetes, loss of mobility and balance, and even death. Moreover, the vulnerability of older people to iatrogenic disease is greater than that of any other age group.

- Older people are more likely to be subject to polypharmacy and harmful drug interactions.

- Their reduced renal function makes the build-up of drug toxicity within the body more likely.
- They have a lower tolerance of high doses.
- Forgetfulness may lead to unintentional self-overdosing.
- Repeat prescriptions can lead to drugs being prescribed for periods far longer than is recommended as safe.

It has been estimated that as many as 10 per cent of older people admitted to hospital are there as a direct result of drugs prescribed by their GP (Age Concern, 1977). Phillipson (1982) suggests that much over-prescription of drugs is a conscious attempt to control the medical demands made on the health service by older people.

Reliance on medicine can therefore be dangerous. Medical and pharmacological competence cannot and should not be taken for granted. New drugs and new medical techniques, frequently introduced as 'miracle' cures, may subsequently be quickly withdrawn after proving to be harmful, and sometimes fatal, in use.

The counsellor can play a role in monitoring the quality, effectiveness and possible iatrogenic affects of medical treatment.

- Is the doctor treating the condition rather than the symptoms?
- Has the doctor diagnosed accurately, or have ageist considerations clouded medical judgement?
- Is the prescribed medication or treatment safe, and what are the likely side-effects?
- Is the current illness the consequence of side-effects of medication or treatment prescribed for former illnesses?
- Are there safer or less extreme treatments that might be more effective?

These questions require some knowledge of medical treatments and their potential iatrogenic effects, and it is not the purpose of this book to go into this subject in detail. A comprehensive outline of drug side-effects is available elsewhere (Blair, 1985; Parish, 1987; Turner and Volans, 1987). You can also ask your doctor for an old copy of the British National Formulary, or MIMS, which they receive regularly free of charge.

However, questioning doctors can be a difficult and often daunting task, given their high social status. Even other professionals, such as social work staff, have adopted a passive or subservient role that is usually limited to obtaining acceptance of medical decisions, and helping people to come to terms with them. However, it is possible to question medical practice without necessarily questioning medical authority or competence. In any case, better doctors will welcome our insight as assistance rather than interference, and will make full use of it.

Too often, carers spend time trying to find residual meaning and satisfaction given a person's current state of ill health rather than looking for its cause and seeking an effective remedy. Yet knowledge of the sick person can often place the counsellor (especially the carer-counsellor) in an ideal position to link illness with diet, exercise or iatrogenesis.

This is not to suggest that good medical advice and treatment are not important. In stressing the social, psychological and nutritional factors that underlie health, it is the dominance of medicalized answers to problems that should be questioned. Moreover, it is the doctor/nurse-counsellor who can most usefully ask these questions, for spending time considering these aspects of ill health is often more helpful than a prescription for drugs.

Alternative medical practice

The counsellor can also propose the intervention of non-conventional or alternative medical practitioners, especially for problems for which conventional medicine has little or no answer. This is relevant to many conditions to which older people are vulnerable, such as arthritis. The medical response is to prescribe painkillers. These relieve pain temporarily, but do not pretend to treat the causes of the disease itself.

The value of alternative medical care for older people remains largely unexplored. However, there is evidence that many alternative therapies can help people suffering from so-called 'incurable' conditions, and it is perhaps time for those responsible for the care of older people to investigate the potential of such treatments as homoeopathy, acupuncture, chiropractic, osteopathy, herbalism and many others (Scrutton, 1992).

Counselling sick people

Maintaining good health is to a large degree under our own direct personal control, even in older age (Scrutton, 1992). Counsellors who have time to investigate such matters as exercise and nutrition may be in a better position than doctors to arrive at an accurate health assessment, and counselling insight can often be more valuable than medical knowledge.

The counsellor should become as acquainted as possible with relevant information from as many professional spheres as possible, and use that information to ensure that the best possible treatment and care are obtained. Counsellors are not nutritionists or medical experts in any field. However, they need to use all of the human resources and information available to them from every relevant quarter to ensure that the best interests of the person are being pursued. The counsellor is not a 'jack-of-all-trades', but someone in the privileged position of being able to see the individual as a 'whole' person. This holistic outlook is extremely important and potentially very powerful. The counselling task is not to understand just one single facet of the person, but to know something about the whole person.

This enables the counsellor to focus upon the potential contribution of medical, social and psychological circumstances to the person's health and well-being. This gives the counsellor a threefold task:

1.   to assess the various factors contributing to the individual's health;
2.   to discuss the significance of these factors with the individual;

3. to help the individual to decide on the most appropriate response to the main factors contributing to ill health.

The emotional impact of illness

The emotional and psychological impact of illness, particularly when it is serious enough to leave the patient weakened or incapacitated, can be enormous. This is especially true when mobility, sight or hearing have been impaired, perhaps after a serious stroke. Heart disease and illnesses such as pneumonia can be equally traumatic. Some older people suffering from these and other major conditions can undergo a significant change in personality, which is often distressing to the people who are close to them.

Counselling can often deal with the personal anger, frustration and eventual depression caused by illness. It can help people to assess the cost to their former life-style, so that they can realistically fight the consequences or else accept and come to terms with them. It can help people to reassess what they are able to do in future, and where necessary to find alternative ways of coping with their life.

When mental health becomes an issue (e.g. in depression, bereavement or grief) or when someone is under severe emotional stress, counselling can try to determine the origins of the problem, and seek to help people to face and come to terms with it.

Disabling illness

Illness that causes frailty or a loss of mobility may have an emotional impact that is every bit as important as its physical effects, leaving the individual not only unable to cope physically, but with an emotional fear of trying to do so. This might include:

- a reluctance to resume walking after a series of falls;
- an unwillingness to return home from hospital, or to return to an independent life.

Counselling can encourage people and seek to renew their confidence, both through dialogue and through practical assistance and support. There are many questions that must be answered.

- What is the nature of their frailty?
- Is it permanent or temporary?
- Is a loss of body weight the 'natural' consequence of old age?
- Or does it result from an illness or nutritional deficiency?

Where illness causes permanent disability, counselling can help people to decide how they can continue living life to the full and with optimum personal fulfilment.

Sensory impairment

Where illness leads to loss of sight, speech or hearing it diminishes people's ability to make use of counselling. Too often sensory impairment results in older people being treated as if they were also mentally impaired. People talk to them as if they were stupid, or as if they had somehow reverted to infancy. There is nothing more annoying to older people. Their need to communicate at an adult level is likely to remain as strong as ever, and in order to communicate, counsellors must be innovative.

- For deaf and aphasic people, it may be necessary to employ pen and paper in addition to speech, and to make more use of bodily and facial cues.
- For blind people, more physical touch may be required. In all cases the need for empathy and positive regard is greatly increased.

Failure to recover

Recovery from illness is sometimes avoided, particularly when older people feel isolated and neglected. Sickness can bring with it a degree of sympathy and attention that is greatly valued, especially by lonely people who may believe that when their health improves they will lose the time and attention that illness has afforded them. The counsellor will meet older people who do not want to get well. As an 'incentive' to recovery, the counsellor might then need to talk to them about ways of increasing their social involvement when they are well.

An increased counselling role?

Counselling sick people is difficult, not least because of their reduced ability to think clearly, make judgements, reach sound decisions, determine on a course of action, and generally fight their own battles. If it is important to question the impact of medical care, it is equally clear, in contrast to other areas of counselling, that it is the counsellor rather than the counsellee who may have to do this. It is often inappropriate to involve sick people, and the counsellor may have to take more direct action in their interests. In doing so, he or she is acting as an advocate on the person's behalf, rather than acting directly according to their wishes. However, where possible, the counsellor should consider the following:

- what the person might him- or herself have wanted had he or she been sufficiently well to make the judgement him- or herself.
- on this basis, the counsellor should seek to defend the person's interests, and not be subservient to the wishes of any other authority.

The importance of health in older age cannot be underestimated. The contents of this chapter have been significantly extended in a book by the same author (Scrutton, 1992), in which the issues of growing old, staying healthy and remaining in control are developed at greater length.

13 Alcohol and drugs

It is often said that if older people have a drink 'it will do them no harm'. This is probably less true than for any other age group. Ageing livers and kidneys lose their ability to cope with alcohol, and older people are therefore more susceptible to its effects. However, ageist attitudes patronize and endanger older people in other ways. It is often said that alcohol is 'the only little pleasure that old people have'.

However true this might be of an occasional drink, alcohol dependence is certainly not pleasurable at any age. Ageism can take this complacency one stage further. Price and Andrews (1982) stated that 'diagnosed alcoholism frequently is not referred for alcoholic treatment because of health professionals' beliefs that the alcoholic is too old to benefit from treatment'. This view is also entirely without foundation.

The causes of alcohol abuse

There are two types of ageing alcohol abusers:

1. those whose drinking started in earlier years;

2. those whose drinking habits started, or have become excessive, in old age.

It is often difficult to determine how long someone has been drinking. Rosin and Glatt (1971) differentiated between the factors causing chronic, long-term alcohol abuse, chiefly pathological personality characteristics such as neuroticism, and the 'reactive' factors that were more relevant to people who start drinking later in life. These factors were major life changes which can often disrupt the lives of older people. They include:

- retirement;
- bereavement and loss;

- loneliness and depression;
- anxiety.

This indicates that excessive drinking is often a response to social distress – an inability to cope with the losses of old age. Alcohol becomes a means of escape from painful feelings and circumstances by people who cannot cope with, and wish to avoid, them. Widowers have been found to form the largest proportion of 'late-onset' alcoholics.

Social distress and alcohol abuse

It is unwise for counsellors to view excessive drinking and alcoholism as a separate issue. Social distress is the fundamental cause of alcohol abuse. Drinking is a symptom of deeper underlying social and emotional causes. Excessive drinking is caused by unhappiness, negative self-image and an inability to cope with stress, and it is on this aspect that counselling should focus.

The counsellor should be alert to the possibility of heavy drinking, and should be aware that the symptoms are often mistaken for signs of normal ageing. He or she needs to look beyond what may at first appear to be a straightforward case of depression or early confusion. When faced with these symptoms, and before such a diagnosis is accepted, or the person is deemed unable to look after him- or herself, the counsellor should check whether there is an alcohol problem.

The physical effects of alcohol

There are many popular myths associated with the consumption of alcohol.

- It is widely believed to have a stimulant effect, and it is said that it 'cheers people up' because its immediate effect is to make the drinker more friendly and outgoing in social settings. In fact, alcohol depresses the central nervous system, and what people believe to be a 'stimulant' effect is in fact the anaesthetizing of the part of the brain that inhibits social behaviour.
- It is believed to have medicinal benefits. There is little or no evidence to support this view.
- It is said to help people sleep, but whilst alcohol may enable people to get to sleep more quickly, it can also lead to waking later in the night.
- It is believed to have a 'warming' effect, whereas in fact it speeds up heat loss from the body, and can aggravate problems of hypothermia.

The main 'benefit' of depressing the central nervous system is to dull the pain associated with loss in old age. This benefit is transitory, wearing off as alcohol is filtered from the body, and leaving the underlying problems intact. As a result, more alcohol is required to dull the pain. Consequently, the desire to drink can become continuous, and the effects of heavy drinking can be drastic.

- Appetite is reduced, resulting in weight loss and nutritional problems.
- The absorption of vital minerals can be affected, leading to vitamin deficiency, with deleterious consequences for both physical and mental health.
- Heavy drinking can lead to cirrhosis of the liver.
- It can cause hypocalcaemia (a deficiency of calcium in the blood), leading to osteoporosis.
- It can cause cardiomyopathy (a chronic disorder of the heart muscle).
- It can also lead to certain cancers, notably of the mouth, pharynx and oesophagus.

Alcohol and prescribed drugs

There is also the danger of alcohol interacting with prescribed drugs. If alcohol is taken with sleeping tablets or painkillers, it can cause excessive drowsiness. A combination of alcohol and anti-arthritic drugs can cause severe stomach upsets.

Reduced renal function

The consequences of heavy drinking are not confined to people with a recognizable drink problem. Problems can arise when older people continue to drink the same amount they consumed when they were younger, for the ageing body loses its ability to cope with alcohol. Alcohol Concern (1987) has suggested that older people who have been regular drinkers may need to reduce their alcohol consumption by half.

Detecting excessive alcohol use

Detecting a drink problem can require considerable tact and sensitivity. Denial is a major factor in alcohol abuse, both with regard to the amount a person is drinking, and whether it is 'a problem'. Older people often have a strong sense of social stigma about heavy drinking, and may consequently be unable or unwilling to talk about the problem. On the other hand, the counsellor may be assisted by many physical signs which suggest that alcohol is a problem, such as finding empty bottles secreted around the home, or observing that someone is found drinking at all times of the day, often alone.

The effects of alcohol on social behaviour are made more severe by the reduced kidney and liver functioning of older people. These effects include:

- a loss of both physical and mental co-ordination;

- weakened judgement;
- slower reaction times;
- an increase in falls and accidents;
- disturbed sleep patterns;
- a possible decline in sexual interest and performance.

Some effects of alcohol that would be considered a problem at any other age can be accepted, unwittingly, as the outcome of 'normal' ageing.

- Incontinence can result from or be worsened by drinking.
- Memory loss and temporary confusion can be interpreted as dementia. Some symptoms of alcohol abuse are similar to those of Alzheimer's disease.
- The symptoms of alcohol misuse are often mistaken for depression.

Supporting the alcohol abuser

Two important questions need to be asked when alcohol abuse is suspected.

Does the person recognize that their drinking is a problem?

One of the myths that surrounds alcohol, perpetuated by well-intentioned people, is that alcohol consumption is beneficial, at least in moderation, for a variety of conditions and complaints. This gives the impression that there are no dangers attached to drinking. However guarded such advice might be, this reasoning is often expanded to justify increasingly heavy and more regular drinking. Alcohol Concern highlighted the need for re-education regarding the potentially harmful effects of alcohol within the ageing body: 'Once given this information and guidance on how to drink more safely, many people manage to cut down without needing special treatment or counselling' (Alcohol Concern, 1987).

Controlling the source of the drink is another important consideration, and this may involve persuading well-intentioned friends and relatives to discontinue their tacit support and not to justify their visits with alcoholic presents.

Does the person want to reduce or stop their drinking?

Often people will not want to stop drinking, seeing alcohol as an acceptable solution to their problems. They may be unwilling to face their feelings and emotions, preferring to drown them in alcohol. When told about the likely consequences of excessive drinking, they may even welcome the prospect of death as an acceptable solution to their everyday problems.

Denial

Faced with denial, the counsellor should abandon the subject of drinking, focusing instead on the person's social and emotional distress. Often the counsellor will need to assure the individual concerned that it is acceptable to grieve over their loneliness, losses and bereavements, to explore their feelings about their life, and to discuss their fears about death. Frequently what is needed is for the person to feel that there is someone willing to be supportive and understanding, to listen to their problems and to discuss alternative strategies for coping with social distress. Every effort should be made to involve the family in giving support in breaking down the denial that is often a feature of cases of alcohol abuse.

A positive approach

The counsellor should stress that alcoholism is a curable condition, particularly when the person's social distress is discussed openly and their problems tackled. In taking a positive stance, it is important for the counsellor to emphasize the personal strengths that the person has available to combat the problem, rather than the weaknesses that led to it in the first place.

Planning withdrawal

In planning to reduce or stop drinking, specialist help may be necessary. Specific, graded and realistically achievable goals should be established. When losing the 'support' of alcohol, the individual will need to fill the gaps left in his or her life, and will require a high level of commitment and support from his or her family and friends. New activities, new relationships and new supports may have to be found. Above all, the person must be certain that this is what he or she wants to do, and be committed to the programme.

Since most older people who have a drink problem tend to be isolated and lonely, some form of social group support may be helpful. The group may consist either of other older people, or of people of all ages with a similar alcohol problem.

After-care

There is likely to be a continuing need for support after alcohol withdrawal has been successfully achieved. Just as it was important to consider alcohol abuse in conjunction with the underlying social distress, it is now important to assess whether these fundamental problems will continue to exist. If they will, then the problems that led to the person resorting to drink may do so again.

Coping with life in old age without alcohol may require an entirely new and improved self-image. Feelings of worthlessness, hopelessness, lack of purpose and depression may still have to be dealt with, or the person may resort to alcohol as a solution again.

Prescription drugs

Older people have lived through what is believed to have been a medical revolution, when 'miracle' drugs appeared to offer a solution to all types of pain and ill health. We now live in a drug-oriented culture, and for some older people this has had a perverse result.

It is prescribed rather than proscribed drugs that have become the main problem for older people.

Many older people are frequently prescribed drugs to relieve their emotional pain and grief. Many will prefer to take them rather than attempt to come to terms with their lives. Drugs, like alcohol, are socially acceptable, and their consumption is encouraged. Ageist attitudes that focus on the depressing nature of old age can encourage this situation.

Drug side-effects can be different to those of alcohol but, like the effects of alcohol, they can be mistakenly classified as the normal symptoms of the ageing process. The same is true when people become dependent upon non-prescription drugs. The causes, consequences and approach to be taken remain relevant, regardless of the drug concerned.

14 Disability and dependence: the emotional and social impact

'Disablist' thinking
The emotional significance of dependence
The limitations of caring
Gradual dependence
Sudden dependence
Reactions to dependence
Incontinence
Dependence and leisure
Sensory impairment
The abuse of older dependent people

The greatest fear that many people have about old age is becoming dependent. The concept of dependence requires consideration. Dominant social attitudes appear to equate older people with 'handicap' and dependency. There is a common image of older people being incapable of living their lives without support, and dependent upon the care and assistance of younger people. Social networks and cultural values may have crucial effects on self-esteem. The ageist attitudes and stereotypes faced by older people can lead them to believe that they will inevitably become incapable, lonely and needy.

Physical function does decline with ageing, and the rate of loss of function accelerates as age increases. However, this is far from the whole picture. Dependency is not an inevitable outcome of old age – part of a natural process of ageing. The main deficit is not a physical one, but one that exists between the mind and the body. When fit, mentally alert older people talk about their age and their experience it is illuminating. Many of them express their surprise at being old. They recognize their age, but never believed that they would become old themselves. Moreover, they do not 'feel old', or perhaps more accurately they do not feel 'old' in quite the way they have been led to expect.

J.B. Priestley said that 'Behind the appearance of age I am the same person with the same thoughts as when I was younger'.

Alex Comfort expressed a similar view: 'Old people are in fact young people inhabiting older bodies and confronted with certain physical problems'.

This is a common insight. It is not the mind that ages but the body, and it is the divergence between the things that the mind is still capable of contemplating, but that the body is not able to do, that is the most difficult process for ageing people to accept. It is the reverse process to childhood, where the mind and body become progressively more able to combine to do things that were once impossible. Children's dependence gradually dissipates until they achieve independence.

In old age, the mind remains able, and personal dignity and pride aspire to remain independent. It is the body that increasingly lets us down.

'Disablist' thinking

People who are disabled, and those who are old, are often considered to be incompetent. People who are both old and disabled are in double jeopardy. Older people from minority ethnic backgrounds may face a third problem, that although they may be both old and disabled, they are not perceived as requiring care! The care needs of minority ethnic communities have been widely ignored because of the comfortable assumption that they will be cared for within the family (Littlewood and Lipsedge, 1989), an assumption that Walker (1994) found was usually incorrect.

Whilst some older people do become dependent, most remain quite capable of leading independent lives to the end. However, ageist restrictions are often placed quite indiscriminately on older people. It is a common belief that older people should not engage in strenuous physical activity. They should not jog or swim, or undertake hard physical work, or travel alone, or even stand for too long. Instead, they should rest, take life at a leisurely pace, and allow other people to provide for them.

This is 'disablist' thinking. It is often successful in preventing older people from doing things, not necessarily because they are unable to do them, but because it is not expected of them. Older people tend to internalize social expectations. Disablist thinking is a safer option for many people who believe that older people are more susceptible to illness, accidents and injuries, or that they may even die. To exclude activity is a less risky and more acceptable option. What is forgotten is that people of all ages take risks – it is a part of normal life, and it helps to keep us alive.

Thus when people become frail or incapacitated, carers often assume rights and responsibilities which are unjustified and which are often deeply resented.

'You shouldn't do this. I'll do it for you!'

The counsellor should also be aware that functional ability does change, and can improve as well as decline (Beckett *et al.*, 1996). Sometimes, older people become ill and lose their ability to cope. Carers take on caring tasks, and if an assumption is then made that care is required because the person is too old, rather than too ill, to care for him- or herself, recovery can be prevented. Carer-counsellors should be aware of this ageist trap, and regularly review what older people can do for themselves – and allow them to do it.

Disablist attitudes become worse when physical disability is mistaken for an inability to think, reason and make decisions. Frail or disabled older people are often treated in this way. They are treated like children and infantilized, although there is no foundation for a comparison with the dependence of children. The emotional impact of, for example, assisting an older person to the toilet is quite different to that of toileting a child. It offends their pride and dignity, which have been developed over a lifetime. Yet carers often embark on personal care tasks without considering the emotional impact on the older person.

Many older people have to come to terms not only with their dependence, but also with the patronizing insensitivity of thoughtless carers.

The emotional significance of dependence

If this is how able-bodied, able-minded people feel, what is the emotional impact of dependence on those who, through illness or other circumstances, find themselves unable to maintain their independence? Older people do gradually lose their ability to look after themselves. Tunstall (1966) asked what triggered older people to become housebound, and concluded that ageing people were often aware of how they were 'expected' to behave as 'old people', but that they did not consider themselves to be old until some 'turning point' was reached. For some, the trigger was a significant bereavement, while for others it was a traumatic fall, or having to ask for help with household tasks. Whatever the event, it triggered an acceptance of being 'old', and hastened a decline into dependence.

When I started social work with older people, the failure of otherwise caring people to understand the emotional impact of dependence was striking. They failed to think beyond the facts of the situation.

- These older people could no longer perform a task.
- As caring people they wished to assist, or to do it for them.

So, acting with the best intentions, they were often surprised by the lack of gratitude they received in return for their care.

If, as carers, we see no further than a physical need, we ignore the emotional significance of caring acts for people at the receiving end. An act intended as 'caring' can seem no more than an imposition on personal pride and dignity.

If older people are struggling with and gradually losing a battle to maintain their independence and pride, it should be recognized that the very act of caring can diminish them further, emphasizing that they are no longer masters of their own lives. It often happens that the more dependent people become, the more reluctant and ungrateful they can appear to be. Failure to understand the emotional significance of dependence can lead to irrational behaviour. People can react to carers with anger and violence, and may reject support and assistance even when they require it. Carers are then surprised that their care is rebuffed with such ingratitude.

Considerable tolerance and understanding are necessary when caring for dependent older people. It is often difficult for able-bodied people to appreciate their feelings, but these have been succinctly expressed by Comerford (1986), a quadriplegic adult who described the effect that even small caring functions can have on someone who is entirely dependent upon them.

These are only small things, and to most people probably irrelevant, but when you depend on another person to perform these tasks then, believe me, the most insignificant detail can become a huge factor in your life, especially if you want to retain your individuality. . . . I know only too well how (residential care), and indeed disabled life in general, can lead to demoralisation and apathy and can cause even the most active bodies and minds to become stagnant and indifferent to all but their own immediate needs. I am no different myself.

(Comerford, 1986)

Even people who appear to acknowledge gracefully the support of carers can still feel diminished, with their pride and independence deeply hurt. Care can produce feelings of hopelessness and despair. It is not surprising, perhaps, that so many older people become depressed. They have lost their role and status in life, and now have only years of dependence to face. Often they sense the burden they have become, which makes the situation far worse.

The limitations of caring

Losing the ability to be independent is a form of personal bereavement. As with all bereavement, feelings of anger, fear, grief, depression and denial may need to be acknowledged before people can come to terms with their situation.

Yet if the act of physical care is not accompanied by a discussion of the problems of dependence, we fail to acknowledge the feelings of dependent people.

Perhaps we are reluctant to discuss such an obviously distressing subject, preferring to concentrate on practical care tasks. The failure to recognize their need to talk can then be compounded when older people, sensing our unwillingness to discuss these matters, repress their feelings.

Caring by 'doing' – often the only care offered to dependent older people – is debilitating. Older people who are consistently assisted with tasks perceive themselves to be less able to cope for themselves. The more care that is offered, the more we create dependency, the more people learn to be helpless, and the less useful or valuable people feel. Thus it is insufficient merely to 'care' for older people in the early stages of them becoming dependent, for care is then either rejected or else accepted with resignation. Dependence and the emotional trauma that can arise from it can affect people in terms of how they see themselves, and how they assess the loss involved. This is confirmed by Shakespeare:

> Reaction to handicap acquired in adulthood is not proportionately related to the objective severity of the handicap. A comparatively mild handicap can cause a severe emotional reaction and a more severe handicap much less reaction. The causal factors in the degree of reaction seem to be what the acquired handicap means to the person in terms of his life style, his job and his interests.
>
> (Shakespeare, 1975)

Shakespeare was writing about disabled people of all ages, but there is no reason why older people should cope differently with increased dependence. People with longer-term disability will have had many years to come to terms with and cope with dependence. Some older people will have spent a lifetime coping with disabilities, and will have 'aged in place'. Younger people, particularly if their disability occurred through an accident or some other misfortune, are likely to receive greater sympathy and understanding. However, older people often receive less consideration. It is felt that they have had their lives, and their dependence is discounted as a 'natural' process of ageing – something they should readily recognize and accept.

Gradual dependence

Dependence associated with ageing is a very gradual process, and disability emerges slowly. It is this imperceptible increase in disability and dependence that can be taken for granted. It is insufficient for carers to undertake caring tasks simply by stating, as we so often do, 'I don't mind doing it for you' or 'You did it for me long enough when I was young'. These comments fail to address the central problem of coming to terms with dependence.

*It is not how **we** feel about offering care, but how **they** feel about accepting it that matters. Well-intentioned caring, devoid of empathy, implicitly informs people that their feelings are unnecessary, even foolish.*

Most older people will want help, particularly from members of their family. However, they will want to maintain their independence and autonomy for as long as possible, and they will not want to feel that they have become a burden.

So what should happen when it becomes apparent that someone can no longer manage independently? To insist that a person continues to fend for him- or herself can be callous and may lead to increased levels of anger and frustration, and enhance feelings of hopelessness by indicating that we do not care and do not want to help them. The dilemma can be overcome by counselling that seeks to determine how the person feels.

- Do they prefer to persevere, however painfully and slowly?
- Are they are ready to accept offers of assistance?

The counselling aim should be to discuss how people feel about their newly acquired dependent status, and how they want practical help to be provided. This demonstrates our willingness to help, but allows people to describe their feelings. If the problem of caring already exists, the issue can be tackled sensitively.

'I feel that you are reluctant to let me care for you. I would like to know why you feel like this, as I am quite willing to do it for you?'

Such discussion can help people to come to terms with their dependence. When the counsellor is aware of the person's feelings they can be dealt with constructively. Feelings of worthlessness or being a burden can be overcome, perhaps by involving ways in which people can 'give' something in return for the care they now require, or by providing care in some other more mutually acceptable way.

When the onset of dependence is gradual and progressive, each stage needs to be discussed. There is a tendency for caring people who see that someone requires additional care merely to add further tasks to the list, without comment or discussion. Frequently they do so in order to avoid unnecessary upset, but their 'secrecy' can often cause offence and anguish.

Carers should never assume that just because they 'do' more for someone, they are necessarily being more helpful.

Sudden dependence

Similar considerations apply when people become dependent after a sudden event, such as a stroke. There may be an initial stage when people readily accept caring input, but when recovery is slow and/or permanent dependence is likely, the person will at some point realize that their condition is long term. At this point, the sudden loss of independence can be devastating.

- It can lead to disorientation and bewilderment.
- Realization can be followed by frustration, anger and depression.

In cases of sudden dependence, there has been no warning or time for preparation, and it can be a loss as unexpected and traumatic as any death. Feelings of loss can affect every aspect of personal life, and the implications for the individual have to be coped with quickly. Most people will find this difficult, and drastic personality changes can occur.

- The docile can become demanding.
- The reasonable can become unreasonable.

Counselling can help people to come to terms with their situation. Again, sudden dependence in older age can be discounted. There is less surprise when a stroke strikes someone at 70 than at 50 years, and there is a mistaken tendency to assume that the trauma is less. Above all, time is required for the person to come to terms with the new reality. Certainly carers should always discuss the provision of care openly and honestly, and take nothing for granted.

Reactions to dependence

It is common for older people to feel depressed and anxious about their loss of independence. Several studies have shown that depression serves to increase the risk of impaired physical function (Hay *et al.*, 1997). There may be a period of denial, especially if dependence is sudden, this being part of a normal grieving process that protects people from the full impact of the shock. Other reactions that can accompany increasing handicap have been outlined by Shakespeare (1975):

- regression, where people behave in an infantile way, perhaps becoming unnecessarily over-dependent;
- increased egocentricity, where people become demanding and intolerant of the needs of others when these are, or seem to be, conflicting with their own needs;
- withdrawal from contact with other people;
- increased use of fantasy as an escape from facing the reality of disability;
- the projection or deflection of their feelings of inadequacy on to other people;
- new identifications (buying expensive possessions, joining 'high-status' groups) in an attempt to restore damaged confidence with impressive new associations.

These reactions are expressions of social distress that can accompany dependence. None of them are necessarily damaging, but they do become matters for concern if they are excessive, or if they last too long. The task of counselling is to help people to recognize and come to terms with their changed circumstances.

Incontinence

For most older people, there is no more depressing or shaming dependence than incontinence. The social and emotional trauma it can cause may be deeply and painfully significant. Incontinence can also lead to the break-down of family care, often because insufficient support is given to carers, or it is given too late.

There is an ageist belief that incontinence is an inevitable part of growing old that has to be accepted. This is not so. Incontinence should never be accepted without thorough investigation. The counselling task should be to investigate, or have investigated, the specific circumstances of the person, for it can often be simply remedied.

- Incontinence can be caused by poor diet.
- It can be caused by lack of exercise or poor mobility, sometimes allied to fear caused by failing eyesight.
- Illness, such as bladder and urethra disorders, can cause incontinence.
- Constipation can lead to incontinence.
- Drugs can also be a contributory factor (night sedatives suppress signals from the bladder to the brain; diuretics increase the frequency of urin-ation).
- Social and emotional problems and personal worries and anxieties can also precipitate bouts of incontinence.
- Incontinence itself can add to personal worries, increasing anxiety and thereby worsening the incontinence problem.

If incontinence has a more permanent cause, it can be managed by a wide variety of measures. These include the use of incontinence aids, regular toileting programmes, and the close proximity of toilet facilities, especially at night. More drastic circumstances may require bladder retraining, medical treatment and even surgery. These measures will not directly concern counsellors, although they may have to pressure agencies to act positively to assist older people.

Dependence and leisure

Dependence often means that a coterie of old hobbies, pastimes and interests have to be reduced or abandoned. Even socializing with friends may be restricted. The counsellor should be aware of the losses arising from depend-ence, and discover what the individual misses most from their previous life. This is particularly important with gradual loss of function, when older people can stop taking part in meaningful activities and tasks without other people being aware of this.

- How, and with what, are such activities to be replaced?
- What physical activity is available to the older person with disabilities?
- What activities will continue to engage a still lively mind?

Counselling can play an important part in this. Indeed, it is an essential feature of caring for older people to avoid the feelings of helplessness and boredom that are experienced by so many dependent older people.

Sensory impairment

Although the main focus of attention has been on physical dependence, the loss of speech and hearing can also create dependence, with similarly drastic results. Such loss also has particular implications for counselling, as this is a skill that relies entirely on the ability to communicate.

Hearing loss

Loss of hearing can create considerable frustration, both for the affected individual and for close friends.

- It can lead to irritation and impatience.
- It can lead to people becoming unco-operative and antagonistic.
- It can lead to feelings of being isolated and not totally aware of what is going on around them.

Hearing impairment often stops people participating in activities that are going on around them, such as ordinary conversation or watching the television. As their hearing deteriorates, people may have to discontinue many activities and interests, including visits to the cinema or theatre, and going to parties, pubs, bingo sessions and much else.

Many carers become exhausted and tire of repeating themselves, even to the point of ending any attempt to communicate unless it is absolutely essential. Hearing loss can embarrass some people. Carers can also become over-anxious, perhaps worrying that deafness will mean that affected individuals are unable to hear traffic on dangerous roads.

Acknowledgement of disability is an important step towards coming to terms with it. Many older people try to avoid this, and try to hide their deafness from others. Many of them dislike wearing hearing aids, or will go to considerable lengths to hide them, as a result of which hearing impairment is not always immediately obvious to other people.

Loss of speech

Loss of speech is usually the result of a sudden illness, such as a stroke. Its onset can therefore be sudden and traumatic, and the condition can be partial or complete. Aphasic people are particularly prone to disablist assumptions about their intelligence. The assumption that physical handicap signifies mental handicap is common. The counsellor must avoid such a conclusion, and assume instead that the person is an intelligent, sensitive and feeling individual. This view is more likely to be correct, but even if it is incorrect, the mistake is more easily remedied.

The results of aphasia for the counsellor are obviously significant. People with speech difficulties can be very sensitive to, and frustrated by, their inability to communicate. Perhaps the greatest barrier to communication is the anxiety and embarrassment felt by many carers. They may be embarrassed by their inability to understand what they are being told or asked, or they may feel that constantly asking someone to repeat him- or herself is unacceptable. Too often, the result is that carers pretend that they can understand, or jump to the wrong conclusions. There is also a tendency for carers to assume that they are being asked to provide physical or practical help, with the result that many older people are brought more cups of tea or taken to the toilet more frequently than they desire!

People with hearing impairment usually appreciate people who are willing to take time to understand them, rather than someone who pretends to do so.

Counsellors need to be aware of their own feelings in this respect. It is important that the counsellor does not pretend to understand. It is better to ask for numerous repetitions and to seek clarification. Most aphasic people will prefer an honest approach, however frustrated they may be with themselves. At least they will realize that someone is genuinely trying to understand them fully.

Communication with deaf and aphasic older people

The problem of counselling aphasic people highlights the importance of listening. Counselling aphasic people means that the listening process is more lengthy, more difficult, and requires not only additional time, but also additional skills. It is important, for instance, that communication difficulties are not compounded by any outside disturbance, whether this be extraneous noise, or any other distractions that might hinder the person's attention.

- Where speech is not possible, word or picture books can be developed which contain key words and information, perhaps enabling the individual to point to the words they wish to use.
- Computers can be helpful, with their ability to construct, store and recall words and phrases at the touch of a button.
- Arrow questioning is a technique which only uses questions that require a 'yes' or 'no' answer. It can be developed for people who are unable to communicate verbally, but can use nods and shakes of the head, eye movements, or squeezes of the hand for communication. Arrow questioning means that the counsellor has to play a more active role in interpreting personal needs. With each hypothesis, the counsellor should ensure that the person can indicate how 'warm' or 'cold' their tentative suggestions are compared to what they want to express, and that they are modified if inaccurate.

More sophisticated systems of alternative communication also exist, including symbol systems such as Blissymbolics, manual signing languages and synthetic speech.

Whatever means of communication is employed, the counselling skills required are identical to those used with people who are able to use verbal communication. Counselling people with speech impairment can be frustrating and time-consuming, but it can also be rewarding. The need to communicate may often be greater as such people may feel more isolated, and have less opportunity to talk about their feelings. As a result, they can be more appreciative of the opportunity to communicate with someone who is willing to do so, and sufficiently interested to develop the appropriate skills to make this possible.

It is important that the counsellor remembers that a warm, reassuring manner, free of patronizing attitudes, remains the best counselling technique for aphasic older people. Through genuineness, empathy and a willingness of the counsellor to devote their time, aphasic people will often relax. This in itself may release communication abilities that were previously restricted by anxiety, unhappiness and a lack of opportunity.

The abuse of older dependent people

The drift into dependence can be a depressing time for older people, and it can be an exhausting time for their carers. Older people become depressed, develop a poor self-image and grow weaker and more dependent, while carers become frustrated and their role becomes more onerous, yet more essential, and their position more powerful.

This is the ideal breeding ground for abusive relationships. Between 3 and 6 per cent of people over 65 years of age report elder abuse or neglect, and abusers are normally family members (see, for example, Pillemer and Finkelhor, 1988; Ogg and Bennett, 1992; Podkieks, 1992). The following are risk factors:

- poverty;
- race;
- functional impairment;
- cognitive impairment.

During a time when older people are living longer, community care policies are keeping them at home longer, and the willingness to fund support services is low on the list of social priorities, the potential for elder abuse is growing. The counsellor needs to listen to older people when they hint at abuse.

Older people can be abused physically, financially or even sexually, and they can be subject to neglect or violence. Where this seems to be apparent, the counsellor needs to take the appropriate action.

- They must discuss the available options with the abused person.
- If the person wishes, the police, health or social service authorities should be notified.
- The carers, who may be struggling, should be supported and thereafter monitored regularly.

Depression, loneliness and loss

Sadness brings with it a fall in energy and enthusiasm, and it slows the body's metabolism. Depressed people develop a negative self-image, viewing themselves as inadequate in some way and unable to cope with their lives. They tend to see problems and difficulties as the result of personal defects, and these – allied with an inability to cope with their circumstances – make them feel unable to achieve any satisfactory sense of fulfilment, happiness and contentment. They view the events and circumstances in their lives pessimistically, and become defeatist in their outlook. Everything becomes too much, and the entire world can seem to be putting insuperable obstacles in their way. They feel increasingly isolated, lonely and rejected.

Such feelings can paralyse people, who may feel that they have no power to change the circumstances of their life. This attitude becomes self-fulfilling. The acceptance of personal incompetence will ensure an inability to alter or modify their circumstances, and this can deepen feelings of hopelessness. The future seems to hold only more problems and pain. Current difficulties, believed to be insoluble, are projected into a future filled with continued hardship, failure and frustration.

Depression in older age

Depression in older people is essentially no different to depression at any other age. However, there is evidence to suggest that depression in later life is more common than is often assumed, some research indicating that it affects more than 44 per cent of people over 65 years old, although it is more often considered to be about 15 per cent (Family Policy Study Centre, 1991). Gurland (1976), examining research into the frequency of depression at various ages, found general agreement that the highest rate of depressive symptoms was in the 65+ age group.

Many older people do not recognize their depression. They are told, or they believe, that it is a symptom of normal ageing, or part of a physical illness. Banerjee and MacDonald (1996) found that 84 per cent of depressed older people were not receiving appropriate treatment.

Depression in older people is usually associated with the many losses of ageing, allied to a loss of purpose and will and an increasing sense of being alone. Old age can be a time when the reasons for living appear uncertain. The prospect of future enjoyment and fulfillment can seem remote, not just because this is how many older people view their condition, but because dominant social ideas emphasize the inevitability of future decline.

Degrees of depression

Depression is experienced at many levels. Mild, temporary depression is something that most people will experience at some time. The starting point may be a feeling of pessimism, not being hopeful about the future, or disappointment that something has either happened or not happened. In mild depression, people are able to view their situation with a degree of objectivity. Often these are cyclical, time-limited feelings – a 'low period' that will pass. Some people may have been prone to recurrent periods of depression, and as they grow older these can become deeper and more frequent. Such depression will often respond quickly to counselling. The time and concern of the counsellor, and the alternative perspectives that can be brought to bear on particular issues, can help to reassure people that not everything in life is bleak and hopeless.

However, older people can become more susceptible to more severe, debilitating and long-lasting depression that is more concerned with despair than disappointment, and more inclined to accept the ageist belief that there are few prospects and little hope in older age. The individual becomes more obsessed with negative thoughts and ideas, and this feeds the underlying causes of depression. The person's preoccupation with current problems makes it difficult for counsellors to focus on more hopeful perspectives. Some depressed people refuse to eat or drink, or to take part in any outside activity, preferring to stay in their homes, perhaps confined to a favourite chair or their bed for most of the day. In extreme cases, people can be unresponsive to anything that does not confirm their negative feelings. They become intent on feeding their depression, and are oblivious to the people around them and the help that they can offer.

The physical and mental effects of depression

Depression in older people can lead to increasing illness, debility, dependence, mental confusion and even death. Hays et al. (1997) found that depressive symptoms and a lack of social support increased functional impairment, and also increased the loss of independence. However, the symptoms of depression are various, most being recognized as abnormal in younger people, but too readily discounted as a normal part of ageing in the case of older people. They include:

- general apathy, even in areas of previous interest;
- a lack of activity;
- loss of appetite, often accompanied by weight loss;
- irritability and prolonged bad temper;
- over-tiredness, and a continual desire to sleep;
- conversely, depression can lead to insomnia;
- a permanent state of sadness, and an inability to see the brighter side of events and situations;
- feelings of physical and mental weakness.

Depression in older people can ultimately lead to mental stress, which is commonly mistaken for the early signs of dementia. Severe depression is often described medically as 'pseudo-dementia', although the two conditions are quite distinct. However, there is some evidence to suggest that depression is a risk factor that can trigger dementia (Bender and Cheston, 1997). Many depressed people feel that they are losing control of their minds. They become anxious and worried, and suffer from a series of fears and delusions. Depression at this level is obviously serious, and can indeed be life-threatening.

The death rates for older people with depression are considerably higher than those for people who are not depressed.

The medicalization of depression

Depression in older people is too often viewed as a medical problem rather than an emotional or social one. Depression has become a mental illness, a link that is reinforced by the tendency of depressed people to complain of some physical ailment. Indeed, many older people prefer to present physical rather than emotional reasons for their state of mind. This can be taken to extreme lengths, with individuals being certain that they have contracted some form of serious terminal illness, such as cancer, when there is little physically wrong with them.

Older people from minority ethnic communities need to be particularly wary of the medical diagnosis of depression (Dein and Huline-Dickens, 1997). Rait et al. (1996) found that existing methods used to screen for depression (and dementia) were developed for western European populations. Different cultural and educational backgrounds can lead to distress being expressed in different ways, and this can influence social performance, test results and the diagnosis of depression. Conversely, depressed older people from non-western cultures have been found to express their depression through physical symptoms, rather than recognizing the actual cause of their distress (Kleinman and Good, 1985). Considerable care needs to be taken when making judgements about the mental health status of people from minority ethnic communities. Dein (1994) found that there has been relatively little research conducted on cultural aspects of old age psychiatry.

The depressed mind can have a devastating effect upon the functioning of the body. Psychosomatic illnesses are real enough. Depressed people may indeed have aching limbs, but the depression itself may either highlight the pain, or actually give rise to it. Too often we fail to reach a correct diagnosis. We focus upon ailments – real or imaginary – and not on the psychological causes of such ailments. The implication is that many physical illnesses associated with old age are best treated not by medication, but by spending time looking at the economic, social and emotional factors that have given rise to depression.

Antidepressant drugs are frequently used in the treatment of depression. There has been an enormous increase in their use, and we have been led to believe that there is no need to feel depressed – that whatever the underlying cause, the tablets will make us well again. This idea is now very much open to question, and the effectiveness of antidepressant drugs is now subject to considerable debate.

- The side-effects of antidepressant drugs are often detrimental.
- The antidepressant effects of drugs are transitory, lasting only until their toxicity is removed from the body.
- The drugs are habit-forming, leading people to believe that they cannot cope with life without them.
- *They reduce the need for people to look at the underlying causes of depression.*
- *They prevent people from developing their inner resources to deal with their feelings.*

Counselling should seek to free depressed people from dependence upon drugs, and emphasize the importance of developing their personal coping skills.

The causes of depression

Counselling should seek to discover the underlying causes of depression. The first task is to ascertain whether personal behaviour and attitudes represent a depressed state of mind by establishing links between behaviour, physical ailments and the wider social and economic background to individual problems. Initially, people may want to talk about their physical and medical problems, but the counselling process should seek to shift attention away from these, moving towards other, more relevant and legitimate areas.

Social and economic causes

A high proportion of the depression that affects older people centres around their economic and social life. Brown and Harris (1978) suggested that all depression has its origins in psychosocial factors, and that life events that had severe, threatening, long-term implications, usually associated with loss, played a major role in depressive disorders. These included:

- separation, or the threat of separation or death of a spouse;
- an unpleasant revelation that forces a major reassessment of a person or an important relationship;
- a life-threatening illness in someone close;
- a major material loss or disappointment, or the threat of this;
- an enforced change of residence, or the threat of it;
- other crises involving loss, such as redundancy.

Murphy (1982), relating the work of Brown and Harris to older people, found that there was an association between major life events, major social difficulties, poor physical health and depression. However, because loss in older age appeared to be more irretrievably hopeless than that in younger people, he concluded that the outcome of major life events becomes more serious with increasing age. Yet not all life-threatening events cause depression. Brown and Harris (1978) explained this by suggesting that these events are mediated by four 'vulnerability factors' whose presence makes it more likely that depression will result, two of which have specific relevance to older people.

1. the lack of a confiding relationship with a spouse or similar partner.
2. the lack of employment outside the home.

The potential social agendas leading to depression are numerous, involving many complex interrelationships between personality factors, life history, recent events, loss and current life expectations. Cumulative loss, isolation, incapacity and dependence, illness and pain are particularly important. Brown and Harris (1978) considered that social class, and related issues of low income and poverty, produce additional pressures which increase vulnerability to depression. People from lower socio-economic classes often have a poorer diet, live in poorer housing, suffer from physical disability, are more dependent and less mobile, and are more prone to serious illness.

Loneliness and loss

Many older people feel lonely. Loneliness can be triggered by the losses of old age which make it difficult to maintain social relationships (see Chapter 11). The feeling of being alone can be deeply depressing, and is made worse if there appears to be no prospect of doing anything about the situation in the future.

Loneliness is a vital factor in depression. Townsend (1963) found that the most isolated older people tended to be unmarried or childless, with few surviving relatives. They often reinforced their isolation by refusing or being unable to participate in social activity by joining clubs or forming new friendships, yet all people need the company and stimulation of friends.

There is no truth in the belief that attachment needs decline with age.

The isolation of older people is a situation from which many feel that there is no escape. Loneliness lowers morale, and dims any hope that they will be able to refill the gaps in their lives. The horizons of life are reduced, and a vicious circle of loss, loneliness and depression tightens. Moreover, for many older people loneliness represents a double or mutual loss.

- It means a reduction in companionship.
- It also means a reduction in their capacity to care for other people.

Illness

Chronic illness can also give rise to depression, and many painful and debilitating diseases are probably a significant cause of depression in older people. Cancer, stroke, hypoglycaemia, rheumatoid arthritis, Parkinson's disease and cerebral arteriosclerosis have all been cited as potential causes of depression. There is also evidence that viral infections and hormonal imbalances can be an important cause. These should be investigated, particularly when the person has no previous history of depression. When illness is a possible cause of depression, medical attention that addresses these ailments can reduce the symptoms.

Iatrogenic illness

Far from being a solution, however, conventional medicine can often be the cause of depression. Many drugs that are commonly prescribed for older people to combat a variety of medical conditions are known to have depressive side-effects. They include:

- analgesics and painkillers;
- corticosteroids;
- cardiovascular drugs;
- appetite suppressants;
- anti-arthritic drugs;
- antibiotics;
- anti-Parkinsonian drugs;
- antipsychotic drugs;
- antihypertensive drugs;
- anticonvulsant drugs.

Indeed, what all of these 'anti-' drugs have in common is an ability to cause or worsen depression, as can alcohol and contact with organic pesticides. The counsellor who suspects that drugs are implicated should consult a doctor who is prepared to check the medication, reassess whether it is vital, and if not, whether it can be reduced, stopped, or an alternative prescribed. The effect of the reduced or changed medication can then be monitored.

Nutrition and depression

Nutrition can also cause depression. The link between mental states and the food we eat is well established. Petty and Sensky (1987) linked depression with food sensitivities or allergies, and although they concluded that these are probably not a common cause, others claim that they account for a considerable amount of depression. They point to evidence linking specific forms of depression with deficiencies of several vitamins, to the importance of a balanced diet, and to the potential effectiveness of vitamin tablets.

- Thiamin (vitamin B_1) deficiency can cause irritability, emotional instability, apathy, poor appetite and tingling in the fingers and toes.
- Thiamin levels in the body can be affected by drinking too much coffee (and coffee is known to cause depression).
- A deficiency of niacin (nicotinic acid), which is readily available in fish, poultry or brewer's yeast, is another known cause of depression.
- Pyridoxine (vitamin B_6) deficiency is associated with explosive and hysterical episodes in otherwise shy people.
- Pantothenic acid is plentiful in a wide variety of foods; it is easily destroyed in processing, but has been used successfully to treat people with depression.
- Vitamin A deficiency, which causes tiredness and difficulties in sleeping as well as depression, is readily treated with cod liver oil.
- High levels of copper can also cause depression, and this trace element is obtained from industrial pollution, cigarettes and copper water pipes.
- Petty and Sensky (1987) suggested that vitamin tablet treatment was an effective way of dealing with depression, whilst advocating caution about taking too high a dose.
- Depression can also be a consequence of low potassium intake, and several studies have found that older people tend to choose a diet with a low potassium content (Dall and Gardiner, 1971; Judge and Cowan, 1971).
- The loss of potassium in older people is closely associated with the use of diuretic drugs.

Weinberg (1972) sought to widen this biochemical appreciation of the importance of food, linking eating with one's state of mind. Food is a key factor in social life and personal pleasure. It represents our first human contact, involving an exchange of love and affection as well as nutritional sustenance. Thereafter, food becomes an important 'symbol of personal security'. Davies (1981) also points out that a vicious circle of depression, non-eating, poor nutrition and deeper depression can occur.

For similar reasons, refusal to eat (or eating to excess) can have a powerful effect on carers. Older people can manipulate their eating habits to draw attention to their personal needs and feelings. These should be tackled so that they can express their feelings openly, and not by such devious means.

A counselling approach to depression

The counsellor should view depression as a response to personal circumstances. It is a state of mind largely determined by the way in which people have learned to interpret their lives. People assume social roles based on assumptions that they have made about themselves and their circumstances. The counsellor's task is to try to unravel this in order:

- to develop a better understanding of how a person is interpreting his or her situation;
- to help the person to modify their current, perhaps distorted view of the world;
- to improve the person's negative self-image.

The task is rarely straightforward. Depressed people can present many difficulties to the counsellor, with negative moods producing negative thoughts, and negative thoughts deepening depression.

- They can be confused, preoccupied, distracted and lacking in concentration.
- 'Normal' desires for sleep, sustenance and even survival can disappear.
- They can be reluctant or unable to place their feelings in an ordered or realistic context.
- They may have little personal motivation or drive.
- They may be unwilling to discuss their feelings, or they may reject help on the basis that 'no one can make their problems easier'.

Only the individual is able to break this vicious circle. Depression is usually overcome when the causes have been honestly faced, and the individual has decided on an active personal response. The counsellor should seek to discuss how they can cope better with their feelings, and how they can clear their minds of depressing past events, or fears about the future. Depression is rarely a response to a single event or situation, but has its roots in feelings that we can no longer cope, and:

- that life is unfair and unjust, or just too difficult;
- that there is no point in continuing to struggle with life.

Depression occurs when people give in and decline to battle further. Initially they may do this to obtain help, or to demonstrate how badly they have been treated, or to express their hurt and pain. Depression is our way of saying that no one should be asked to face such odds. Whilst this is understandable, it becomes a problem when it is carried to extremes, or continues too long. For example, grief is natural. However, if it persists for an abnormally long period, the counsellor may have to challenge the person about whether their grief arises from their circumstances, or whether it has not become a chosen or preferred state of mind. There is a time when depression becomes a state of mind in which people are looking for sympathy rather than resolution.

However, sympathy alone is not sufficient. The lives of many older people can certainly be depressing enough to warrant sympathy, but there has to be a personal desire to overcome depression. It requires a level of personal commitment. When people find it difficult to talk, the counsellor may have to adopt a more direct approach, taking the initiative in clarifying the issues and problems that underlie depression, and opening them up as legitimate areas for discussion. In doing this, it is important that the counsellor emphasizes that depression is a response to specific circumstances, and to the way in which the person thinks about him- or herself. Ultimately, conquering depression will depend upon the person's ability and resolve:

- to struggle;
- to accept reality and face up to problems;
- to accept that matters can improve, and determine to do something about the situation.

The counsellor needs to be able to engage the depressed person, and their response is vital. There is a danger of reacting negatively to the 'negativity' of depressed people, but the counsellor cannot afford to do this. It is important at all times to empathize, to feel how they feel, and to understand better what is causing them to feel hopeless. One approach is to view depression as grieving over shattered dreams.

- *'It sounds as if you had dreams and pictures about your life that have been shattered. Can you tell me about them?'*
- *'It seems that life has not turned out in the way you expected. Is it possible to create new dreams, or to adapt old ones so that they can fit with the new situation?'*
- *'Is it possible for you to create a new identity?'*

This approach relies upon the power of hope, a hope in the future, dreaming a new or at least an adapted dream.

Counselling seeks to help sad people to rediscover some hope, some value and some meaning in life. Hope is something we all need, however old we are or however empty our lives might appear to be.

Suicide

When life appears to be without worth or significant meaning, thoughts of suicide can arise. Suicide is the ultimate act of depression. It is common for older people to feel that they are a burden, and that they do not want to be a nuisance to anyone. It is also common for older people to look forward to dying, perhaps in order to be reunited with loved ones. Annual suicide figures indicate that a significant number of older people take their own lives, and that suicide rates rise with age. It is also known that a higher proportion of older people succeed in suicide attempts, and fewer older people seek assistance before they act (Pearson *et al.*, 1997). There are significant differences in suicide rates between different cultural groups. This is accounted for by their religious beliefs, and the differential support provided for elders (Dein and Huline-Dickens, 1997).

However, people who take their own lives openly perhaps represent only the tip of the iceberg. It is difficult to know how many people who are facing the prospect of old age lose the will to live, and may refuse to eat, abuse their medication, or in some other way subtly contrive to terminate their own lives.

Depression is a common precursor to suicide (Dennis and Lindesay, 1995). Geldard (1989) places suicidal people in three overlapping categories:

1. people with a poor quality of life, with little or no possibility of improvement. This can include older people who are in constant pain, seriously disabled, chronically ill, or who for any reason feel that they have little to live for;

2. people who have recently suffered a traumatic loss, and who are going through a period of severe bereavement;

3. people who use suicidal talk or behaviour to attract attention and manipulate the behaviour of other people.

The threat of suicide is often a cry for help rather than a statement of serious intent. Several studies have shown that a high proportion of older people who were admitted to hospital after an attempted suicide had told someone about their intention. Primary-care physicians typically do not recognize or treat adequately depression among older people (Pearson *et al.*, 1997). Suicide attempts often follow a series of emotional and social events that have led to feelings of social alienation. The threat of suicide constitutes a strong signal of social distress, and should always be treated seriously. When older people talk about 'ending it all' or 'doing away with themselves', they should not be ignored, for such threats can develop into active suicide attempts.

However, denial is a common response to the suicidal feelings of older people. Their social distress is too often met by attempts to persuade them that they are wrong, and that there is 'someone or something for them to live for', even when the person is convinced otherwise. Denial can often result from certain moral objections – for example, the belief that people have no right to take their own lives. It is important that counsellors, as individuals, do come to terms with their own beliefs in this matter. However, within the counselling process, denying the personal feelings of a distressed person is not only futile but also dangerously counter-productive. Their feelings have to be addressed. Not to do this can increase the likelihood of a suicide attempt. It is no time for side-tracking or delaying discussion, whatever the attitude of the counsellor.

There are dangers in both over-reacting and under-reacting. In dealing with depressed people, it is important to distinguish between:

•   those who are expressing strong feelings of distress or resignation; and
•   those who are actively intent on suicide.

It is important to listen closely to what the person is saying. Rarely do people say that they are contemplating suicide directly. More usually, it is approached obliquely, by talking about their general dissatisfaction with life and living. The counsellor should seek to discuss such statements and their meaning, and they should not be afraid to ask for clarification, however directly.

- *'Does it feel so bad that you might consider killing yourself?'*

Only a small proportion of depressed people actually try to commit suicide, and it is usually possible to provide help and support long before this. Naturally, the possibility of suicide, when depressed people decide that they no longer wish to continue living, is very real. Without doubt the person who is genuinely thinking of 'ending it all' requires immediate help.

However, to over-react to the dangers of suicide is often to miss the real point. The counsellor should ensure that threats of suicide are not a means of attracting attention or obscuring other, more difficult agendas. Where this is so, it is these agendas, and not the suicide threat, that should be opened up and discussed.

When dealing with a suicidal person (however serious they may be), the counsellor will require help and support for his or her own personal feelings. This should be actively sought. It is not that the counsellor should withdraw from or relinquish the task. You might be the right person, by virtue of your relationship with the person. However, you will need someone to share your doubts and fears, and to discuss how you might best deal with the ongoing situation. Sometimes, when a person is deeply psychologically disturbed, it might be important to refer them for skilled professional counselling.

Furthermore, the counsellor should not assume responsibility for what an individual does or does not do. Ultimately, any action that a person takes will be something that he or she has decided upon, regardless of counselling skills. The counsellor does have an influence, but it is necessarily limited. Discussing this can be part of counselling, namely that what the person decides to do will ultimately be his or her own choice. This places the responsibility where it properly belongs, and it can also help to deal with subsequent feelings of guilt in situations where, despite the best efforts of the counsellor, someone decides to take his or her own life. Geldard (1989) said that once he had decided that he was not responsible for the decision 'Should I kill myself or not?', then he maximized the chances of change occurring in suicidal thoughts:

> Most if not all suicidal clients have some degree of ambivalence towards dying. After all, if a client was one hundred per cent convinced that she wanted to kill herself, she probably wouldn't be talking to a counsellor, she would just kill herself. Exploring the client's ambivalence is the key to successful counselling of such people.
>
> (Geldard, 1989)

This ambivalence can also be the subject of counselling.

- What are the costs and benefits of living?
- What are the costs and benefits of dying?
- How do they compare?

In raising these questions, the counsellor inevitably opens up much more than the subject of suicide, namely the very issues that have led an individual to contemplate suicide in the first place.

One common issue is anger and revenge. The threat of suicide can represent, in the strongest and most extreme way, how futile the person's life has become. Through the threat of suicide they seek to blame and punish other people for the things they have done (or failed to do) that have made life so meaningless. In such situations, paying direct attention to the threat can miss the real point and purpose of the communication. It is their anger and desire for revenge that need to be confronted. Why are they trying to punish other people? What have they done to deserve such a response? Such inquiries can sometimes reveal very significant information.

Dementia and confusion

Dementia and confusion are terms used to describe people who no longer have full control of their mind. For most older people, the prospect of dementia is the most deeply feared and significant of all losses – the loss of one's very self. Thus it is important to stress that confusion is an aberration, not a feature of the normal ageing process. Whilst normal ageing does bring with it some limited physical decline, this does not normally have a dramatic effect on personality or mental function. It has been estimated that 6 per cent of people over 65 years of age have definite dementia, although that figure rises to 38 per cent for people over 90 years (Jacques, 1992). However, the unavoidable truth is that whatever causes confusion, the impact can be devastating, affecting our thinking, feeling and reasoning, and leading to a deterioration in memory, concentration and reasoning.

The fear of dementia means that we often choose not to use the word. It is important to differentiate between two terms. *Dementia* arises from a variety of brain diseases, whereas *confusion* is a symptom of dementia, but has other causes, such as intense grief, infection and depression. Confusion manifests itself in many ways:

- disorientation in both time and space;
- a decreased ability to concentrate;

- behaviour that can change through an inability to control impulses and therefore to conform to moral norms;
- wandering and aimless behaviour;
- the memory fails to register, store and retrieve information, often involving a failure to recognize familiar people in its later stages;
- speech becomes incoherent or incomprehensible;
- the ability to express emotion gradually disappears.

The question for counsellors is whether there is value in counselling confused older people. Traditional attitudes would suggest that as confused people do not understand or remember what is being said to them, and we cannot understand what they are saying, there is no point.

If confusion is regarded solely as a psychomedical condition, that is a likely or even inevitable consequence of ageing that leads to death, then counselling confused people may appear to be pointless. However, there is a wider, more comprehensive understanding of 'confusion' which suggests that counselling can play a role, perhaps in preventing the condition, and certainly in caring for people who suffer from it. It is this wider definition that must be sought.

Medical definitions

The medical view of dementia focuses on a group of degenerative organic brain diseases that impair memory, thinking and behaviour. These are untreatable, irreversible, progressive and terminal. This medicalized clinical view sees dementia as an illness, and defines it in purely neuropathological terms. It identifies two main types of dementia.

Multi-infarct dementia

This is caused by a failure of the blood supply to the brain, due to small strokes or the narrowing of the arteries. These blockages lead to small failures in parts of the brain. The onset of this form of confusion can be sudden, and its course unpredictable and patchy, largely depending upon the regions of the brain that are damaged.

Alzheimer's disease

In Alzheimer's disease, the brain cells degenerate gradually. The cause of the disease remains unexplained, but it has been blamed variously on low levels of neurotransmitters (brain chemicals), the presence of aluminium and other metals, head injuries, and a slow-acting virus. The onset and progress of the disease are gradual, and the condition is considered to be irreversible.

Questioning medical orthodoxy

These medicalized descriptions are important. They describe the symptoms, look minutely into the biochemistry, and investigate the physical condition of confused brains.

However, they are limited by their failure to consider the wider circumstances that can produce confusion.

The concentration on neuropsychological factors is a classic example of medicalization. The tendency to study social problems and transform them into disease entities reflects the dominance of medicine, and also society's general unwillingness to consider other environmental and social causation. This has two main outcomes.

1. 'Dementia', the disease, becomes the explanation for all confusional states. Certain facts are selected (that brain cells die progressively throughout life, and that older people often become forgetful) and these are combined to explain matters that do not necessarily follow (that the normal process of brain cell loss leads to dementia).

2. The onset of a mild confusional state is viewed as a medical problem. Any alternative approach that seeks to identify the complex network of social, emotional and environmental factors which can produce the condition is discounted.

Without denying the existence of 'disease', it is important to question the priority given to the medical view. Post-mortem examinations have failed to prove any significant difference between 'confused' and 'normal' brains. The brains of dementia sufferers have been shown to contain deposits of 'neurofibrillary tangles' that accumulate within cells, and 'senile plaques', which are patches of degenerating nerve terminals. The problem is that the links between these physical features and dementia are inconsistent. The brains of many dementia sufferers do not contain these features when they should, and the brains of non-dementing people have them when they should not. Verwoerdt (1976) confirms this: 'There appears to be no consistent relationship between intellectual deterioration and organic brain changes (especially in the milder cases)'.

In any case, even if research did find a consistent neurological pattern, it would still beg several essential questions.

• Why do some people become confused/develop dementia while others do not?
• What factors trigger confusion/dementia?

There are other reasons to question the apparently straightforward link between changes in the brain and confusion in old age.

• Cohen and Faulkner (1984), comparing different age groups, found that memory varies according to what is being remembered. In certain matters (e.g. birthdays, anniversaries, answering letters) older people are significantly better than younger people.

- Many younger people have developed dementia, and their brains have been found to have developed 'senile plaques'.
- Not everything that confused/dementing people say and do, at every minute of every day, indicates a confused/demented mind. Even deeply confused people can display flashes of lucidity and understanding which indicate that they have a greater awareness of their surroundings than is normally assumed.
- Minority ethnic groups need to be particularly careful about diagnosis. Rait *et al.* (1996) found that screening tests are 'Eurocentric', constructed for use by a white/western population group, and that for people from different cultures, using different languages, their value can be limited and they may even be dangerous.
- 'Environmental' causation has been found by Mortimore (1988), with poor education, inadequate nutrition, alcohol abuse, smoking and exposure to toxic substances increasing the probability that plaques, tangles and infarctions associated with dementia will develop. This implicates social class, poverty, place of residence and country of birth as potential causal factors.

More attention needs to be given to the social and emotional factors that either underlie, or can be the precursor of confusion/dementia. Psychiatric medicine itself is deeply split with regard to the nature of mental illnesses, including dementia. Orthodox psychiatrists provide closed definitions which imply that causes and cures can be found within clinical settings. Others consider 'mental illness' to be a subjective judgement made about people whose behaviour deviates from the norm. Goffman (1968), Scheff (1966), Szasz (1976) and others have criticized vague medicalized definitions of mental illness, and point to alternative explanations based on social, emotional and environmental experience. They imply that effective treatment can be found only by addressing these wider concerns.

The core problem of medicalized attitudes, especially when considering how best to care for confused/dementing people, is that when someone has developed confusional symptoms, it tends to set them apart from other people, making them appear not fully human (Kitwood and Bredin, 1992).

The social creation of confusion/dementia

In the first edition of this book I suggested that a wider social understanding of the origin and nature of confusional states was vital. A social perspective does not deny the existence of dementia as a disease, but it does question whether it is always, or solely, a psychomedical condition. Monsour and Robb, in a review of the literature, concluded:

> that old age is basically a reflection of an aging person interacting with and reacting to the psychosocial and environmental demands. Because the exact mechanism of biological aging remains in doubt and because brain changes do not necessarily result in mental impairment, the

assumption that organic causes give rise to wandering in old age must be questioned. It is, therefore, reasonable to assume that manifested behavioural patterns in old age, whether intact or distorted by illness are, to some degree, rooted in the previous years of a person's life.

(Monsour and Robb, 1982)

More recently, Kitwood (1989, 1990, 1992) has suggested that a dynamic interplay between neurological and social–psychological factors offers a less deterministic, more comprehensive explanation of these disorders, and argues that this view fits more closely with the experience of individuals who care for people with confusion/dementia. The addition of a social perspective to the condition leads to different questions being asked.

- Why do most older people not suffer from confusion?
- Why do the brains of some people deteriorate more rapidly than those of others?
- Why do the arteries of the brain narrow in some older people and not in others?
- What are the environmental, social and emotional causes that have led to the significant increases in dementia witnessed over the last 100 years?

The medical view of confusion/dementia was first challenged by Meacher (1972) who, after outlining the literature of the 1950s and 1960s, concluded that a complex range of causes were implicated, none of which was entirely proven. He adopted a classification that explained confused behaviour as a *logical reaction* to the emotional stress of social isolation, powerlessness and segregation. Whereas most people can cope with the pressures and demands of social life, others cannot. Their unhappiness generates behaviour that is labelled 'antisocial', 'inappropriate' or 'unacceptable'. This 'abnormal' behaviour is then interpreted an an 'illness'.

If this is so, it may be possible to persuade people, through involving them in activity and counselling, to re-engage, or at least not to lose all contact with social reality. Eleftheriades (1991) describes a project with people suffering from severe dementia that stimulated their behaviour, and improved their communication. One conclusion drawn by that author was that people with dementia can utilize their brain if they choose to do so.

Confusion: the emergence of the person

The strongest trend in research on confusion/dementia since the publication of the first edition of this book has been the 'emergence of the person'. Personhood has become a topic of considerable importance (Goldsmith, 1996). This includes the person's sense of self, his or her rights, and the value gained by concerning oneself with the perspectives of the individual (Downs, 1997). The assumption that people with dementia experience a steady decline in personality and identity has been challenged (Kitwood and Benson, 1995). Mills and Coleman (1994) used counselling and reminiscence work to demonstrate that confused/dementing people retain important aspects of personal awareness. It is now recognized that the essential humanity of the person remains, that people do not consist of memory alone, but that they remain people with feelings, imagination, desires and will (Cohen and Eisdorfer, 1986).

This work demonstrates an increased interest in the potential of using counselling, and other psychotherapeutic techniques with confused/ dementing older people. It is no longer sufficient to assume that confusion arises from untreatable organic mental impairment, and that there is little purpose in talking to them. Counselling can help to locate the 'person', and thereby provide a personal dimension to care strategies, while at the same time seeking to discover the social causation of confusion, by asking important questions.

- Is confusion the result of social, emotional or environmental factors that have made life intolerable?
- If so, what were these factors?

If these factors have led to the organic/medical condition of dementia, then this suggests that counselling can provide a valuable preventive, perhaps even curative role in the condition. In responding, the counsellor, perhaps in association with skilled medical assistance, will need to consider all of the potential social, emotional and environmental causal factors.

Possible social links with confusion/dementia

What are the social factors that might contribute to confusion/dementia? Bergmann and Jacoby (1983) looked at research evidence and found that six categories of older people appeared to be most vulnerable to confusion:

1. those over 75 years of age and living alone;
2. those who had recently suffered bereavement;
3. those recently discharged from hospital;
4. those requiring home-help and community services;
5. those requesting residential care;
6. those planning to give up their homes.

These connections highlight certain areas (living alone, bereavement, the effects of medical treatment, the loss of independence, and so on) that are central to counselling older people, indicating that effective counselling undertaken at a time of crisis might be a powerful preventive tool.

Ageism and social distress

Ageist social attitudes anticipate that older people will lose control over their minds. Such attitudes can become self-fulfilling. 'Learned helplessness' (Lubinski, 1991; see also p. 32) describes the condition that arises when older people are not expected to make decisions for themselves, and when we focus on what people cannot do rather than on what they can do for themselves. This can make the prospect of older age seem so unbearable that older people can become unwilling to maintain contact with reality.

However, although ageism can create resignation, people do not become confused just because they expect to or we expect them to. Although we need to rescue older people from ageist expectations, there are many features of social life that can be instrumental in creating, developing and reinforcing confusion. Living into older age may have become too difficult or too painful to bear so, rather than experiencing it, they refuse to cope. They disengage mentally and enter a world of their own, filled only with what they want to have there. There is evidence to support such a view.

- Socially distressed people, perhaps experiencing bereavement or isolation, can exhibit behaviour that is often mistaken for confusion, and which can lead to confusional states. Depression is often diagnosed as confusion.
- It is known that some biochemical and hormonal features of psychological disturbance are generated by social trauma (Petty and Sensky, 1987). This provides a link between confusional states, the biochemical changes found in confused brains, and stress arising from social circumstances.

Social class

Confusion has a strong social-class component, older people from lower socio-economic groups having higher rates of confusion/dementia. This suggests that one of its most powerful social origins is the struggle against poverty and hardship. Many older people have fought poverty throughout their lives, and its heavy burden can eventually take its toll on the human condition. The daily stress of managing on insufficient income, poor diet, inferior health care and unhealthy working and living conditions creates the right circumstances for mental stress. It is not unlikely that psychological withdrawal, confusion and dementia may follow. Similar links have already been made between poverty, social neglect and other forms of mental illness, such as schizophrenia.

Anxiety and stress

However, confusion/dementia is not restricted by social class. Anxiety and stress are classless. Stress-induced behaviour is usually irrational – we do things we would consider untypical and foolhardy in more relaxed times, we let ourselves down, we feel sorry for ourselves, we wallow in our troubles and consider the world to be an unfair place, and we become antisocial. One well-known response to high levels of stress is to withdraw and to seek solace elsewhere.

Perhaps one 'advantage' of old age is that withdrawal becomes acceptable. Ageism has made it legitimate. Whereas the desire to die is not a practical possibility, the demise of the mind – a kind of 'mental suicide' – is easier. Whilst confusion should not be viewed as a voluntary state, consciously chosen by people who cannot cope with life's realities, it may none the less provide a convenient means of escape.

Loneliness

The prospect of social isolation is daunting. The ability to communicate with other people is an important factor in maintaining sanity (isolation may also arise from deafness, blindness and aphasia, and the effects of these conditions should not be underestimated). Communication, in its many forms, engages our bodies and minds and helps to keep us active, involved and lucid. In contrast, the harsh effects of solitary confinement are well known, and its symptoms can be legitimately related to confusion in older people.

However, there is another form of 'isolation', even for older people who are in regular contact with other people. This is the isolation that arises from a perceived lack of concern and understanding, when their feelings and what they say appear to be unimportant, their complaints are brushed aside or trivialized, and their feelings are discounted as unnecessary or silly. Many older people may feel that no one cares whether they live or die. This is not how life used to be, when there were people who cared about them. The 'old days' are remembered with fondness. By comparison, today is anathema. It is perhaps significant that, in the initial stages of confusion, people will forget the present, whilst they remember the past with great clarity.

Dependence

Growing dependence can also play a part in the social creation of confusion/ dementia. We have seen how the loss of independence can signify a damaging blow to pride and morale. Each loss in coping ability necessitates an emotional adjustment, and this can cause some older people the deepest distress.

Fear

Ageing can be a frightening process, particularly when it is allied with growing dependence and increasing loneliness. Fear can impact on the mind to produce irrational and obsessional behaviour. It can cause panic and undermine our ability to cope with everyday life. Older people can be afraid because they live in a world that has changed out of all recognition from the one in which they were nurtured. They may fear illness and death, burglary and mugging, or falling. There is good reason for older people to be afraid, and thus to suffer the detrimental effects of this on both body and mind.

Relocation

Unwanted moves into hospital, sheltered accommodation or residential care may also contribute to confusion/dementia. Social upheaval happens more frequently to older people. They lose control of their lives. Becoming dependent can mean relinquishing the right to make decisions. The loss of independence, moving to unfamiliar surroundings, and the stress that these changes cause can lead to confusion/dementia. Confused behaviour may then be induced, maintained and perpetuated by the institutional care provided by hospitals and residential homes.

Given a combination of these social circumstances, it is perhaps unsurprising that some older people refuse to stay mentally lucid. When people are unable to resolve their difficulties, there is an understandable tendency to withdraw. The 'confused' or 'demented' mind may be a more comfortable state than the world of social reality. It is easier to allow other people to assume responsibility when one feels unable to cope. In this sense, the drift into confusion/dementia can be viewed as an understandable, even rational decision.

Possible health factors and confusion

Illness

The brain, especially the ageing brain, is a sensitive instrument that can be affected by a variety of external influences. Mild confusional states can accompany an illness at any age. Confusion is a well-known feature of fever, but acute confusional states can arise from many illnesses, including:

- chest infections;
- heart failure;
- high blood pressure;
- pneumonia;
- urinary tract infections;
- constipation.

Indeed, any illness that causes constant pain can cause confusion (Wattis and Church, 1986). Verwoerdt (1976) mentions epilepsy and liver disease, and Gray and Wilcocks (1981) describe the effects of hydrocephalus and syphilis.

Hormonal imbalance

Older people are susceptible to metabolic disorders that can cause confusion. They arise from an imbalance in the body of hormones produced by the endocrine glands, or by malfunction in the kidney or the liver. Hypothyroidism (a lack of thyroid hormone) produces tiredness, constipation and an intolerance of cold, as well as a confusional state that can be mistaken for

Alzheimer's disease (Wattis and Church, 1986). Pernicious anaemia causes confusion when the amount of oxygen carried by the red blood cells to the brain is reduced. Insulin from the pancreas, calcium from the parathyroid gland and urea from the kidney have also been implicated (Gray and Wilcocks, 1981), as have prostate gland trouble and weak kidney function.

All of these potential causes of confusion suggest that, when someone appears to be developing signs of confused behaviour, it does not follow that this represents the onset of dementia. Recovery can be assisted with simple medical attention.

Iatrogenic medical intervention

However, medicine can also be a problem. There are a considerable number of drugs, commonly used for older people, that are known to produce confusional states. Wattis and Church (1986) produced a long list, including the following:

- sedatives;
- antidepressants;
- tranquilizers;
- benzodiazepines (especially long-acting varieties);
- sleeping pills;
- barbiturates;
- digoxin;
- digitalis-based drugs;
- steroids;
- non-steroidal anti-inflammatory drugs;
- anti-Parkinsonian drugs;
- antihistamines;
- diuretics.

Indeed, most drugs can cause confusion because of their potential inter-actions with other drugs (including alcohol). Older people are particularly susceptible because their kidneys do not eliminate drugs so efficiently, making a build-up of toxicity more likely. Alongside a sympathetic doctor, the counsellor should check the currently prescribed medication with a view to withdrawing or changing the offending drugs.

Nutritional factors

The link between nutrition and confusion is well documented (Gray and Wilcocks, 1981; Wattis and Church, 1986).

- Thiamin (vitamin B_1) deficiency can cause rapid delirium associated with changes in the nerves, and a sudden and profound loss of memory.
- Vitamin B_2 deficiency can be mistaken for Alzheimer's disease.
- Folic acid, potassium, vitamin B_6, protein, iron and calorie deficiencies have been linked with confusion.

- Research at Southampton University has linked Alzheimer's disease to aluminium in water supplies in certain areas. If this is correct, the drinking of tea (which has a high aluminium content) becomes a possible contributory factor.
- Statistics linking social class and poverty with higher rates of confusion/dementia suggest potential nutritional links.
- The consumption of certain foods (liver and fish) can be helpful in preventing the onset of dementia (McDerment and Greengross, 1985).

The role of the counsellor

The social creation of confusion/dementia may be unproven, but is supported by arguments that are probably as sound as the medical model. The social model has the advantage that it explains why some people develop confusion in older age, while others do not. It also offers an opportunity for counselling intervention.

Counselling of confused people has been restricted by ageism and medicalization, both of which assume that confusion is an inevitable and irreversible part of growing old. Even the limited view that counselling may be able to prevent or contain confusional states is difficult to justify, but this should not prevent concerned people from attempting to use it as an approach.

The re-emergence of 'the person' is the starting point for counselling. Gardner (1993) stresses the need for assessment, goal-setting, developing and implementing strategies, and evaluation. In doing so, he adapts general counselling principles to people suffering from confusion but, as he says, when counselling people with brain dysfunction, some techniques are less applicable and require alteration. In the early stages, counselling is possible, but as the disease process progresses, their ability to engage diminishes.

We know little about the personal experience of confusion/dementia – what it 'feels' like, or how people feel about our reactions to them. Until recently, confused people were considered to be unable to give an explanation. However, books are now being written by people in the early stages of dementia. McGowin (1993) stated that we need to find ways of enabling people to live with the disease by helping them to focus on their strengths rather than their losses. Davis (1989), who suffered and eventually died of Alzheimer's disease, made an important statement:

> I want to shout, 'Be gentle with your loved ones. Listen to them. Hear their whispered pain. Touch them. Include them in activity meaningful to them'.

Information

When there is an early diagnosis of dementia, should information about the person's condition be disclosed or withheld? Goldsmith (1996) rehearsed the arguments for and against early disclosure, including the difficulties of accurate assessment. Most of the literature would appear to be in favour of disclosure, but fear of the condition is considerable, and there is a tendency to secrecy based on several grounds:

- the uncertainty that exists about diagnosis and prognosis;
- the absence of treatment or any hope of improvement or recovery;
- the distress it might cause;
- the ability of the person to understand and cope with the knowledge;
- the inability of family members to cope with the knowledge.

However, secrecy prevents people from being able to plan ahead, put their affairs in order and make known their wishes for the future while they are still able to do so. It also denies their right to know, especially when the person will already be aware that something is wrong. It prevents us from learning about how the early dementia sufferer feels, and what he or she is experiencing. Downs (1997) points to research which indicates that 'people with dementia want a range of information about its effects ... about services and supports, and about adjusting to dependency in the caring relationship'. If our response to dementia is to value people and have empathy with them, it is difficult to support withholding of information.

However, information should not be provided without considering the potential pain that the information will engender.

It now appears that even demented persons experience and feel threatening losses, and it would appear that the process of dementia creates an environment which fosters uncertainty and the lack of safety. This could mean that demented persons are struggling with emotional problems which have been hitherto underestimated.

(Meisen, 1992)

People suffering from dementia probably pass through a normal process of grief (Solomon and Szwarbo, 1992). This should not be surprising, unless we believe that sufferers lose their humanity at a very early stage. They may not pass through the entire process, never reaching the stage of reorganization (see Chapter 17) because of the progressive disorganization of their minds.

Recognizing symptoms and assessing causation

The counsellor should try to assess whether social or health factors underlie the confusion/dementia. When this seems to be a possibility, they should become the focus of attention. If the condition has a medical cause, this should be investigated by enlisting the help of medical personnel. Some studies have found that 15 to 30 per cent of dementia cases are treatable (Ropper, 1979). In this respect it is fortunate that the changes in early confusion/dementia can be gradual, as time is available for finding and enlisting support.

Addressing the social causes of confusion

It is common for confusion to be triggered by recent events, losses and bereavements. Sometimes a series of traumatic events may have occurred over a short period of time. Confusion is often the result of extreme unhappiness. It is important that the counsellor does not believe that confusion is a 'happy' state of mind that is best left alone. The main premise when counselling a confused person should be that the person's past social and emotional problems have not always been resolved, and that they may have withdrawn from reality as a result. It follows that confusion can be effectively dealt with only if these problems are tackled.

Empathy

In the early stages of confusion/dementia it is important that the counsellor seeks to understand how the person feels, and tries to locate the 'person within'. The earlier in the process this is done, the greater the understanding that can be achieved. Confusion varies in its impact, and responses will vary between people. There is no one condition or one response, as each person requires an individual understanding.

It is important to be realistically optimistic. People with dementia can learn simple things, even if it is only that 'this person is kind and cares about me', and they do have feelings. It is too easy, as with most disabilities, to assume that we know best. Davis (1989) is again helpful here:

I was alone, cut off . . . what was in my mind? Blackness and darkness of the worst kind. As soon as I let go of my concentration to try to fall asleep, there was nothing there. This vacuum was filled with terrifying blackness.

Davis told us many things, for example that he could not stand too much 'stimulation' because it made him tired, that walking helped him reorientate himself, and that his dreams made him fearful and anxious. We can only respond to these matters if we are aware of them.

Communication

Counselling seeks to help people to make sense of their present reality. It aims to help them to come to terms with their life, accept it as it is, and reassume personal responsibility for it. To achieve this with people in the early stages of confusion/dementia means that they need to face up to and resolve the problems which beset them. Counselling skills are vitally important if this is to be achieved (Kitwood, 1993; Goldsmith, 1996).

However, additional skills are required. Davis (1989) describes how his wife, Betty, makes the crucial point that you should never begin speaking to Alzheimer's sufferers before being absolutely sure you have their attention, for otherwise they may miss the crucial early parts of what you are saying. Kitwood and Bredin (1992) have made several other recommendations.

- Remember that the person's mind may be working more slowly than yours, not that it is not working at all.
- Speak slowly and clearly, with a deep rather than a 'squeaky' voice.
- Place yourself in front of the person, so that there is facial contact and lip movements can be seen.
- Smile, and give praise for understanding.
- Keep words simple and sentences short.
- How you speak, as well as what you say, is important. It may be important to speak firmly (especially if the person is deaf), but not to shout (as this may give an impression of anger or hostility).

Confused people have difficulty in responding to what is said. This is not necessarily because they do not understand what we are saying, or do not appreciate our attempt to communicate meaningfully with them. The counsellor should not be afraid to repeat questions, kindly and gently, or to persevere in focusing on crucial issues.

As the disease progresses, communication has been likened to conducting a conversation with someone who is speaking a different language. However, the importance of continuing to communicate has been succinctly outlined by Killick (1997), who describes it is 'a matter of life and death of the mind', and says that failure to overcome the difficulties can have serious consequences, which include:

- a sense of isolation and disempowerment in the confused person;
- a sense of hopelessness in the carer;
- a tendency to deny personhood to the confused person.

Killick's article deals with understanding the apparently nonsensical words and phrases used by people with dementia, and the skill required to do so, although the techniques have only recently been studied, and understood. A few examples are given here.

- Wanting to go home can be a way of saying that they do not know where they are.
- Calling for their mother may be a way of asking for love, care and attention.
- Crying without apparent reason may be grieving the loss of their mind.
- Aggression may be the result of frustration – their inability to do what they want to do.
- Wandering and restlessness may be concerned with a search for past connections, perhaps with parents or children.

Such interaction can demonstrate that, as dementia deepens, confused people do retain abilities, however limited they may be. The counsellor should become a translator, patiently seeking reason from what may appear to be irrational language and behaviour, and should offer words of understanding or explanation with which the confused person can identify.

Another frustration can be a person's apparent inability to remember what has been said, even only minutes earlier. Memory impairment can make communication a non-ending repeat of the same conversation. It is important that the counsellor is able to hide his or her frustration, as this will not assist either the communication or the caring relationship. When memory loss reaches this stage, there is often little point in repetition, and it might be important to consider using reminiscence or validation techniques, rather than continuing to communicate about current concerns.

Non-verbal communication

There are simple non-verbal aids that can be used with confused people, especially in the early stages of dementia. As the value of language decreases, and the objective remains to make the person feel secure, then it becomes important to develop these techniques.

- Appropriate touch can be important, as it conveys warmth and care. It can range from a reassuring holding of hands, to cuddles, to formal massage (Goldsmith, 1996).
- Diaries, notepads and scrapbooks can be used to stimulate memory, assist communication and reduce frustration.
- Life-history books can be written that contain basic facts and information, photographs and other memorabilia from the person's life. These can be used to remind them of the reality of their past, and to generate discussion about former loved ones.
- Activity constitutes vital communication. Confused/dementing people are too often left to sit in one place, often on the basis that they appear to be content doing so. Their passivity and somnolence are both caused by confusion/dementia and, if allowed, can deepen the confusional state.
- Social contact is also important. The absence of companionship can both cause and deepen confusion. Involvement in the discussion, argument and debate of normal relationships can provide the intellectual 'stimulation' that confused people need in order to avoid further decline.
- Art and music can be used both as stimuli and as a means of self-expression (Pollack and Namazi, 1992).
- Massage and aromatherapy can be used for enjoyable sensual stimulation, and for their calming effects.
- Woods and Ashley (1995) have used tape-recordings of relatives' voices on personal-stereo equipment as therapy that meets the attachment needs of dementing people.

Taking time

Work with confused/dementing people is time-consuming, and progress can be imperceptibly slow. There are no quick or easy solutions. Our one-dimensional medicalized approach has produced none, and we have become negatively fatalistic. If counselling is to play a role, it has to be a patient one, with realistically moderate expectations. Even maintaining stability can constitute success, especially for people whose drift into confusion has been rapid. If it does nothing else, counselling can investigate intellectual function in order to see what remains. Goldsmith (1996) emphasized that people had different personalities before they developed dementia, and that there are different illnesses that cause dementia, so that an enormous number of variables are involved. Assessing the effects of dementia, both in terms of the losses incurred and, more importantly, in terms of the personality that remains, is a time-consuming task, but an essential one if the person is to be credited with an identity.

Caring

People suffering from confusion/dementia require care, and it is their identity that ensures this care is personalized. However, as carers receive little response from confused people, it is often assumed that care, kindness and warmth are not appreciated. Davis (1989) stated:

> Sometimes Betty [his wife] would hear me crying or even screaming in my sleep. She would hold me, speak soft words of reassurance to gently bring me back to reality. How precious was her touch at those agonising times.

Confused people can experience a profound sense of emptiness or absence related to the potential future loss of self, which causes them deep despair and terror. Medicalized responses often neglect these feelings, replacing them with extended assessments and the absence of support (Bender and Cheston, 1997).

The basic principles of caring, which are often taken for granted when dealing with other people, apply equally to those suffering from confusion/dementia.

- Treat them as 'normal' people, not as people with a mental illness.
- Spend time with them, not rushing them or taking over from them because they are unable to think concisely, logically or quickly.
- Smile, and use appropriate touching for reassurance.
- Communicate using your normal voice intonation.
- Avoid the tendency to agree with everything they say, or to dismiss what they say as meaningless.

> I don't bite. I am still the same person. I just can't do my work anymore. I know that one of these days I will not be in here anymore, but for now, maybe for another year or two, I am still home in here and I need your friendship and acceptance.
>
> (Davis, 1989)

Although the parts of the brain that deal with memory and thought processes are usually affected, those that deal with feelings are not.

Most people who care for confused/dementing people are convinced that their feelings do not change. They should not be patronized, as so often happens, and their need for love and affection remain undiminished. Marples states that:

> Throughout the course of dementing illness, the individual remains sensitive to the attitudes of those around him. He detects insincerity, along with the irritation and impatience caregivers try to suppress. Although the senile person may not be in sufficient control of his behaviour to act wilfully, he is able to respond to others' feelings and act out his frustration.
>
> (Marples, 1986)

The full security and support of the counselling relationship need to be offered, even in the later stages of dementia. Perhaps ultimately this will provide a basis from which the person may feel sufficiently 'safe' to renew contact with their difficult and uncomfortable world:

> In my rational moments I am still me.
>
> (Davis, 1989)

Behaviour changes

Behaviour can change as dementia develops. It is often assumed that this is a result of the disease, but it is important to realize that people suffering from dementia can experience the same stress or frustration that would cause behaviour problems in ordinary people. However, behaviour change can often become a problem for carers, whose own needs for care and consideration can become a vital issue. They may need help in understanding the reason for the behaviour change, to enable them to continue with their caring.

Dignity

Dementia sufferers will ultimately become totally dependent, and will barely resemble their former selves. They can become very pliable, and in caring for them we can speak to them and make them do things that they do not like, or would not want to do. Davis stated his objections clearly and decisively:

> There is still a part of that vital person living inside that sometimes helpless-looking body, a person who deserves to be treated with dignity. Just because a person is incontinent or requires feeding does not give some eighteen-year-old twit the right to call them 'dearie' or 'sweetie'.
>
> I cannot stand the beat of rock music or the bounding around of even senior citizen aerobic exercise classes. Human dignity demands that I

have the right of refusal for any activity or entertainment that I do not perceive as entertaining.

(Davis, 1989)

Again, the danger is the assumption that 'the person' is no longer there, so it is not important what is done with them because they have no feelings.

Terror

People suffering from dementia can feel real terror at the prospect of mental decline. Bender and Cheston (1997) liken the needs of people informed of their dementia with those of individuals informed that they have HIV and AIDS, and adds that whilst the latter can expect counselling and other support services, these forms of support are rarely available to early dementia sufferers.

Delusions and hallucinations

Confused/dementing people can suffer many delusions and hallucinations, which can take many forms. Many people believe that their parents are still living, that their children are still 'children', or that carers are people from their past. Often, in the interests of 'reality', these experiences are considered to be unimportant. However, Meisen (1993) explains this behaviour by reference to attachment theory (see p. 125), as a response to the 'strangeness' and therefore the danger of their situation, and their need for emotional security. Kitwood and Bredin (1992) confirm that these delusions have meaning, and that if carers listened carefully they might catch a sense of the feelings being conveyed. Their recommendation is sound.

respect the 'reality' of the person you are caring for, even though it is different from yours. If you are struggling hard to bring them to your sense of reality, ask yourself why you are doing it. Are you simply trying to relieve your own sense of discomfort? Are you trying to uphold your authority? If what you are doing really does have a point – if it really does add to their well-being – that's fine. But if not, relax and let things be. In any case, always accept and respect each person just as they are.

(Kitwood and Bredin, 1992)

Apathy

Confused/dementing people often appear to lose interest in the world, and become apathetic and lacking in motivation. This is frequently attributed to their condition. However, Bender and Cheston point out that it is becoming clear that social and personal factors may also be involved, and that apathy can result from having their social roles withdrawn.

their social interactions do not allow them to maintain a sense of themselves as lovers, helpers, carers, teachers or whatever. It is not simply that there is no place for them to perform, even marginally, in these roles, but that there is no place or permission for them to talk about themselves as occupying these roles. The ultimate result of this situation may be the fending off of the dementia sufferer, who then becomes totally displaced.

(Bender and Cheston, 1997)

The counsellor has to be more pro-active, taking greater initiative in interacting with confused people than is normally required in the counselling process.

Techniques to assist the counsellor

Reality orientation

Reality orientation (RO) is one approach to working with older people suffering from mental confusion or dementia. As its name implies, the technique seeks to maintain confused people in or return them to the existing world of reality. RO confronts confused people with reality. It is a behaviourist technique based on the idea that behaviour is learned, and can therefore be unlearned.

1. It recognizes that the person's mind is no longer functioning in the real world, but in a confused and unrealistic personal world.

2. It interprets confused behaviour as 'inappropriate'.

3. It seeks remedy by insisting on behaviour that is more in line with reality.

4. It utilizes a variety of techniques to draw attention to reality, such as:
   - the correct day, month and year;
   - the correct time;
   - the nature of the weather;
   - the place, and the people who are present.

5. Work often focuses on well-known objects, asking people simple questions about their colour, shape, feel and usage.

6. It seeks to maintain concentration for as long as possible.

7. Questions are repeated until the correct answer is given.

8. Correct responses are rewarded.

9. Incorrect responses are punished, perhaps by a withdrawal of privileges.

RO can be practised individually or in small groups, and as the technique is considered to become more effective with increasing frequency, it is undertaken as often as time permits. Twenty-four-hour RO is considered ideal, and has been undertaken in some hospitals and specialized units for confused older people where the total living environment can be devoted to it.

RO is a narrow technique whose impact is cold and inflexible. By seeking to grade behaviour as 'appropriate' or 'inappropriate', and standardizing rewards and punishments in response to that behaviour, RO is considered to be a scientific methodology (and thus attractive to some people). However, the 'science' of RO justifies an impersonal technique that seeks to cajole unwilling minds back into the present. It discounts the presence of 'meaning' in so-called 'inappropriate' behaviour. It also stops people communicating their feelings and wishes, and so prevents us from finding meaning in their behaviour. On those grounds, it should be dismissed as a method of counselling and caring for confused older people.

The counsellor needs to understand why someone is unwilling to face reality. Whilst RO sets out to modify 'inappropriate' behaviour, counselling seeks to understand the reason for it.

Reminiscence

Reminiscence is a method of working with confused people that has many advantages over RO. Our sense of self-esteem and identity is based on our past, and reminiscence acknowledges that the person retains a sense of their inner world, and uses a variety of aids to prompt memories in order to affirm a sense of self.

- It focuses on what a person *can* do rather than on what is no longer possible.
- It focuses on times when people were in full possession of their mental faculties, and so can help to establish psychological integrity (Bender and Cheston, 1992).
- It enables the counsellor to concentrate on a more pleasant past, rather than on a painful present.
- It can engage people in joyful rather than sad exchanges.
- It enables the counsellor to gain knowledge about 'the person' behind the illness.

Gibson (1993) states that it is plausible to assume that if knowledge of our past is important to our sense of well-being in the present, it must be important for people with dementia to try to hold on to their past. Coleman (1986) suggests that reminiscence can represent a means for people to communicate feelings which, if expressed directly, would be difficult for them (and/or their carers) to handle. For example, when confused older people speak to their 'parents' rather than to their sons or daughters, this may be because it is safer for them to do so.

Several studies on the outcome of reminiscence (Kaminsky, 1988; Gibson, 1989; Fielden, 1990; Gibson, 1994b) have demonstrated positive results, including increased sociability, less isolation, improved appetite and mood, reduced restlessness and agitation, and less challenging behaviour.

Carers can also be encouraged by being able to engage in positive and meaningful communication, and gaining access to skills and abilities previously believed to be lost. Although specific responses can sometimes appear to be irrelevant, and confused people may be unable to use words to describe their feelings, through their smiles, body language and other gestures they can give a powerful indication of how they feel. This allows carers to enter their increasingly isolated and apparently strange world.

The animation that can arise from such positive experiences between confused people and their carers can be important, particularly when relationships have become one-directional and filled with sadness. Positive reminiscence can help carers to rekindle their energy, moving them from a wearing and thankless caring task to one in which there is a level of mutual communication. Gibson sums up the challenge to family and professional carers:

> How may we become sufficiently acquainted with the person with dementia's old familiar landscape as to be able to recognise the landmarks? How may we show our willingness to join them on their journey through this landscape, walking with them as companions for at least a little part of their route? If we are to tolerate seemingly bizarre and often difficult behaviour, we have to extend our understanding and increase our tolerance to their pain. A detailed knowledge of the person's past becomes the means by which we extend our capacity to venture, to explore, to remain a travelling companion for more of the journey and postpone for a time the parting of the ways.
>
> (Gibson, 1993)

Validation

Validation is an approach to communicating with and understanding older confused people by affirming their sense of reality. Its starting point is similar to counselling, emphasizing the importance of listening, empathy, building trust, being non-directive and non-judgemental, having unconditional positive regard for the person, and being genuine. It assumes that what the person says and does has meaning. However, in one very important respect, validation differs from counselling.

It is based on the belief that confused older people have withdrawn from the world of reality, and that carers should not seek to bring them back from their own perceived world.

Naomi Feil (1992), who developed and pioneered the method, states that to bring the person back from their perceived world is counter-productive, as it destroys the relationship of trust. In validation, there is no belief that through self-awareness a confused person can be returned to reality. Validation is counselling without the prospect of change or personal growth. The objective of validation is to empathize, not to give insight, and to respect the person, not to confront him or her with reality. It is to treat disoriented people with understanding and respect. Feil says that 'clock time' has gone. The person is governed by the past and its memories. Daughters become mothers, sons become fathers, and every action and every incoherent statement is concerned with the past. It is possible, by listening and validating, that we can confirm these meanings.

Feil makes use of Erikson's life stages, but adds a seventh and final stage, which she describes as *'resolution versus vegetation'*. In this stage, the task is to resolve the past, whilst failure to do so leads to vegetation. Older people who have failed to resolve their feelings in earlier stages now resolve to bury themselves in the past and to die in peace, untroubled by the realities of the present world. When older people enter this final life stage, Feil describes four stages of retreat into unreality:

1. *malorientation* – when the person is unhappily oriented to reality;
2. *time confusion* – when the person suffers a loss of cognitive capacity;
3. *repetitive motion* – when these actions replace speech;
4. *vegetation* – a total inward retreat.

At each stage there are different ways of responding. It is not the intention to go into these here, but they have been clearly laid out by Feil (1992). However, in general terms, to 'validate' is to acknowledge that the feelings of the confused person are true.

> They need someone to listen to validate their feelings. If no one listens, they withdraw to vegetation. With no stimulation from the outside world, they become one of the living dead in our nursing homes. The validation worker listens, knowing that there will never be complete resolution.
>
> (Feil, 1992)

Moreover, validation is necessary regardless of the degree of personal disorientation. Only by validating their feelings is it possible to restore any vestige of self-worth, reduce stress and justify living, however marginally, in the real world. If we try to do otherwise they will withdraw and drift further into a vegetative state. Through validation, confused people are more likely to resolve unfinished business, maintain communication and prevent further progressive disorientation.

Validating does not mean that we agree with their disorientation. Feil states that disoriented older people do know the truth, and feel patronized by someone who agrees with them. However, validation does demand that we do not deny them. Confused people want others to listen to them, to try to understand what they are saying and doing. When we do so, they respond.

Confused people will not 'return' to the present or work out their problems in any way. They have been ravaged by the losses of old age, and do not want to return. Confusion – living amidst the nostalgia of the past – is an easier option. The present holds no advantage for them. Validation permits them to stay where they are, and is their way of coping with the end of their lives.

Feil is also clear about who is helped by validation. The dividing line is a person's ability to think cognitively. It is useful for the disoriented 'old-old', namely people who have led normal lives and functioned reasonably well until they were overpowered by the cumulative losses of old age. They may have failed to pass successfully through one or more of Erikson's life stages, and they may or may not have permanent damage to their brain, but they show by their behaviour that they do not want to understand, to be aware, or to be brought face to face with reality.

Conversely, validation is not for someone who is oriented, or for a mentally handicapped person, or someone with a history of mental illness, or indeed for a person who has suffered recent trauma. These people can be helped by counselling. Nor does Feil believe that validation is for people with organic brain disease, such as younger people who have been struck down by Alzheimer's disease. She convincingly suggests that disoriented 'old-old' people and the younger Alzheimer's sufferer do not have the same disease. The 'old-old' may develop the plaques and tangles typical of Alzheimer's disease, but autopsies show that the physical condition of the brain is not the sole determinant of behaviour. Some older people develop the typical plaques and tangles of Alzheimer's disease but continue to lead fairly normal lives right up to their death.

The onset of dementia demands something else – a social/emotional trigger. This can occur when there are too many physical and social losses, and the person retreats. Dementia in this sense is a choice, not a medical condition. It is the individual who determines how he or she reacts to his or her situation.

Caring for carers

The carers of confused people can easily despair and become frustrated. Caring for older people with dementia is probably the most challenging task of all. The personality of the individual can change fundamentally, they can display difficult behaviour, and there may be few rewards for the task of caring. The communication barriers that this creates can lead to carers attending to only the person's most basic needs. This can increase the sense of isolation and depression in both carer and confused relative.

Carers can experience psychological stress and physical fatigue, and entire families can be disrupted (Marples, 1986). This can lead to anger, bewilderment, feelings of inadequacy and resentment and, in extreme circumstances, to violent physical abuse of confused people. Certainly in cases of severe dementia the most important task that counselling can perform is to support the carers, rather than to engage in more direct but more speculative work with confused people.

The 'empty chair' technique can be useful when working with carers. The chair replaces the person, and enables the carer to talk as if their loved one was present. They can thus seek to conclude unfinished business.

Family work can also be helpful. Dementia is a condition that usually impacts on the whole family. Complex and difficult decisions have to be made about the care of confused relatives. Within the family there can be conflicting ideas about how best to respond, and difficulties can arise from this. The process of decline can generate even more stress, producing dysfunction within even the healthiest families. Family work can assist in reaching agreement on how to proceed, and thereby improving the care that they are able to provide for the confused person.

At some stage it has to be recognized that the individual is no longer competent to make their own decisions, and that carers might need support in making them. This can often be best achieved by going over what the person might have wanted if he or she was still able to make decisions him- or herself.

Particular mention must be made of people and families from minority ethnic communities who suffer from dementia. Patel et al. (1998) reported that they are diagnosed later, and are at a disadvantage in obtaining community care services. Even those who receive such services discover that such services are neither sensitive to their ethnic origins nor appropriate to their needs.

Bereavement and grief ◼ 17

Bereavement results from significant loss, often associated with the death of close friends and relatives. There are, however, many other forms of loss, many of which have been discussed in earlier chapters. These include:

- loss of employment;
- loss of the parenting role;
- loss of health;
- loss of mobility and independence.

These aspects of loss in older age can be as important, if not more important, than death. This chapter will focus on bereavement arising from death, but a wider consideration of bereavement in older age can be found in Scrutton (1995).

For most of our life, bereavement is something that happens to other people. We do not live with a full consciousness of the possible traumas of the future. The possibility crosses our mind, perhaps impinging at times, but we are reluctant to dwell on the subject. It is always some time away – something to deal with later.

However, older people spend more time pondering their losses. Often they are discouraged from doing so by younger people who believe that this is too morbid to warrant consideration. Such an attitude is wrong. Older generations are closer to bereavement in all its forms, and death is no longer a distant prospect for them. Indeed, the experience of feeling close to bereavement can be quite vivid for older people, especially those who live in sheltered accommodation or in residential care, where it surrounds them with relative frequency. However, even in these places the tendency to deny the social realities of older age is often evident.

The denial of death

Reticence about death has always been a feature of modern western society. Traditional religious belief and social customs attempted to help people to come to terms with personal loss, but their rituals and the belief structures that underlie them are no longer so powerful (Gorer, 1965). People from minority ethnic communities may have quite different beliefs and expectations about death, but they may find that they are not taken fully into consideration, and that younger generations of their family do not take them as seriously as they might like. Regardless of background, it is important that the cultural aspects of bereavement and death are taken fully into consideration by the counsellor. Green and Green (1991) have comprehensively covered the religious, ethnic and cultural aspects of death and dying.

However, it is important that counsellors understand the problems and limitations of all approaches to bereavement taken by all religions. They rely upon theological ideas about an *afterlife* in order to deal with the pain suffered *in this life*. It is believed, for example, that loved ones have gone to a 'better place', where there is 'no suffering', and where we shall 'meet again'. Whilst this 'other-worldly' emphasis may be temporarily helpful to someone struggling to come to terms with the absence of a loved one, it is essentially a philosophy of denial. The individual has to continue living, and to restructure his or her life in this world.

However deep the personal conviction, there is little in such ideas that soothes present pain and the new social reality. The decline of religious ritual is regretted not so much because it was ever particularly effective, but because we have failed to replace the social and emotional contact it provided with anything else.

> *Bereavement is a selfish emotion, albeit a necessary one. Grief may be **about** another person, but essentially it is **for** ourselves and our own needs.*

The family is another important cultural element in social responses to bereavement, providing the basis for ongoing support and a sense of continuity. However, the family is no longer such an integrated and supportive institution. Its traditional role in caring for dying people and the bereaved helped people to develop an acceptance of death, provided a firm basis for the renewal of life, and represented its continuation. Moreover, the decline of the family can be as true for families from minority ethnic backgrounds as for any others.

The sanitization of bereavement

Many deaths occur among older people and their families. A typical bereavement takes place after an illness, during which members of the family, to varying degrees, have provided care both for the now deceased person and for those who were likely to face the greatest bereavement at their death. Thus the issue of how best to deal with the situation before, during and after the event arises regularly, but when it does so, people often feel unprepared and uncertain about what to do.

Alongside traditional rituals and ceremonies, much of our former knowledge of what to do, what to say, and how to support bereaved people has also declined. The older, more uncertain and diffident etiquettes have been replaced by an embarrassed certainty, represented by efficient bureaucratic responses – initially the medical profession, and then firms of undertakers.

- The process of dying often takes place outside the home, in a hospital or hospice.
- When a death occurs at home, the body is removed within hours.
- The body is laid out in a chapel of rest.
- Viewing the body can be avoided entirely.

These professional services seek to relieve bereaved people of responsibility. Their task is to carry out the necessary process efficiently, and also to try to assuage the emotions. The aim now is to avoid the feelings of grief, and to ameliorate the pain and distress of bereavement. Formality seems to have replaced emotion. It is felt best that a 'depressing' situation is quickly forgotten. The result is that dying has become a lonely and dehumanized event. The importance of actively involving bereaved people in the process is discounted.

Even the words associated with 'death' have become taboo. To talk openly about death is often considered to be in bad taste – an indication of morbid interest or curiosity. The less said about the subject the better, and to avoid it we hide behind other, meaningless phrases.

- 'He's gone', 'passed away'.
- 'At peace', 'at rest' or 'sleeping'.
- 'Gone to a better place'.

Even the trite remarks associated with death rarely reassure. 'Death was a blessing' because 'at least they did not suffer'. Such euphemisms do little to remedy feelings of loss, and succeed only in paying homage to the social process of denial. Indeed, such reassurance gives the impression that death should not be accompanied by pain or suffering on the part of those who remain.

The right to grieve

Those who bemoan the passing of tradition miss the point. It was not belief or ritual that was important, but the opportunities that they provided for friends and relatives to pay their respects, and to provide comfort and reassurance. The loss of tradition has left bereaved people, particularly older people, in a social vacuum, and it is this that counselling can help to dispel.

The desire of carers to protect bereaved people from grief is a mistake. For older people, especially if they are already troubled, ailing or frail, it can be even worse. When a person's life seems to be surrounded by loss and grief, the tendency to protect them from further pain can be seen as a kindness. Indeed, this is a recurring feature of the lives of many older people whose carers seek to protect them from traumatic events and circumstances, including:

- refusal to allow them to view the body of the deceased;
- refusal to allow them to attend the funeral;
- keeping them ignorant of important social events;
- relatives who insist that they move out of their homes 'for their own good';
- people who have been placed in residential care within days of suffering loss.

All this is usually done 'in their own best interests'. To be living happily with a loved one, and then to find oneself uprooted and alone in strange surroundings, is trauma extended to monumental proportions. It is designed to create mental infirmity in even the strongest of wills, and it is done to people who are closer to their own death, and all that this implies, than their misguided carers. They would have been aware of the imminence of death, and they might have welcomed the opportunity to discuss it.

One suspects that a daughter who emigrated without telling her ageing mother until she had left in order to spare her the distressful farewell scenes, and the family which did not tell their mother about the death of her son, did so to prevent their own pain rather than the pain of the older person.

Consequently, many older people are denied the right to grieve. The result is that they may continue to grieve for many years, paying a heavy psychological and emotional price for being 'protected' by kindness. Many older people become confused, and their confusion can be dated from the time when their loss was handled inappropriately.

No carers have the right to deprive bereaved people of their pain.

Pain may be a strange 'right', but grief following trauma can only be postponed, not avoided. Just as death is a normal part of life, so is the hurt and pain we feel at having to live without a close friend and companion. The bereaved person will experience troubled emotions, and we will be conscious of their suffering. We will want to protect them from it, but by 'protecting' them we deny a necessary process, and we can plunge them deeper into grief. Grief is undoubtedly painful in the short term, but by facing and coming to terms with it, there comes a healing power that enables the bereaved person to survive, and to re-establish their life. The pain of grief will subside, but first it has to be experienced.

Patterns of normal grieving

The experience of bereavement will vary greatly. Some bereavement, for example that from unhappy or unfulfilling relationships, can bring feelings of relief and emancipation. The loss of more important relationships, especially those of longer duration, will be more difficult. Even so, the degree to which loss will affect different people will vary according to their personality and the amount and quality of the remaining social supports. People who make relationships more easily, and who have a wide circle of friends, will tend to cope better.

The recovery time will vary. Some people are able quickly to repair the damage to their lives, while others will spend long periods in mourning. These variations mean that it is probably unwise to talk about 'patterns' of grief. However, some underlying knowledge of the process is helpful, and Parkes (1972) has proposed four stages of 'normal' grieving.

Shock and numbness

The process begins with the initial shock, followed by a period of numbness. Parkes found that this was the most common response to death, and could last for anything from a few hours to many days. Numbness is the body's natural tranquillizer, necessary to shield the bereaved person from the intensity of the immediate pain of losing a loved one.

Yearning

This is followed by a period of yearning and protest, during which the bereaved person is preoccupied with the deceased person, and suffers considerable pain and anguish. It is a period of great sadness, fear, self-reproach and guilt. This is often mixed with anger and self-pity. During this time, the bereaved person constantly goes over the events leading up to the death, and the circumstances of the death itself.

Depression

Bereaved people may then experience considerable depression and disorganization. They may be restless, aimless, listless, apathetic, lacking in concentration and unable to sleep. They may feel hopeless, with a general lack of purpose, and they may lose their appetite. This can be a period of social withdrawal and loneliness, with deep anxiety about their future without the deceased person.

Reorganization

The final stage is one of reorganisation, in which depression gradually subsides and an interest in normal activities begins to re-emerge.

Patterns of abnormal grieving

Although generalized pathways through grief do exist, recovery does not always follow these patterns. Sometimes bereaved people feel that they are 'going mad' with grief. Whilst feelings of intense grief are normal during the weeks after bereavement, if such behaviour is still continuing a year or more after the event, it indicates that the bereaved person is not coming to terms with their loss. They may believe that they hear the deceased person. They may set a table or cook a meal with them in mind. A room, or a person's belongings may be kept as a 'memorial'. The bereaved person appears to be unable to resume normal life. Many people may continue to experience grief several years after bereavement. Indeed, bereavement can and often does lead to serious psychiatric disturbance. Parkes and Weiss (1983) identified three common patterns of abnormal grief.

Sudden and unexpected bereavement

When the loss is sudden or unexpected, the main problem is shock and disbelief, and this can delay recovery, causing a stubborn persistence in grieving that prevents bereaved people from feeling free or able to initiate new relationships.

- They cannot accept the full reality of loss.
- They withdraw from social contact.
- They persist in the belief that the dead person remains present in their life.
- They harbour strong feelings of self-reproach and despair.
- They maintain a continuing 'obligation' to the deceased.

None of these feelings protect the person from loneliness, anxiety or depression. The process of recovery and the recommencement of social functioning can be seriously delayed. This is considered to be an abnormal response.

The reaction of bereaved people who had some warning of their loss was found to be quite different. Death in such circumstances might bring an end to suffering or the heavy responsibility of care. They will have had time to prepare, and if the time was used positively, they may have already achieved some of the grieving tasks. Their grief may not necessarily be less painful, but it does tend to be less disabling, and recovery has been found to be quicker. Schulz *et al.* (1997) also found that it gave time for family support systems to be mobilized to assist those left behind.

Ambivalent grief

The degree of closeness and interdependence within a relationship determines the degree of loss experienced. The quality of the lost relationship is an important factor. Close, loving relationships are harder to lose, and grief can be intense. However, grief is not quite so simple. Within good relationships there is likely to be less guilt and less unresolved business. More tempestuous relationships, whilst outwardly less fulfilling, still fulfil important personal needs, and whilst separation may appear to bring a quieter life, this is not always either wanted or appreciated.

Parkes and Weiss (1983) found that, whilst the immediate reaction to the loss of an ambivalent relationship may be one of relief, as time passes feelings of intense despair can emerge. Whilst relationship conflict may have produced real anger and hostility, these feelings coexisted with attachment and affection. They also found that ambivalent relationships were often formed between people who had difficulty in establishing more satisfactory attachments.

The outcome of bereavement can produce abnormal grief when the survivor becomes self-reproachful, or when they feel compelled to make some form of restitution for the failures of the relationship, but can find no satisfactory way of doing so. Their delayed grief can lead to delayed recovery.

Chronic grief

Chronic or intractable grief lasts for an excessive duration and never reaches an entirely satisfactory resolution. It was associated by Parkes and Weiss (1983) with highly dependent relationships, defined as relationships in which the individuals were unable to function adequately without the social and emotional presence, support or help of the partner. Grief is not delayed, but it is associated with high levels of yearning and intense feelings of helplessness. It can continue for abnormal lengths of time.

Factors leading to abnormal grieving

The likelihood that a person will experience abnormal grief reactions is heightened by the existence of four main factors (Parkes, 1985). Where there is a significant combination of these factors, abnormal grief becomes more likely, counselling becomes more important, and the task is more difficult.

Type of death

Problems arise when bereaved people feel that there is reason for personal blame for the death, or when the death is sudden, unexpected or untimely, or when it occurred in circumstances that were mismanaged, horrifying, or involved great suffering or pain. Deaths following 'stigmatizing' illnesses, such as suicide, AIDS or even severe dementia, can also affect recovery.

Characteristics of the lost relationship

The loss of a very close relationship, particularly the death of a spouse or child, can lead to abnormal grieving, although abnormal grief is more likely to occur when the relationship was either dependent or ambivalent.

Personal characteristics of the survivor

Grief was found to exacerbate existing personality characteristics, including:

- low self-esteem;
- insecurity and over-anxiety;
- ill health, including mental illnesses;
- physical disability;
- self-reproach;
- an inability to express personal feelings.

An ability to develop new interests and friends is an important factor in recovery.

Social circumstances

There are several social factors that can make a person prone to abnormal grieving:

- an absent or unsupportive family;
- detachment from traditional support systems;
- unemployment;
- dependent children;
- low socio-economic status;
- unresolved past losses;
- a lack of opportunity to grieve.

If people from minority ethnic and cultural groups are unable to follow their time-honoured rituals adequately, this can also lead to poor outcome.

Recovery from bereavement – a counselling approach

Worden (1983) looked at the grieving process in a more dynamic way, outlining four mourning 'tasks' that people need to achieve successfully. Counselling can assist people through these tasks:

1. to prevent denial, and accept the reality of loss – counselling can help to confirm an awareness of the reality of the loss for the person;

2. to experience the pain of grief – counselling can help the person to experience their feelings fully;

3. to adjust to a new environment in which the deceased person is missing – counselling can help the person to overcome impediments to adjustment;

4. to withdraw emotional energy from the deceased person, and to reinvest it in other relationships – counselling can enable the person to feel able to withdraw from past relationships, and to feel comfortable investing in new ones.

As people pass through these four tasks, they should be reassured that their grief is normal, that it will pass and that life, although changed, will continue.

However, it is important that this is done in such a way as not to deny or diminish the pain that they feel currently. The counselling task is to enable people to feel, and to feel safe about feeling.

The counsellor needs to be aware that reflecting on death can lead to the development of a variety of fears and worries, which are often worse for older people who live alone, or who are depressed. These include:

- the fear of a lonely and isolated death;
- a feeling of abandonment and annihilation;
- questions and fears about what follows death;
- fear of what the moment of death will be like.

Understanding, support and encouragement are the contributions that the counsellor can make at this stage, whilst time alone can do the rest.

Anticipating bereavement

Support offered to older people prior to bereavement can assist subsequent recovery. This is possible during a long illness or a slow decline to death. People who have watched a loved one die gradually will have gone through an exhausting experience, both physically and emotionally, but at least they will have had an opportunity to prepare for the outcome. Some people are able to take that opportunity, but many more fail to do so. There are several ways in which counselling can help to prepare older people for loss.

First, it can be used to ensure that the person is receiving accurate information, and is not either being misinformed or failing to accept the likelihood of what is to occur. This can enable the person to complete many tasks that might otherwise become a matter of regret at a later stage.

- People can be encouraged to share their memories – both good and bad – and to relive them for the final time.
- Messages of sorrow, remorse, thanks and love can be exchanged.
- Restitution can be made for failures or ambivalence in the relationship.
- People can be actively involved at all stages of the dying process.
- Potential problems and anxieties following death can be anticipated.

Support, listening and acceptance

Following bereavement, important decisions about the availability and required level of care need to be made. There are two extreme responses:

1. a tendency to leave bereaved people alone (often because being in the presence of grief is too uncomfortable for us);

2. an insistence that they are never left alone (to prevent isolated mourning, or for fear that the person might harm him- or herself).

The correct level of support is usually a sensible balance between these two extremes, and it should be based upon the expressed wishes of the person concerned.

Openness is vital. The counsellor should make it known, by both word and action, that death is not a taboo subject and that they are willing to talk about the person's feelings. The counsellor can ask about the death, how it happened, its cause, and how and when they found out. They can discuss the details of the funeral, and their wishes about its conduct. All of this indicates a willingness to discuss difficult areas, if and when the person wishes to do so.

In the early stages, the counselling task is to listen and understand. Counsellors will have to be able to cope with many feelings, including:

• distress and fearfulness;
• anger and feelings of unfairness and injustice;
• denial;
• hopelessness and despair;
• desire for personal death

The bereaved person's feelings have to be dealt with sensitively, and they should never be denied. Bereaved people cannot be told how they should react, how they should feel or what they should do. The counsellor must not understate or belittle the significance of the loss. The only amelioration to suffering at this stage is often to reassure the bereaved person that someone is there who is prepared to spend time with them.

Bereaved people must have sufficient time to grieve. However, the idea that people should recover quickly is common. It is also attractive, because it makes life easier for those less involved with the loss, who have to witness their distress. The length of time required is difficult to quantify. Worden (1983) suggests between 3 months and 1 year after the death, but there are no rules. The important anniversaries within a relationship can be a problem long after the event.

Older people may have difficulty finding alternatives to grief. Younger people will return to work and find other interests that help to take their minds off their loss. They may be too busy to allow grief to consume their time, but such avenues are often unavailable to older people.

Facing reality

An acceptance of the reality of loss should be a primary counselling objective. This is possible only by full involvement with and in that reality. Many bereaved people will try to avoid the intense distress of grief, through drugs, alcohol, or engaging in activity. These can serve to deny the event temporarily, or to assuage overwhelming and unremitting feelings of loss and sorrow.

The counsellor should not allow any pretence to get in the way of accepting loss. Bereaved people should not be soothed or cheered up. Many people will believe that they will be reunited in another world. If this is a feature of their religious belief it can be important that they hold on to it. However, the counsellor needs to focus on readjustment to the reality of the present world. It may be necessary to remind the person about what has occurred. The bereaved person needs to express his or her emotions, to cry if necessary, and to grieve fully. This can seem cruel, but only by talking about their pain and only by going through grief can people come to terms with the new and painful reality, and recommence their lives as best as they can, and as they see fit.

The purpose of counselling should be to help the bereaved person to explore their feelings and to express them openly. One technique which has been found to be valuable in this respect is to ask them to make a list of their losses. This can help people to identify those things that the deceased person provided – not just the obvious ones, such as companionship, but more detailed ones such as driving the car, keeping the garden tidy, doing the shopping, cooking the meals, escorting them to social events, accounting for money, and so on.

Accepting a new reality does not involve forgetting the past or denying the importance of what has happened. It means recognizing that a fundamental change has taken place that has deeply affected their life. Just how their life has been affected, and what to do about it, is the task that is faced in counselling.

Our desire to protect vulnerable older people from grief often becomes a problem. It is dangerous to deny older people the right to view the body, to attend the funeral, or to continue to live in the family home, yet this is frequently done.

Medication is another problem. Drugs can tranquillize the pain of bereavement, dulling the immediate awfulness of the new reality. In some situations it may be felt that it is necessary to prescribe such drugs but, as a general rule, medication should be avoided. Grief has to be faced, and the effect of tranquillizers is transitory. When decisions are taken to give medication, it should be remembered that delayed grieving is known to reduce the prospects of long-term recovery.

When a counsellor enters a situation in which these decisions have been made, the person may need to be taken back through the pain of loss, perhaps involving discussion with relatives, visits to the grave, and recounting and reliving the circumstances of the death.

Social expectations

In grief counselling, the interchange between bereaved people and social expectations should be borne in mind. Parkes (1985) stated that mourning is determined in part by social expectations, but that the response to the mourner will also, to some extent, be determined by his or her behaviour.

- Some people will believe that they are not grieving sufficiently. They will feel unable to cry, and this will make them feel guilty.
- They may not feel a sense of loss as deeply as they think they should.
- They may be preoccupied with hallucinatory images and visions of the deceased person.

Often this can result from the disbelief and numbness that follow the initial shock, when the bereaved person finds it difficult to accept what has happened. The counsellor must assure them that what they are going through is a normal process through which they will eventually pass. They should be told to 'feel' whatever they feel without apology, and to respond in whatever way they wish, and not to be concerned with stereotypical images about what is right and wrong behaviour.

Conversely, many people will worry about expressing the depth of their feelings. This arises from the belief that we must not 'wallow' in self-pity, that too much grief indicates that we are not in control, that we are feeling sorry for ourselves, that getting hysterical is unnecessary, and that we must pull ourselves together. To fail to do this might bring social disapproval. Again the counsellor has to assure the bereaved person that to cry, to talk about the loss, to express feelings of sorrow, and to mourn in whatever way they feel, is not only normal, but acceptable and necessary.

Anger is a common reaction, but is often misunderstood or frowned upon. The person may project negative, hostile attitudes towards the deceased person, often on quite irrational grounds (for example, of being 'abandoned'). However irrational they may be, such feelings are normal. Yet to speak or feel badly about the dead goes against social expectations. Bereaved people can feel that such thoughts should be disqualified, however real they may be, and this can lead to strong feelings of guilt.

Self-blame is also common. Are we in some obscure way to blame for the death? Did we do everything possible? Perhaps we should have done this, or not done that. If only we had been more sympathetic, if only we could tell them what we felt for them, if only . . . and so on. Often detectable in such guilt is the idea that other people may blame the bereaved person for their omissions or commissions.

Grief can be alienating. It can alter our responses to both people and situations. Anger can often be displaced, and friends and relatives may be blamed for failing the deceased, or for failing us in some way. No one understands. Life has become empty, and no longer has meaning. We become blinded by pain. Such anger and recrimination alienate other people, who refuse to be accused of such irrational charges, and consequently withdraw. The bereaved person then becomes even more isolated. The counsellor has to understand such behaviour for what it is, and to help the person see what they are doing, and why, and that they are, in part, responsible for their increased loneliness.

Often bereaved people question their sanity. They cannot concentrate, they are restless and irritable, and they do not associate these feelings with their grief. There are many feelings which can persuade people that they are going mad. Hallucinations, and acting as if the deceased person is still present, are common. The counsellor should ensure that the bereaved person understands that these are natural and understandable responses to bereavement, and enable them to discuss such matters openly.

Re-emergence from grief

There is no definitive end to grief – no time before or after which grieving becomes acceptable or unacceptable. Each person has their own pace. Nor is re-emergence from grief a linear process. The journey will consist of periods of progress and re-integration, and periods of regression. Many older people say that 'you never get over the death of a loved one, you just get used to it'. Time will just reduce the intensity, frequency and duration of grief.

Anniversaries are often significant times when sadness and grief return. Worden (1983) also identified a period 3 months after the event as being important. At such times the bereaved person will appear to be making little progress towards recovery, apparently intent on maintaining their sadness and pain. However, as long as they continue to move towards recovery, the overall rate of progress is not important. What is significant is that people should not deny what has happened, and shelter from their feelings behind drugs or alcohol.

Loss severely disrupts the regular pattern of life, and this can only be restored by the person's own inner resources and resolve. Survivors have to renew some sense of their place in the world, to make sense of something that appeared 'senseless', and come to terms with an experience that originally seemed to threaten their existence. They have to find new meaning both in the past and in the present.

However, bereaved people have to do this themselves. If they do not want to adapt to their new reality they can become trapped by their own thoughts, and impervious to life around them or the efforts of carers to help and support them. Many bereaved people assume a 'sick' role. Their grief is seen as a medical condition, to be treated with antidepressants and tranquillizers. Medicalized grief prolongs the grieving process. Counsellors must be aware of the dangers of prolonging grief, and concentrate on supporting people to reconstruct their own lives.

The process of recovery begins when people begin to withdraw from their emotional ties to the deceased. Their preoccupation with the old relationship begins to wane, and new opportunities are sought. Reminiscence can be used to assist this process. Bereavement is a time when reflection on personal history, particularly the relationship with the deceased person, can be a helpful – if painful – experience. Reminiscence, remembering shared times, can help bereaved people to appreciate the importance and meaning of the relationship. It can help them relive aspects of the past, so that they can grieve over those things which will never be again. The use of old photographs, letters and other memorabilia can assist the process. Grief is a time of intense struggle between the conflicting claims of the past and the future, conflicts that can be resolved by consolidating what remains meaningful and significant from the past, and discovering some meaning for the future.

Counselling bereaved people has to be a compromise between the needs of the past and those of the future. To concentrate too much on the past and what is gone can tend to diminish the importance and prospects of the future. However, to concentrate too much on the future might tend to belittle the past, and lead to guilt about relinquishing it too easily. The guiding principle should be the wishes of the individual, and the pace that is set should be one with which they are able to cope.

The ultimate goal should be to assist bereaved people to live their lives in the absence of the deceased. Where progress towards this seems to be blocked, Worden (1983) suggests that the counsellor should try to identify which one of the four grief tasks has not been successfully completed (see above, p. 206). This will indicate the area of the process that has been avoided or neglected, and this should now receive further attention.

The process of reconstruction

Death destroys the certainty about the stability of former life-styles. There may be a need to establish new relationships and to develop new forms of behaviour. Such change will loosen the bonds with the deceased person. Many bereaved people will feel that to do this is disloyal. Reconstruction can also be difficult when bereavement has developed feelings of isolation and alienation. Bereaved people may believe that no one else can understand how they feel or what the loss means to them, so they do not want to go out, meet new people or embark upon new activities.

Even former associations with people and places can be abandoned. Old relationships can remind people that they are now alone. They visit friends alone, when once they used to be accompanied, and old activities can be abandoned for similar reasons.

Many bereaved people also discover that social organization is geared towards 'couples' rather than single people. Older people may be reluctant to spend unaccompanied evenings in public places, particularly older women.

- They will not accept invitations from couples or men.

- They may experience a loss of social status as a widow or widower.
- There is often a considerable loss of pension income.

The outcome can be that life for older people after bereavement becomes increasingly lonely and isolated, and this can suggest a bleak future. However, the counsellor should seek to present a more optimistic view, and work on the opportunities available for developing their social life. Encouraging people to seek new friends and activities will help to avoid a depressing and defeatist view of the future. As time passes, people can be encouraged to reconstruct their lives and, in particular, to fill the gaps which have been left by the bereavement.

The establishment of special bereavement groups can be helpful both in dealing with these feelings, and in helping people to commence the process of social re-integration. By sharing grief with others who have lost important individuals, group members can support each other through the different aspects of the problems:

- to see the irrationality of some of their behaviour;
- to see that other people share their feelings;
- to help each other out of depression and resignation;
- to search for new perspectives in life;
- to join forces with other group members to rebuild their lives.

It is often said, correctly, that time is a great healer. Many bereaved people discover that the absence of a life-long partner can open a new stage of life in which they undertake new tasks, either because they have to, or because they are no longer prevented from doing so. They may find that they now have the freedom to pursue different interests, making the post-bereavement period a liberating experience. Counselling can help to make it so.

18 Preparation for death

There is never a good time to prepare for death. We are either fit and healthy and it does not appear to be relevant, or we are too ill to concentrate on it, or it approaches too quickly and we have insufficient time. Consequently, many older people die without wills, or with important unfinished business. We, and those around us, are unprepared for an unavoidable event that should have been talked about, but which was always (for whatever reason) avoided.

The avoidance of death

The counsellor of older people should never knowingly allow this situation to occur, and so must try to overcome the social constraints that consider death to be an inappropriate subject for discussion. Older people often make comments about their own death, and we often fail to respond, ignoring the possibility that they may need to discuss their death. If an older person says 'I have not got long to go', this probably means that they have a desire to talk about their death, who will be there, who will miss them, how they will be remembered, and what will happen to them. Too often such comments are ignored, or the person will be told that he or she is wrong, even though we all know that it is true. The reason for such avoidance is an integral part of our cultural attitudes to death. Butler compares westernized attitudes with those of oriental cultures.

> The Western concept of the life cycle is decidedly different from that of the Orient, since they derive from two opposing views about what 'self' means and what life is all about. Oriental philosophy places the individual self, his life span and his death within the process of human experience. Life and death are familiar and equally acceptable parts of what self means. In the West, on the other hand, death is considered outside of the self. To be a self or person one must be alive, in control

and aware of what is happening. The greater and more self-centred or narcissistic Western emphasis on individuality and control makes death an outrage, a tremendous affront to man, rather than the logical and necessary process of old life making way for new.

(Butler, 1974)

Culture and religion are important considerations when one is talking about death (Neuberger, 1987). An elderly Sikh who believes in reincarnation and a devout Christian will require counselling that is sensitive to their respective traditions, as these are the source of their personal understanding and beliefs about death.

Dominant western attitudes towards death are unhelpful. We ponder whether we should tell dying people that they are going to die. The idea that imminent death can or should be kept from a dying person is strange. Most people know when they are dying, regardless of whether they are formally told. They know how they feel, or they sense the atmosphere and attitudes of people around them. Avoidance can lead to farcical situations where both dying people and their carers are aware of the truth, but unable to face each other with it (Davis, 1979).

The failure of honesty reinforces death as a taboo subject that is not to be discussed even with dying people themselves, and takes T.S. Eliot's oft-quoted remark 'Mankind cannot bear too much reality' to ridiculous extremes. If death is seen as taboo, counselling dying older people will continue to receive low priority. The neglect of older people is based on seeing old age as decline, and death as an outrage. Counsellors should see death as an integral part of life and – although the final part – no less important for that, certainly for the person concerned.

Talking about death

The counsellor should always seek to be open. It is a counselling task of some courage and skill to be able to discuss terminal ill health in a way that carefully and gently confirms the realization that death is imminent. Ideally, it should be done by people who are close to the person.

However, the difficulties can be overstated. Dying people are often less sensitive about the issue than we are. Older people face death as a close prospect. Often they welcome the opportunity to discuss the impending event, but will defer to the 'sensitivity' of those around them, who so obviously wish to avoid doing so. Binstock and Shanas (1985) refer to several studies that showed older adults were more willing to talk about death than any other age group. Thus older people require little encouragement, and often supply us with ideal openings.

- 'You don't need to worry about me, I'll be dead soon!'
- 'Life just isn't worth living any more, I'm so tired of it.'
- 'I wonder if I will join [a loved one] when I die.'

Older people often muse on the value and purpose of their own lives, and why they should continue living. Such remarks are intended as an opening bid for discussion, but too often they are dismissed.

* *'Don't be silly, you'll outlive us all!'*

Yet such remarks may hold important agendas that the counsellor should encourage and utilize.

* Do such questions indicate that the person wishes to talk about, or be reassured of, their value and importance?
* Do they indicate despair about their social role, and a desire to discuss their feelings of self-worth?
* Is the person concerned about death, or do they feel that it is imminent, or require reassurance that they are still healthy and well?
* Is the person concerned about the nature of death, and whether it will be a peaceful process or a lingering and painful one?

Their casual remarks provide an opportunity to ask questions, and to encourage them to express their worries or feelings. They should receive a considered response, and preferably one that opens rather than closes discussion.

Euthanasia

Some older people, especially those in significant pain or distress, may welcome the prospect of death. Certainly it is likely that the counsellor of older people will meet the issue of euthanasia at some point.

The debate

Euthanasia has always been opposed by religion, especially two major world religions, namely Judaism and Christianity. Dominant attitudes continue to reinforce these traditions, even though it is undoubtedly practised, in all but name, throughout the western world. In some countries, notably The Netherlands, more liberal attitudes have developed. Whilst it is not intended to debate the issue fully here, it would be wrong to discuss counselling about death without reference to the issues.

There have been many well-publicized cases of people who have genuinely wished to take their own lives and sought assistance to do so. Derek Humphry helped his wife to die, and then wrote a moving account in his book *Jean's Way* in 1978. James Haig, a tetraplegic, made several attempts to end his life, and eventually killed himself in 1983 by setting fire to his home. These examples can be multiplied a hundredfold, both by those who successfully end their own lives with or without assistance, and by many thousands more who would like to do so.

Why should this be so? And does modern social life make euthanasia more attractive to older people?

Advances in medical science mean that we can now prolong life, often beyond the point where it has any meaning or value to the individual. When this artificial prolongation of life is considered alongside the trend that undermines and denigrates the role and value of older people, the increasing acceptability of euthanasia becomes clearer.

This powerful cocktail of social experience can lead people to grow tired of life, which can become an undignified and meaningless process. They actively want to die, and may require assistance to do so.

Many people claim that there is a 'right to die' (Humphry and Wickett, 1986), and that people should be able to decide when to end their life. The Voluntary Euthanasia Society, in a 1985 survey, claimed that the majority of people in this country now favour euthanasia if it is sought in order to relieve unbearable suffering and pain. Other religious and medical bodies continue to argue against it, fearing that once it was legalized, euthanasia would not remain 'voluntary', but could be used to eliminate groups of people considered to be 'troublesome' or too expensive to keep alive. The taint of eugenics has handicapped the euthanasia argument since the excesses of Fascism in the 1930s and 1940s, a view that is reinforced by a powerful medical establishment which insists on viewing death as a failure.

Thus the euthanasia debate is destined to continue, and it is unlikely ever to be resolved entirely. Euthanasia will remain illegal, but is likely to gain support, especially from older people. It will be practised, albeit illicitly and under another name.

This is the dilemma that counsellors will face. They will want to talk openly with older people about their feelings, but they will be offered little practical support or assistance. The question for the counsellor is simple.

When faced with a person who expresses a desire to die, how is the counsellor to respond?

Reasons for wanting to die

The first reaction should be to discuss the reasons that have led the person to want to die. It is important that counsellors understand that the desire for death can often arise from feelings and situations that are unconnected with a wish to die.

- The person may be experiencing temporary trauma or stress.
- They may be suffering from deeper, longer-term depression.
- They may be demanding attention, and may feel that this is the only way to receive it.
- They may want relief from pain or chronic illness, and know no other way of achieving it.

Counselling, allied with other forms of caring intervention, can help to alleviate the desire for death in many of these scenarios.

For depressed or disillusioned older people, this can be what is required. The counsellor can present them with reasons why they should not feel that death is the only option:

- other people do care for them;
- they are valued and important;
- there is, or can be, meaning in their lives.

The individual might welcome such positive remarks, and may be encouraged out of transitory feelings of depression and move on to a more optimistic outlook on life. Clearly, if this is so, counselling can be invaluable.

A genuine desire for death

It is also important to accept that some people do genuinely want to die. It may become clear that the person is quite rational, and has fully considered what he or she wants to do. Then the counselling task is to listen. People who feel this way may face a variety of problems that have reduced the importance of living:

- being totally inactive, or feeling entirely worthless and useless;
- becoming a burden on other people;
- losing mental control;
- having rapidly deteriorating health, and terminal illness.

If a person feels that life has become meaningless, and that they have no desire to continue living, then the counsellor should try to understand and empathize. Where this is so, the counsellor cannot and should not continue to resist or deny euthanasia as a genuine expression of the way they feel.

The question that then arises concerns whether the counsellor should collude with, or even listen to, wishes that are unlawful. If the request is a passive one, 'just leave me to die', it will raise many important moral and emotional issues. If the request is an 'active' one, 'please assist me to die', the issues become even more important. At the end of the day, it is impossible to continue to ask why the person feels this way. And it is not 'counselling' to deny that this is what they want.

Essentially, it is the same dilemma that the counsellor faces when asked to assist in the solution to other problems. Euthanasia is different only in that it is illegal to be actively involved in killing someone, and it concerns the taboo subject of death and all the contentious ethical and moral questions that surround it.

There is no straightforward answer to an issue that juxtaposes personal commitment to an individual against the law of the land. Resolution has to be a personal decision. It is a situation where the counsellor will benefit from personal counselling, perhaps with a friendly priest or doctor who is prepared to discuss the issues involved. There are three courses open to people faced with a request for active involvement in another person's death.

1. The legal option is to refuse to co-operate, yet this can be an uncomfortable position for a counsellor to adopt, particularly if their empathy with the feelings and circumstances of the person is strong. Even so, it is possible for the counsellor to explain their position in reasonable terms so that the person is able to understand why they cannot acquiesce to their requests.

2. The 'passive' response would be to encourage medical staff and others to discontinue efforts to support or prolong life.

3. The 'active' response would involve acting criminally – that is, taking steps that lead directly to death. The fact that someone has expressed a desire for death, even after counselling, is no excuse in law. Someone who takes such action must do so in accordance with his or her conscience, and in full knowledge of the potential legal consequences.

It is important to reiterate that counselling older people should be about life, and enabling people to enjoy it right up to death. The essentially optimistic approach to counselling older people advocated in this book should remain. Yet whilst it would be nice if counselling could persuade all older people, all of the time, that life is worth living and should be lived as fully as possible right to the end, this is not always realistic. Counselling sometimes has to deal with a well-reasoned and reasonable desire for death, and with both its inevitability and its consequences.

Supporting the dying person

The dying person has many needs. Some of these are medical, such as the alleviation and relief of pain. However, it is important to realize that dying is not just a medical matter. Clearly there is a need for correct medical assistance, but only in a minority of cases are dying people best supported by medical staff in a medical environment. People usually wish to be where they feel safe, relaxed and at home, normally with the friends and relatives they know and trust, and with whom they have good personal relationships. These are the people who will have looked after them, and who are most likely to honour and respect them in their final days.

Counselling can provide considerable comfort and support for the dying person. The counsellor needs to respond sensitively to the dying person's needs, which include:

- where they wish to be;
- who they wish to be with;
- discussing their anxieties, and helping them to come to terms with imminent death;
- talking about their fears and their feelings of loneliness;
- discussing their religious and spiritual requirements, and ensuring that someone attends to them.

Counsellors can do even more than this if they try to maintain the dying person's responsibility for controlling his or her own situation. Carers have a tendency to assume control. This not only emphasizes and reinforces dependency, but can make people feel more dependent than they often need to be. The counsellor should try to ensure that the dying person maintains as much normality as they want for as long as possible. When decisions have to be taken, the wishes of the dying person should be given precedence.

The process of dying

Kubler-Ross (1970) studied the process through which dying people often pass when they are aware of their impending death. She found five distinct stages that characterize people's reaction to dying.

1. Denial

The first reaction is often one of disbelief and denial. The dying person is not prepared to accept the fact that he or she has only a limited time to live. Kubler-Ross says that this is more typical of someone who is informed prematurely or abruptly, thereby emphasizing the need for a careful counselling-based approach to disclosure. Denial serves an important purpose, as it provides time for the person to come to terms with an unwanted and unacceptable idea.

Disclosure might spur the person to fight the illness, and this has been known to bring about remission of many conditions. More often denial does not last long, particularly in the case of older people who are normally aware of their physical condition. Some are quickly ready for personal death. Yet whilst people are in denial, counsellors should neither play along with this, nor over-stress a too painful reality. Instead, they should create an open but sensitive atmosphere in which reality and truth can quietly take precedence over avoidance and deception.

2. Anger

Anger can replace denial. This can be a difficult stage to handle. Everything is wrong – the bed, the food, the room temperature, too many or too few visitors, and so on. Such anger, whilst normal, can be disconcerting. It is normally directed towards those who are closest to the dying person – relatives, friends, medical staff, and even God. The care provided may itself provoke anger as it highlights the dying person's illness and reinforces their growing dependency. Many friends can be lost during this stage, but it is important to cope without withdrawing care and approval. Empathy is vital if the counsellor is to understand the feelings, thoughts, frustration and fears that the dying person is experiencing.

3. Bargaining

Bargaining often represents the realization by a dying person that there is important unfinished business. Time is required to complete such business, so they seek 'remission' for good behaviour, thoughts, deeds or promises. Often this is allied with a tendency to see their illness as a punishment for past misdemeanours, leading to promises to do everything they consider to be 'good' in return for more time. Often implicit in this behaviour is a sense of guilt for the things they have not done, or have failed to achieve in their lives.

Counselling should treat bargaining in a similar way to denial – not accepting the bargain as a possibility, but seeking to promote discussion about why time has become so important, and what needs to be done about the matters that are causing concern.

4. Depression

The effort expended in denial, anger and bargaining may eventually subside into depression. The person begins to experience a sense of grief for all those things that they will never know again:

- their job;
- their home and hobbies;
- their relatives and friends;
- anything else that has been important in their lives.

This is an important period, essential to the dying person and those who will be bereaved by his or her death. Counselling can give the dying person an opportunity to express many things, including:

- their feelings;
- the things that are left undone;
- their worries about the people they will leave behind.

There should be no attempt to breed false optimism, for this is quickly seen through. Dying people are losing everybody and everything that is important to them. False optimism can result in a loss of trust and confidence. It is our ability to listen, to understand and to respond sympathetically that is important. If this is done, the dying person can pass to the next and final stage of the dying process.

5. Acceptance

If they have sufficient time, dying people do become resigned to their fate, and are neither angry nor depressed about it. The agitation of the previous stages will have been resolved, and it can be a time of relative peace, although not necessarily one of happiness. The person may feel able to say 'goodbye' to loved ones, and perhaps offer them words of reassurance and comfort. This should be encouraged, as it is often extremely important to those who are left behind, assisting them through the process of bereavement. Often it will be a time of increasing weakness and sleep, when the dying person may wish to be left alone, in peace, except perhaps for a few treasured friends.

The struggle is over. No further counselling will be required.

Bibliography

Age Concern (1977) *Profiles of the elderly. Vols 1–3.* Mitcham: Age Concern.

Alcohol Concern (1987) *Alcohol and older people.* Unpublished leaflets. London: Alcohol Concern.

Argyle, M. (1987) *The psychology of happiness.* London: Methuen.

Atchley, R.C. (1976) *The sociology of retirement.* Chichester: John Wiley & Sons.

Banerjee, S. and MacDonald, A. (1996) Mental disorders in an elderly home care population: associations with health and social service use. *British Journal of Psychiatry* **168**, 750–56.

Barclay Report (1982) *Social workers: their role and tasks.* London: MacDonald and Evans/National Institute for Social Work.

de Beauvoir, S. (1972) *Old age.* London: Deutsch/Weidenfeld and Nicolson.

Beckett, L.A., Brock, D.B., Lemke, J.H. *et al.* (1996) Analysis of change in self-reported physical function among older persons in four population studies. *American Journal of Epidemiology* **143**, 766–78.

Benbow, S., Egan, D., Marriot, A. *et al.* (1990) Using the family life cycle with later life families. *Journal of Family Therapy* **12**, 321–40.

Bender, M.P. (1997) Bitter harvest: the implications of continuing war-related stress on reminiscence theory and practice. *Ageing and Society* **17**, 337–48.

Bender, M.P. and Cheston, R. (1997) Inhabitants of a lost kingdom: a model of the subjective experience of dementia. *Ageing and Society* **17**, 513–32.

Bergmann, K. and Jacoby, R. (1983) The limitations and possibilities of community care for the elderly demented. In *Elderly people in the community – their service needs.* London: HMSO, 141–67.

Berne, E. (1968) *Games people play.* Harmondsworth: Penguin.

Binstock, R. and Shanas, E. (1985) *Handbook of aging and the social sciences.* New York: Van Nostrand Reinhold.

Blair, P. (1985) *Know your medicines.* Mitcham: Age Concern.

Bosanquet, N. (1978) *A future for old age. Towards a new society.* Aldershot: Temple Smith/New Society.

Bowen, M. (1978) *Family therapy in clinical practice.* New York: Jason Aronson Publishers.

Bowlby, J. (1980) *Attachment and loss: loss, sadness and depression.* London: Hogarth Press.

Braithwaite, V.A. and Gibson, D.H. (1987) Adjustment to retirement: what we know and what we need to know. *Ageing and Society* **7**, 1–18.

Brecher, E. (1993) Love, sex and ageing. In Johnson, J. and Slater, R. (eds), *Ageing and later life.* London: Sage.

British Medical Association (1986) *All our tomorrows: growing old in Britain. Report of the BMA's Board of Science and Education.* London: British Medical Association.

Brown, G.W. and Harris, T. (1978) *Social origins of depression.* London: Tavistock.

Buchanan, K. and Middleton, D. (1994) Reminiscence reviewed: a discourse analytic perspective. In Bornat, J. (ed.), *Reminiscence reviewed: evaluations, achievements, perspectives.* Buckingham: Open University Press, 61–73.

Butler, R.N. (1963) The life review: an interpretation of reminiscence in the aged. *Psychiatry* **26**, 65–76.

Butler, R.N. (1974) Successful ageing and the role of the life review. *Journal of the American Geriatrics Society* **22**, 529–35.

Butler, R. and Lewis, M. (1988) *Love and sex after 60.* New York: Harper and Row.

Cohen, D. and Eisdorfer, C. (1986) *The loss of self: a family resource for the care of Alzheimer's disease and related disorders.* London: W.W. Norton.

Cohen, G. and Faulkner, D. (1984) Memory in old age: 'good in parts'. *New Scientist* **11 October**, 49–51.

Coleman, P. (1994) Reminiscence with the study of ageing: the social significance of story. In Bornat, J. (ed.), *Reminiscence reviewed: evaluations, achievements, perspectives.* Buckingham: Open University Press, 8–20.

Coleman, P.G. (1986) *Ageing and reminiscence processes.* Chichester: John Wiley & Sons.

Comerford, S. (1986) Reasons to be cheerful . . . *Community Care* **4 December**, 18–19.

Corey, M.S. and Corey, G. (1987) *Groups: process and practice.* Monterey, CA: Brooks Cole.

Crosby, I. and Traynor, J. (1985) *In our care. A handbook of workshop activities for those caring for older people.* London: Help the Aged Education Department.

Cummings, E. and Henry, W.E. (1961) *Growing old. The process of disengagement.* New York: Basic Books.

Dall, J.L.C. and Gardiner, H.S. (1971) Dietary intake of potassium by geriatric patients. *Gerontology Clinics* **13**, 119–24.

Davies, L. (1981) *Three score years . . . and then? A study of nutrition and well-being of elderly people at home.* London: Heinemann.

Davis, L. (1979) Facing death. *Social Work Today* **10**, 16.

Davis, R. (1989) *My journey into Alzheimer's disease. A true story.* Amersham: Alpha.

Dein, S. (1994) Reading about cross-cultural psychiatry. *British Journal of Psychiatry* **165**, 561–4.

Dein, S. and Huline-Dickens, S. (1997) Cultural aspects of ageing and psychopathology. *Ageing and Mental Health* **1**, 112–20.

Dennis, M.S. and Lindesay, J. (1995) Suicide in the elderly – the UK perspective. *International Psychogeriatrics* **7**, 263–74.

Dixon, J. and Gregory, L. (1987) Ageism. *Action Baseline* **Winter 1986–1987**, 21–3.

Downs, M. (1997) The emergence of the person in dementia research. *Ageing and Society* **17**, 597–607.

Doyle, L. (1983) *The political economy of health.* London: Pluto Press.

Eleftheriades, S. (1991) Remember, remember . . . *Social Work Today* **25 April**.

Erikson, E.H. (1965) *Childhood and society.* Harmondsworth: Penguin.

Estes, C.L. (1979) *The ageing enterprise.* London: Jossey-Bass.

Estes, C.L. (1986) The politics of ageing in America. *Ageing and Society* **6**, 121–34.

Exton-Smith, A.N. (1971) Nutrition of the elderly. *British Journal of Hospital Medicine* **May**, 639–45.

Eweka, I. (1994) Counselling for old and elderly people: time for positive action. *Counselling* **November**, 196–8.

Family Policy Study Centre (1991) *An ageing population. Factsheet No. 2.* London: Family Policy Study Centre.

Feil, N. (1992) *V/F validation: the Feil method. How to help disoriented old-old.* Cleveland, OH: Edward Feil Productions.

Fielden, M. (1990) Reminiscence as a therapeutic intervention with sheltered housing residents: a comparative study. *British Journal of Social Work* **20**, 21–44.

Freud, S. (1905) *On psychotherapy.* London: Hogarth Press.

Gardner, I. (1993) Psychotherapeutic interventions with individuals and families where dementia is present. In Chapman, A. and Marshall, M. (eds), *Dementia: new skills for social workers.* London: Jessica Kingsley, 16–39.

Geldard, D. (1989) *Basic personal counselling: a training manual for counsellors.* London: Prentice Hall.

Gibson, F. (1989) *Using reminiscence: training pack.* London: Help the Aged.

Gibson, F. (1993) The use of the past. In Chapman, A. and Marshall, M. (eds), *Dementia: new skills for social workers.* London: Jessica Kingsley, 40–62.

Gibson, F. (1994) *Reminiscence and recall.* London: Age Concern England.

Gibson, F. (1994b) What can reminiscence contribute to people with dementia? In Bornat, J. (ed.), *Reminiscence reviewed: evaluations, achievements, perspectives.* Buckingham: Open University Press, 46–60.

Gibson, H. (1992) *The emotional and sexual lives of older people.* London: Chapman & Hall.

Gillies, C. and James, A. (1994) *Reminiscence work with older people.* London: Chapman & Hall.

Goffman, E. (1968) *Asylums: essays on the social situation of mental patients and other inmates.* Harmondsworth: Penguin.

Goldsmith, M. (1996) *Hearing the voice of people with dementia: opportunities and obstacles.* London: Jessica Kingsley.

Gorer, G. (1965) *Death, grief and mourning in contemporary Britain.* London: Crescent Books.

Gray, J.A.M. (1982) *Better health in retirement.* Mitcham: Age Concern.

Gray, M. and Wilcocks, G. (1981) *Our elders.* Oxford: Oxford University Press.

Green J.B. and Green, M.A. (1991) *Dealing with death.* London: Chapman & Hall.

Greengross, W. and Greengross, S. (1989) *Living, loving and ageing: sexual and personal relationships in later life.* London: Age Concern.

Gurland, B.J. (1976) The comparative frequency of depression; in various adult age groups. *Journal of Gerontology* **31**, 283–92.

Halmos, P. (1978) *The faith of the counsellors.* London: Constable.

Havighurst, R. (1972) *Developmental tasks and education.* New York: David McKay.

Hay, J.C., Saunders, W.B., Flint, E.P., Kaplan, B.H. and Blazer, D.G. (1997) Social support and depression as risk factors for loss of physical function in late life. *Ageing and Mental Health* **1**, 209–20.

Hazan, H. (1994) *Old age: constructions and deconstructions.* Tel Aviv: Cambridge University Press.

Heap, K. (1977) *Group theory for social workers.* Oxford: Pergamon.

Humphry, D. and Wickett, A. (1986) *The right to die.* London: Bodley Head.

Illich, I. (1977) *Limits to medicine.* Harmondsworth: Pelican.

Jacques, A. (1992) *Understanding dementia.* Edinburgh: Churchill Livingstone.

Johnson, P. (1985) *The economics of old age in Britain. A long-run view 1881–1981.* Discussion Paper 47. London: Centre for Economic Policy Research.

Judge, T.G. and Cowan, N.R. (1971) Dietary potassium intake and grip strength in older people. *Gerontology Clinics* **13**, 221–6.

Kaminsky, M. (1988) All that our eyes have witness: memories of a living workshop in the South Bronx. In Disch, R. (ed.), *Twenty-five years of the life review*. New York: Haworth.

Kaye, R. (1993) Sexuality in the later years. *Ageing and Society* **13**, 415–26.

Kelly, G. (1955) *Psychology of personal constructs*. London: Norton.

Killick, J. (1997) Communication: a matter of life and death of the mind. *Journal of Dementia Care* **September/October**.

Kitwood, T. (1989) Brain, mind and dementia with particular reference to Alzheimer's disease. *Ageing and Society* **9**, 1–15.

Kitwood, T. (1990) The dialectics of dementia with particular reference to Alzheimer's disease. *Ageing and Society* **10**, 177–96.

Kitwood, T. (1992) Towards a theory of dementia care: personhood and well-being. *Ageing and Society* **12**, 269–87.

Kitwood, T. (1993) *Frames of reference for an understanding of dementia*. Bradford: Bradford Dementia Research Group, University of Bradford.

Kitwood, T. and Bredin, K. (1992) *Person to person: a guide to the care of those with failing mental powers*. Loughton: Gale Centre Publications.

Kitwood, T. and Benson, S. (1995) *The new culture of dementia care*. London: Hawker.

Klein, W.H., Le Shan, E.J. and Furman, S.S. (1965) *Promoting mental health of older people through group methods*. New York: Manhattan Society for Mental Health/Mental Health Materials Centre.

Kleinman, A. and Good, B. (1985) *Culture and depression*. Berkeley, CA: University of California Press.

Kubler-Ross, E. (1970) *On death and dying*. London: Tavistock.

Landreth, G.L. and Berg, C. (1980) *Counselling the elderly*. Springfield, IL: Charles C. Thomas.

Littlewood, R. and Lipsedge, M. (1989) *Aliens and alienists*, 2nd edn. London: Unwin Hyman.

Lubinski, R. (1991) *Dementia and communication*. London: Decker.

McDerment, L. and Greengross, S. (1985) *Social care for the elderly*. Surbiton: Social Care Association.

McEwen, E. (ed.) (1990) *Age: the unrecognised discrimination*. London: Age Concern England.

McGowin, D. (1993) *Living in the labyrinth: a personal journey through the maze of Alzheimer's*. San Francisco, CA: Elder Books.

Marples, M. (1986) Helping family members cope with a senile relative. *Social Casework: Journal of Contemporary Social Work* **October**, 490–98.

Martin, P. (1987) Psychology and the immune system. *New Scientist* **19 April**, 46–50.

Masters, W.H. and Johnson, V.E. (1966) *Human sexual response*. Boston, MA: Little, Brown and Co.

Mayer, J.E. and Timms, N. (1970) *The client speaks*. London: Routledge.

Meacher, M. (1972) *Taken for a ride*. Harlow: Longman.

Meade, K. (1986) *Challenging the myths. A review of pensioners' health: course and talks*. London: Pensioners Link.

Means, R. (1986) The development of social services for elderly people: historical perspectives. In Phillipson, C. and Walker, A. (eds), *Ageing and social policy*. London: Gower, 87–106.

Medley, M. (1976) Satisfaction with life among sixty-five years and older. A causal model. *Journal of Gerontology* **31**, 448–55.

Miesen, B. (1993) Alzheimer's disease: the phenomenon of parent fixation and Bowlby's attachment theory. *International Journal of Geriatric Psychiatry* **8**, 147–53.

Mills, M.A. and Coleman, P. (1994) Nostalgic memories in dementia: a case study. *International Journal of Ageing and Human Development* **38**, 203–19.

Minois, G. (1989) *History of old age: from antiquity to the Renaissance*. Oxford: Polity Press.

Monsour, N. and Robb, S. (1982) Wandering behaviour in old age: a psychosocial study. *Social Work* **September**, 411–15.

Mortimore, J.A. (1988) Do psychosocial risk factors contribute to Alzheimer's disease? In Henderson, A.S. and Henderson, J.H. (eds), *Etiology of dementia of Alzheimer's type*. Chichester: John Wiley & Sons.

Murphy, E. (1982) Social origins of depression in old age. *British Journal of Psychiatry* **141**, 135–42.

Myles, J. (1984) *Old age in the Welfare State: the political economy of public pensions*. Boston, MA: Little, Brown & Co.

Neuberger, J. (1987) *Caring for dying people of different faiths*. London: Lisa Sainsbury Foundation.

Norman, A. (1985) *Triple jeopardy: growing old in a second homeland*. London: Centre for Policy on Ageing.

Norris, A. (1986) *Reminiscences with elderly people*. London: Winslow Press.

Ogg, J. and Bennett, G. (1992) Elder abuse in Britain. *British Medical Journal* **305**, 988–9.

O'Leary, E. (1996) *Counselling older adults: perspectives, approaches and research*. London: Chapman & Hall.

Parish, P. (1987) *Medicines – a guide for everyone*. Harmondsworth: Penguin.

Parkes, C.M. (1972) *Bereavement: studies of grief in adult life*. London: Tavistock.

Parkes, C.M. (1985) Bereavement. *British Journal of Psychiatry* **146**, 11–17.

Parkes, C.M. and Weiss, R.S. (1983) *Recovery from bereavement*. New York: Basic Books.

Parsons, T. (1949) *Essays in sociological theory: pure and applied*. Glencoe, IL: Free Press.

Patel, N., Mirz, N., Lindblad, P., Amstrup, K. and Samaoli, O. (1998) *Dementia and minority ethnic older people: managing care in the UK, Denmark and France*. Russell House Publishing.

Pearson, J.L., Conwell, Y., Lindessay, J., Takahashi, Y. and Caine, E.D. (1997) Elderly suicide: a multi-national view. *Ageing and Mental Health* **1**, 107–11.

Petty, R. and Sensky, T. (1987) *Depression. Treating the whole person*. London: Unwin Hyman.

Phillipson, C. (1982) *Capitalism and the construction of old age*. Basingstoke: Macmillan.

Phillipson, C. and Walker, A. (1987) *Ageing and social policy: a critical assessment*. Aldershot: Gower.

Phillipson, C., Bernard, M. and Strang, P. (1986) *Dependency and interdependency in old age – theoretical perspectives and policy alternatives*. Beckenham: Croom Helm/British Society of Gerontology.

Philpot, T. (1986) Elderly people in Japan. Respect due? *Community Care* **12 October**, 16–18.

Pillemer, K. and Finkelhor, D. (1988) The prevalence of elder abuse: a random sample survey. *The Gerontologist* **28**, 51–7.

Podkieks, E. (1992) National survey on abuse of the elderly in Canada. *Journal of Elder Abuse and Neglect* **4**, 5–58.

Pollack, N.J. and Namazi, K.H. (1992) The effect of music participation on the social behaviour of Alzheimer's disease patients. *Journal of Music Therapy* **229**, 54–67.

Price, J.H. and Andrews, P. (1982) Alcohol abuse in the elderly. *Journal of Gerontological Nursing* **8**, 16–19.

Proctor, H. (1981) Family construct psychology: an approach to understanding and treating families. In Walrund-Skinner, S. (ed.), *Developments in family therapy*. London: Routledge & Kegan Paul, 350–66.

Rait, G., Burns, A. and Chew, C. (1996) Age, ethnicity and mental illness: a triple whammy. *British Medical Journal* **313**, 1347–8.

Reichard, S., Livson, F. and Peterson, P.G. (1962) *Ageing and personality*. New York: John Wiley & Sons.

Renshaw, D. (1991) Sexuality. In Sadavoy, J., Lazarus, L. and Jarvik, L. (eds), *Comprehensive review of geriatric psychiatry*. Washington, DC: American Psychiatric Press.

Rogers, C. (1951a) *Client-centred therapy*. London: Constable.

Rogers, C. (1951b) *On becoming a person*. London: Constable.

Rogers, J. (1986) *The taste of health*. London: BBC Publications.

Ropper, A.H. (1979) A rational approach to dementia. *CMC Journal* **3 November**, 1175–90.

Rosin, A. and Glatt, M. (1971) Alcohol excess in the elderly. *Quarterly Journal of Studies on Alcohol* **32**, 53–9.

Sargent, S. (1980) *Non-traditional therapy and counselling with the ageing*. London: Constable.

Scher, M. (1981) Men in hiding: a challenge for the counsellor. *Personnel and Guidance Journal* **60**, 199–202.

Scheff, T.J. (1966) *On being mentally ill*. London: Weidenfeld and Nicolson.

Schulz, R., Newsom, J.T., Fleissner, K., Decamp, A.R. and Nieboer, A.P. (1997) The effects of bereavement after family caregiving. *Ageing and Mental Health* **1**, 269–82.

Scrutton, S. (1990) Ageism: the foundation of age discrimination. In McEwen, E. (ed.), *Age: the unrecognised discrimination*. London: Age Concern.

Scrutton, S. (1992) *Ageing, healthy and in control: an alternative approach to maintaining the health of older people*. London: Chapman & Hall.

Scrutton, S. (1995) *Bereavement and grief: supporting older people through loss*. London: Arnold.

Shakespeare, R. (1975) *The psychology of handicap*. London: Methuen.

Sherman, E. (1981) *Counselling the aging. An integrated approach*. New York: Free Press.

Simmons, L.W. (1945) *The role of the aged in primitive society*. New Haven, CT: Archon Books.

Social Services Inspectorate (1998) *They look after their own, don't they? Inspection of Community Care Services for black and ethnic minority older people*. London: Department of Health.

Solomon, K. and Szwarbo, P. (1992) Psychotherapy for patients with dementia. In Morley, J.E., Coe, R., Strong, R. and Grossberg, G. (eds), *Memory function and aging-related disorders*. New York: Springer.

Sterns, H.L., Weis, D.M. and Perkins, D.E. (1984) A conceptual approach to counselling older adults and their families. *Counselling Psychologist* **12**, 55–61.

Stewart, W. (1992) *A to Z of counselling, theory and practice*. London: Chapman & Hall.

Stuart-Hamilton, I. (1994) *The psychology of ageing.* London: Jesssica Kingsley.

Szasz, T. (1976) *The myth of mental illness.* London: Harper and Row.

Thienhaus, O.L., Conte, E.A. and Bosmann, H.B. (1986) Sexuality and ageing. *Ageing and Society* **6**, 39–54.

Thompson, P. (1978) *The voice of the past: oral history.* Oxford: Oxford University Press.

Thunhurst, C. (1982) *It makes you sick. The politics of the NHS.* London: Pluto Press.

Tobin, S.S. (1991) *Personhood in advanced old age.* New York: Springer.

Townsend, P. (1963) *The family life of old people.* Harmondsworth: Penguin.

Townsend, P. (1979) *Poverty in the UK.* Harmondsworth: Penguin.

Townsend, P. (1981) The structured dependency of the elderly: creation of social policy in the twentieth century. *Ageing and Society* **1**, 6–28.

Tudge, C. (1986) *The food connection.* London: BBC Publications.

Tunstall, J. (1966) *Old and alone.* London: Routledge and Kegan Paul.

Turner, P. and Volans, G. (1987) *The drugs handbook.* Basingstoke: Macmillan.

Tyler, L.E. (1969) *The work of the counsellor.* New York: Appleton-Century-Crofts.

Verwoerdt, A. (1976) *Clinical geropsychiatry.* London: Williams and Wilkins.

Walker, A. (1994) *Age, race and ethnicity: a comparative approach.* Buckingham: Open University Press.

Walrund-Skinner, S. (1977) *Family therapy. The treatment of natural systems.* London: Routledge and Kegan Paul.

Wattis, J. and Church, M. (1986) *Practical psychiatry of old age.* Beckenham: Croom Helm.

Weinberg, J. (1972) Psychologic implications of the nutritional needs of the elderly. *Journal of the American Dietetic Association* **60**, 293–6.

Whitbourne, S. and Hulicka, I. (1990) Ageism in undergraduate psychological texts. *American Psychologist* **45**, 1127–36.

Wilson, R.A. and Wilson, T. (1963) The fate of the non-treated postmenopausal woman. *Journal of the American Geriatrics Society* **March**, 347.

Woods, P. and Ashley, J. (1995) Simulated presence therapy: using selected memories to manage problem behaviors in Alzheimer's disease patients. *Geriatric Nursing* **16**, 9–14.

Worden, W.J. (1983) *Grief counselling and grief therapy.* London: Tavistock.

Index

Page numbers given in **bold** refer to a chapter or a section.